MW00564294

Parenting the DIFFICULT Child — Linda

Linda Rice has written an extremely readable book for counselors and struggling parents. I know of no other book that addresses the problem of Reactive Attachment Disorder (RAD) biblically. Linda goes beyond external manifestations of a child's behavior and deals with the heart issues that Scripture emphasizes (Heb. 4:12). It is a very practical book. I highly recommend it.

> – Dr. David Tyler, Director
> Gateway Biblical Counseling and Training Center
> author of *ADHD: Deceptive Diagnosis; Deceptive Diagnosis When Sin is Called Sickness*
> *Self-Esteem: Are We Really Better Than We Think?*

I am more than happy to recommend this book. It is, so far as I am concerned, the only Scriptural effort of any substance to understand and deal with the so-called problem of RAD (Reactive Attachment Disorder). In the book, Ms. Rice clearly sets forth the current non-Christian thinking on the subject, with a critique of the same. She offers a Nouthetic explanation of the problem and a biblical approach to dealing with it. The book is thorough, informative and practical. If you need help in this area, here is the place to turn.

> – Jay Adams, Author, Co-Founder of the National Association of Nouthetic Counselors (NANC) (renamed the Association of Certified Biblical Counselors, 2013)

Although I would not place my children in the RAD category, I have found Linda's book to be practically applicable to my own parenting. Her book answers questions like the following. "How can I honor God by parenting?" "How do I apply God's principles to my own life while applying them to my children's lives?" I am truly blessed to have had the privilege of reading these pages. Her book is compassionately heartfelt, truthfully informative, scripturally based, and refreshingly inspiring.

> – Sandy Skelton, Mother

Parenting the
DIFFICULT
Child

A Biblical Perspective on
Reactive Attachment Disorder

Parenting the

DIFFICULT
Child

Linda J. Rice

SeedSown Press | U.S.A.

Parenting the Difficult Child
A Biblical Perspective on Reactive Attachment Disorder
By Linda J. Rice

ISBN: 978-0-9850431-3-1

Published by: SeedSown Press | U.S.A.
Printed in the United States of America

For information, contact: SeedSownPress.wordpress.com

Scripture taken from the *New American Standard Bible* Copyright © 1960, 1962, 1963, 1968, 1971, 1973, 1975, 1977 by the Lockman Foundation. Used by permission.

Book design by Susan Sylvia | www.StaircasePressDesign.com

This book contains information and counsel regarding child rearing. It is not intended to offer medical or legal counsel.

Publisher's Cataloguing-In-Publication Data:
   Rice, Linda J.
     Parenting the difficult child : a biblical perspective on reactive
     attachment disorder / Linda J. Rice. -- O'Fallon, Ill. : SeedSown
     Press, c2012.

       p. ; cm.
     ISBN: 978-0-9850431-3-1
     Includes bibliographical references.
     Summary: Reactive Attachment Disorder (RAD) is a
psychological label for children with extremely antisocial behaviors.
Adoptive children are especially prone to develop it. This book
approaches RAD from a biblical perspective, to offer
encouragement and guidance for the angry child's parents and
siblings who may themselves struggle with difficult emotions.--
Publisher.

     1. Attachment disorder in children--Treatment--Religious
aspects--Christianity. 2. Antisocial personality disorders--
Treatment--Religious aspects--Christianity. 3. Attachment behavior
in children. 4. Children--Family relationships. 5. Parent and child.
6. Sibling attachment. 7. Counseling--Religious aspects--
Christianity. 8. Family psychotherapy--Religious aspects--
Christianity. 9. Child psychotherapy--Religious aspects--
Christianity. I. Title.

RJ507.A77 R53 2012
618.92/8588--dc23   1210

Acknowledgements

What a great debt I owe to those who have influenced me toward the Lord and the rich salvation I enjoy in His care. I also owe much to those who have stood beside me through this writing project.

First thanks go to our kind and wise God for giving us His Word! What a treasure it is! "For the Lord gives wisdom; from His mouth come knowledge and understanding" (Prov. 2:6). I thank Him also for graciously granting to me wise instructors like John Street, Stuart Scott, Wayne Mack, and Lou Priolo, who placed into my hands biblical tools for applying God's Word to daily living and problem-solving. As I used those tools, the Bible reshaped my view of what is today called Reactive Attachment Disorder.

I thank my friends, Tara Barndt, Connie Cummings, Zella Halstead, Sandy Skelton, and Amanda Daniels for reading the manuscript and giving wise direction. My editor, Ann Burt, was invaluable. Hannah McDowell and Katie Powner helped also.

Heather Rice was a patient, tenacious, analytical, and dedicated editor. She improved the manuscript untold times. God promises to bless children who honor their parents (Eph. 6:1-3). May that promise be abundantly fulfilled in her life.

I thank my husband, Mike, who remained the steady captain of our ship as we raged through turbulent waters in child rearing, and who brightened us all with many comedic moments. How often he has patiently listened, given me wise counsel, and encouraged me in life and in this writing project.

Contents

Contents

Introduction

Through the years it has taken to write this book, I have been praying that God will use it in the lives of those who read it. That means you. I want you to gain hope and to increase in understanding of His truths regarding what is called Reactive Attachment Disorder (RAD). I want you to benefit by practical applications in parenting and gain skill in practically loving your child who displays the characteristics of RAD and your other children so that you might better please the Lord. But before proceeding, let me tell you a little about myself as it relates to RAD.

Three years after we married, the addition of our first-born added joy to our family. When we then adopted, we were hopeful of blending the other two, ages two and four, into our joy. That was not to be. At first, we thought that enough love and careful parenting would solve the problems in our precious children's lives. We weren't expecting a problem-free life, but their absolutely befuddling behaviors were overwhelming. Our parenting seemed ineffectual.

Have you ever noticed that when you put a puzzle together you can sometimes fit a piece into a spot and even though it seems not quite right it fits well enough that you leave it there? Later, you discover where it really fits. This is how my understanding of RAD has changed.

I went on a hunt for answers. It seemed that all sources set the puzzle pieces of our children's behaviors into a picture called, at that time, Attachment Disorder. The basic idea is that a lack of attachment to another person in infancy causes the constellation of behaviors that we were seeing. The explanation made sense to us. We adjusted our parenting practices, consulted a psychologist to check out our parenting, and spent thousands on an educational consultant and hearing therapy (for brain organization). We were not perfect parents, but we persevered in love and consistent discipline.

Meanwhile, as I studied chapter by chapter through the Bible, I began to notice Bible passages that contradicted the presumptions and goals that psychologists viewed as true. I also began to see inconsistencies between psychologists' teachings and what I observed in my adopted children's behaviors. Psychologists proposed that a RAD child has low self-esteem while what I saw was selfishness, which is pride, which is actually high self-esteem. I gradually observed too many instances when I could not attribute my child's behavior to a helplessness to some psychological disorder. Behaviors were being turned on and off at will through deliberately considered and determined choices. Those puzzle pieces needed a closer examination.

Parenting difficult children can be draining. Gradually, my fatigue and anxiety escalated to insomnia, depression, panic attacks, and then prolonged grief when I perceived that I was losing a relationship that I desperately wanted. I felt hopeless and longed for relief.

How could I, who claimed to follow Jesus, find myself in this condition? What I eventually came to realize was that I was not handling stress and fears God's way. As I later studied biblical counseling, I saw how I had failed to follow the direction given by God in His Word, how that led to depression, and how to change. The Bible changed my life. I also noticed that a verse here and a verse there, verses everywhere rang true regarding my observations of children who behave according to the RAD model.

Still, in the back of my mind I argued. What about the research? What about evidence from brain, genetics, and behavioral studies? When I decided to seek answers, I found that psychologists' puzzle pieces were out of place and God's Word fit them together perfectly. This book is a result.

Parent, you are not alone. Like you and me, many have slogged through the confusion, frustrations, feeling of impotence, desperation, futility, loneliness, despair, hopelessness, the temptations to anger, fears, guilt, worries, and depression, and the tremendous ache of loss and grief. With compassion for you and me in our difficulties, God says,

> No temptation has overtaken you but such as is common to man, and God is faithful, who will not allow you to be tempted beyond what you are able, but with the temptation will provide the way of escape that you may be able to endure it (1 Cor 10:13).

God is faithful! He provides the way of endurance with grace and joy. In His Word I found the way out of depression and I have been off of the antidepressant for several years. Though at times fear and depression still tempt me, by His grace they no longer rule me. His Spirit truly enables obedience to the truth that frees (Gal. 5:16; John 8:32).

Where Can We Find Certain Hope?

From early on, while I agreed that the Bible is the ultimate authority, I didn't see how the Bible related sufficiently to my troubles or to RAD. Thanks be to God, my eyesight was the problem.

God says that His Word is sufficient counsel for godly living in relationships and in difficulties. That is a prodigious and revolutionary claim. Both Peter and Paul recorded this truth and never backed away from it. Paul told Timothy that Scripture held the wisdom that led to Timothy's salvation. He said that Scripture teaches how to live, reproves wrong living, corrects back to the right path, and trains to make right living on that path a habit. By these functions, it equips a person "for every good work" (2 Tim. 3:15-17). That pretty well covers all of life. Peter said that God's Word lacks no truth or principle that we need for how to live in a godly way (2 Pet. 1:3; *see also* Pss. 1 and 19). What hope! What psychological theory can compete?

Am I saying that the Bible is relevant? Yes, I am saying that the Bible is *totally* relevant. It is totally relevant, perfectly clear, preeminently authoritative, and absolutely sufficient for our relational problems. That means that the Bible is also THE definitive work on Reactive Attachment Disorder. As this book unfolds, you will see what I mean.

How could God not have something to say about Reactive Attachment Disorder? He is Creator. Of all experts, wouldn't He be the One to have not just the most effectual solutions, but to have *the* illuminating, *the* substantive, and *the* effectual truths?"

Because God is omniscient, what can men have experienced that God would not know and understand? Since God is all-wise, what interpersonal problem could men have that God would not know all aspects of its solution? Since God is about redemption and reconciliation, what necessary information about that solution would He have left out of His Word? His Word was given for the very purpose of accomplishing a person's full redemption and reconciliation with both God and other men. The Bible gives hope for change beyond anything the world can offer (1 Cor. 6:9-11; Phil. 4:13).

Why Does Our Viewpoint Matter?

Reactive Attachment Disorder is an increasingly frequent diagnosis of extremely alienated and antisocial children. Their behaviors are so extreme, irrational, and destructive at such young ages that they mystify parents and professionals. Due to their behaviors, it is not unusual for parents to send them to some other residential care for a period of time prior to the legal age of adulthood. These children comprise some of the most difficult cases that the psychological community faces.

Secular and Christian psychologists propose that the core problem of RAD is lack of attachment to any caregiver. It occurs in reaction to neglect, mistreatment, and repeated separations (such as in foster care and adoptions) in early infancy, and develops from unmet needs, a broken bonding cycle, and disorganized brain development. Unattached children are considered pathological (sick), developmentally delayed, and brain damaged so that they have no conscience and are unable to be intimate, to trust, or to feel remorse.

According to the Bible, RAD children are not pathological. While brain development may have some influence, the cause of their morally wrong behaviors is not developmental delay or brain damage. They do trust and do have a conscience. Children who display the behaviors fitting the RAD label have reacted out of the selfishness of their hearts to tragic and painful circumstances with sinful fear and anger. They want to control their environment in order to gain safety, justice (perverted to revenge), and autonomy, which they crave. Self-sufficiency (self-trust) produces obstinate rebellion and alienation. Their desires, perceptions, choices, and behaviors become unrelenting habits.

Do genes or physiology have a role? The jury has yet to render its decision. While I will apply biblical principles to explain RAD, the fact remains that it is not always necessary to know an explanation or an exact cause of something before changes can be made to solve the problem. Physiological or not, the symptoms are behavioral and the Bible holds solutions for behavioral problems.

Although Scripture offers sufficient counsel (Ps. 19:7-8), psychologists' theories on attachment, called "attachment theory," dominate even in the Christian community. It has so permeated Christian psychology that leading Christian psychologists suggest that attachment theory should be the model for all counseling because it makes sense of every counseling issue, whether misbehaviors, depression, or marital relationships. They say that because a proper attachment develops the "foundation of empathy," it even "lays the groundwork for prayer." Therefore, attachment should be the paradigm through which we understand people of all ages.[1]

These Christian psychologists are elevating attachment theory to be the model for Christians to use for understanding and counseling people. Such a proposal shoves God's Word to the back seat and sets one of the world's theories in the driver's seat of solving people's problems. Considering that these two drivers steer in opposing directions, this is a serious switch for a Christian (Ps. 1; 2 Tim. 4:3-4). Nevertheless, desperate Christian parents often turn to the secular community because they find an appealing wealth of empathy, explanations, support groups, literature, and residential treatment facilities.

How you view the child labeled with RAD is vital because the model you choose will determine your expectations, vocabulary, goals, and methods. Therefore, on this topic of RAD, it is time to take God at His Word and put on the biblical perspective of a child who behaves according to the characteristics of the label. The behaviors are real. At issue are the cause and solution.

What is My Goal?

The goal of this book is not to present one more theory to explain RAD or a psychological therapy for a cure. The world does not need one more man-made theory. My goal is to examine the true and reliable counsel of our beloved Creator. I want to make parents, family, friends, and counselors aware of what the Bible says about the child, why he does what he does, how he thinks, the role of emotions, and how to change.

Furthermore, remembering how hard it was for us to watch our other children suffer innocently or struggle with temptations, I include in this book chapters to comfort and aid struggling parents and siblings. These are not intended to be comprehensive, but a steerage in the right direction. I want to give hope and share some of God's foundational principles relating to the unique temptations thrown at you and the siblings.

I remember my desperate hunger for answers and finding, seemingly, only one main viewpoint available, that lack of attachment is the root of RAD. More recently, I found this view still predominant. There are some secular psychologists who dissent and a few of their arguments are briefly summarized in Chapter 21. What I couldn't find at all was a book or website offering a biblical perspective. Therefore, I wrote this book to provide that perspective. This is not to say that a biblical view is just one among many viable options. I am convinced that God's view is the only viable option.

How is This Book Arranged?

This book is arranged in three major parts. Part 1 presents the Bible's explanation of the mentality, cause, and solution.

Part 2 presents the "how" of what parents must think and do to help their RAD child and other children think and behave in a godly manner. Several of the chapters in part 2 list suggestions for practical ways to help parents implement the truths taught in the chapter.

Part 3 contains psychologists' descriptions and theories on RAD which are in popular use today. It delves below the surface of the explanation to the rationale from which the theories developed. Then it challenges those views with biblical truth for you to consider. One chapter highlights inconsistencies in the theory, some faults in the behavioral research, and insufficiencies noted by secular psychologists. Another summarizes precautions regarding therapy programs.

Because of the extremeness of the behaviors, the topic of Reactive Attachment Disorder can lead to sensationalism. Worst-case scenarios do happen, but most children are not worst-case. Therefore, I utilize illustrations of varying degrees. The introductory case study of Mrs. DeSpare and Donnie is a hypothetical composite from several sources and does not describe any one child or parent.

Terminology is important because words shape our perceptions, thoughts, and behaviors. A doctor's diagnosis determines his prescription. In the same way, if we want to arrive at the biblical solution to our children's problems, we need to apply biblical terminology. The Bible does not use the term "Reactive Attachment Disorder" nor group that set of behaviors as a distinct unit like psychologists do, yet this is our subject. Therefore, I will lean on biblically accurate descriptive terms like "angry" or "alienated" but also use the term "RAD" to stay focused on a circumscribed group of behaviors which is the topic of this book.

Another Word of Hope

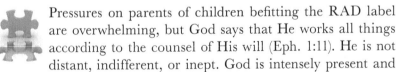 Pressures on parents of children befitting the RAD label are overwhelming, but God says that He works all things according to the counsel of His will (Eph. 1:11). He is not distant, indifferent, or inept. God is intensely present and effectually involved for our good and His glory (Rom. 8:28-29). Parenting God's way is not accomplished by following man-made theories. It is accomplished by following God's Word by the power of His Spirit and with the help of His people in the church.

A biblical view of the child must be the foundation for parenting him. The church, while respecting secular men's efforts and astute observations, should apply the truth of God's Word to the topic, reject false etiological theories, and present the hope that God's Word offers (1 Pet. 3:15). By holding a biblical view, family, children's workers, church friends, counselors, and leaders can all support parents and siblings more effectively.

For the child labeled with RAD, Scripture offers the hope of a new heart through salvation and principles for change. For parents and siblings, it instructs on how to live wisely with the child. The Holy Spirit has the power to change the seemingly unchangeable child and to enable the parents and siblings to rejoice in trials and respond in ways pleasing to God.

The biblical model leads to a Person. It does so because "from Him [Christ] and through Him and to Him are all things. To Him be the glory" (Rom. 11:36). Christ is glorified when people are made new by being reconciled to Him (2 Cor. 5:17-19). So the goal of the biblical model does not settle for a child who behaves better. It aims for the far higher goal of each family member repenting to Christ and becoming more like Him in right relationship with Him.

Footnote

1. Tim Clinton, *Counsel CDs: Attachments: Why You Love, Feel, and Act the Way You Do*. Host, Tim Clinton. Guest, Gary Sibcy. Based on the book, *Attachments: Why You Love, Feel, and Act the Way You Do: Unlock the Secret to Loving and Lasting Relationships*, by Tim Clinton and Gary Sibcy, Counsel CDs (American Association of Christian Counselors).

Part 1: Viewing RAD Through the Lens of the Bible

A child who behaves in a manner which would lead to a diagnosis of Reactive Attachment Disorder is in a pitiable condition. It is likely that he has been abused, or at least neglected or moved from home to home. His methods of coping usually stir others not to the compassion he needs, but to fearful and angry reactions that add confusion to the family dynamics.

You may have already heard what psychologists say about RAD. A biblical view is radically different. God says, "For My thoughts are not your thoughts, nor are your ways My ways" (Isa. 55:8).

As our Maker, God knows how we tick, how we break, and how to fix the brokenness. Since God is the expert, we cannot settle for less than examining His Word to see what He says about RAD.

Part 1 lays the lens of God's Word over Reactive Attachment Disorder in order to gain a biblical perspective of the causes so that biblical solutions might be identified. We will start by defining the subject. Then we will shape our understanding of the subject through application of biblical principles.

Chapter 1

How Psychologists Identify RAD

"We knew it would be challenging, ... but we were totally unprepared for something like this."[1] These words are from Danielle Alexander in *USA Today*, September 14, 2005, in reference to her three-year-old son adopted from Russia. After his arrival in the States, he began hitting his sister, purposely urinating in various rooms of the house, and vandalizing furniture. Months later, he showed only a little improvement.

The newspaper article relates that several U.S. parents have been charged with killing their adopted children. "In each of the criminal cases, the parents' lawyers have argued that the defendants lost control as they tried to cope with unruly children who are beset by hard-to-fathom troubles."[2] The article noted that pre-adoption experiences often lead to what is called Reactive Attachment Disorder (RAD), in which the child is unable to bond with adoptive parents. Victor Groza, a social work professor quoted in the article, estimates that about 20% of children adopted from overseas may need lifelong help.

Children who behave according to the pattern labeled "RAD" are raging storms that blow chaos into a household and keep it turbulent. Their parents often become disillusioned, then frustrated, then hopeless. They ask questions like:

- Why is my child so strange as to reject my affection?
- How can my child have no remorse? How did he end up with no conscience?
- How can I get my child to behave?
- What do I do when I have disciplined with the right attitude, type, and amount, and still the child is insubordinate? How do I discipline someone who laughs at pain and loss?
- How do I protect the siblings? How do I help them cope?

- * What do I do when I feel that I am in danger from my own child?

- * Will my child ever become loving and cooperative? When will he get enough love?

- * How do I get relief?

- * Where can I get help for my child?

Meet Mrs. DeSpare

One afternoon, Mrs. DeSpare consults Pastor Helpin about behavior problems in her ten-year-old son, Donnie. Pastor Helpin is surprised. He knows Donnie as a cheerful, lovable little guy, never troublesome, and always cooperative with his teachers. The DeSpares are known as solid, growing believers with orderly, pleasant children.

Mrs. DeSpare opens. "Donnie set his curtains on fire last night. I'm worried."

Pastor Helpin says, "That certainly sounds extreme. Tell me what is going on."

His request opens a flood of words. "Most mornings, he refuses to get out of bed, and then he dawdles over dressing and breakfast. He nearly misses the bus for school. He gets irate if I expect him to put dirty clothes in the hamper or to make his bed.[3] He constantly argues over anything and everything.

"When I sit him in a corner until he is ready to converse respectfully, he spends his time distracting the other children from their homework. So I send him to his room. He stomps and slams the door and opens it and talks loudly and curses us. He throws things against the walls. He yells at us through the air ducts. Lot of times I've heard him talk to himself, like he's coaching himself, convincing himself that we are mean and plotting revenge against us.

"When I call for supper, he stomps down the stairs, but then suddenly puts on a cheerful grin and sweetly sets the table. At the dinner table, when the rest of us are talking and giggling, he remains stone-faced. If we talk seriously, he bursts out in hysterical laughter that he is helpless to stop. We ignored it for months, but each time he kept on for the rest of the meal and supper cleanup. Everybody was tense. So now, we send him to his room as soon as he starts. It hasn't stopped the laughter but at least the rest of us can enjoy a conversation.

"He mumbles so much that I find myself constantly saying, 'What?' But when he is angry, he speaks as clear as a bell. Unless he is angry, he won't look me in the eye. Or he bats his eyelids. He'll do without rather than ask for information, but he asks all kinds of nonsense questions. He outright told me that instead of trying to learn, he spends our homework time planning how to get me angry. How can I help a child like that!?"

Mrs. DeSpare's voice rises a notch. "Things are disappearing, but no one seems to know who is doing it, and Donnie is the only one with things not stolen. Food disappears from the kitchen and there is writing on the furniture, but Donnie knows nothing about it.[4] He is a superb liar. He eavesdrops. He startles us from behind doors. He listens through the air ducts, and watches us through picture glass on the walls. He prowls the house at night. The other children and I have awakened to find his face hovering over ours. We don't feel safe.

"He bullies his younger siblings and hits them if they don't cooperate. We don't keep a pet anymore because our last two cats were found dead in the garage. It was pretty obvious they'd been strangled.

"People don't understand. At church, Donnie is adorable. He hugs people like he just can't get enough of them. Teachers say he is the sweetest boy they've met. People even ooh and aah over him in front of the other children. But, he makes the ride home from church miserable for us.

"People tell me it's just his age, a faze. Well, Donnie's phase has lasted for seven years now, ever since we adopted him. I feel like others don't believe me or think I am overreacting."

Mrs. DeSpare wrings her hands. "The Donnie you know is not the one we know. Sometimes he is sweet and cooperative. Then he rebels when I tell him to do something. But then he does something nice for us other than what we wanted and gets angry if we don't praise him for it. It's like he sets us up. Anything but obedience. Do you think he might have two personalities?

"Discipline doesn't faze him. If I take away a favorite toy, he shrugs his shoulders. When we spank him, he laughs. His pain tolerance is amazing. He surprised the doctor by picking at an oozy, ingrown toenail like it was gum on a sock. He never flinched when the doctor lanced it. He even baits me for discipline, then snickers when I deliver it." Raising her hands, she asks, "How can I deal with that?"

She shakes her head. "He is never sorry. Never. If he apologizes, it is phony. It doesn't matter if we discipline or praise; it is a lose-lose situation for us. We have no parenting tools left.

"I admit to having yelled sometimes, but I keep working on using godly responses. And I've noticed that the more self-controlled and gentle I have become, the worse he is getting. The other children are scared of him. Twice, we have found knives stolen from the kitchen and hidden in his room. The other day when he was furious, his glare shocked me. It was almost fiendish and his pupils turned black. I didn't know that was possible. I wondered if he has a demon. Lately, he has threatened me. He's like a swelling volcano, and I wonder when he'll explode.

"I feel so drained! He battles for control literally from first thing in the morning until bedtime, unless he's out playing. But then he often tries to cause trouble for the other kids, and I have to deal with that sometimes. It's getting harder to get out of bed in the mornings when I know that the first moment I see him he'll be glaring at me or snapping at me. No agency will help us.

"The doctor says he has something called Reactive Attachment Disorder, but I don't know what to think. Please help us."

Mrs. DeSpare went to the right place for help, her church. Pastor Helpin sees that the first thing she needs is hope. While he shows her Bible truths that offer hope, we are going to take a closer look at Donnie so as to define and describe our subject.

How is RAD Diagnosed?

Donnie DeSpare manifests many characteristics of a pattern that psychologists have labeled Reactive Attachment Disorder. Psychologists use a variety of terms for the child: unattached, character disordered, dissociated, antisocial, or a "RAD." RAD is listed in the *Diagnostic and Statistical Manual of Mental Disorders (DSM-IV)*, which the American Psychiatric Association uses for diagnosing behavioral disorders.

According to the *DSM-IV*, "the essential feature of Reactive Attachment Disorder is markedly disturbed and developmentally inappropriate social relatedness in most contexts that begins before age 5 years and is associated with grossly pathological care."[5] In other words, these children do not relate to others in a normal way and their behavior is related to severe mistreatment in the care they received when very young. There are exceptions; some children form stable relationships in spite of abuse.

The *DSM-IV* lists two subcategories, inhibited and disinhibited. The inhibited type persistently fails to respond or initiate normally, resists being comforted by others, may be hypervigilant (intensely watchful) toward others, or fluctuates between avoidance and overdone approach. The disinhibited type lacks selectivity in the choice of the person he targets for attachment. He shows excessive familiarity and charm with relative strangers but offers highly ambivalent responses to family. So, in various social situations, even at a very young age, the RAD child behaves in ways noticeably inappropriate and abnormal for his age.

Many children display obnoxious and defiant behaviors. How is RAD distinguished from common childhood defiance and teen-aged rebellion? The *DSM-IV* provides three distinguishing criteria.

* Attachment – There is a lack of attachment, exhibited by disturbed social relatedness.

* Timing – Onset of symptoms of abnormal behavior begins prior to age five.

* Cause – It forms in the environment of pathological, not supportive, care.

The "grossly pathological care" comes in various forms. The primary caregiver persistently disregards the child's basic physical needs and/or emotional needs, as in cases of parental neglect or abuse, or in an extended hospitalization of the child. Or primary caregivers change repeatedly so that no stable attachment can form, as in foster care. It is presumed that these conditions are responsible for the "disturbed social relatedness."[6] Authorities at Chaddock, a residential facility specializing in treatment of RAD in adolescents, state that anxiety or drug use during pregnancy may cause attachment problems to begin even in utero.[7]

What does the label "RAD" *not* describe? It does not describe the abused child who still forms attachments and is not markedly maladjusted. It is unlike disorders such as autism, which develop within a relatively supportive setting. Although it can present like Attention-Deficit/Hyperactivity Disorder (ADHD), it is different in that children with ADHD will form attachments. The label is not applied to children with mental retardation or brain damage. Neither does it describe rebellion which develops in the teen years.

To distinguish teen-age rebellion from RAD, Chaddock staff look at the first three years of life. Chaddock's view is that generally good children who later rebel have demonstrated intimate attachments in the early years and rebel for other reasons, such as the use of rebellion as the cultural method of separation from parents to gain adulthood. RAD children have had trauma early in life, have not attached since infancy, and have demonstrated their extreme negative behaviors and attitudes from prior to age five.[8]

Stanton Samenow, author of *Before It's Too Late*, distinguishes autonomy from rebellion. The teen who rebels violates specific standards, wanting his way in opposition to how he has been raised. The antisocial child is not necessarily rebelling against rules. He has already determined his own standards and way of life, and rebellion just happens to be one action necessary when authorities cross him.[9] While not a vital point, it highlights the RAD child's attitude of autonomy: he is not rebelling against any one set of standards. He considers himself out of relation to any authority but himself and under no obligation to any way of life but his own.

The *DSM-IV* lists behavioral criteria in broad terms. Because of this vagueness,[10] practicing mental health professionals have supplemented specifics to aid in diagnosis.

What are Typical RAD Characteristics?

Following is a compilation of behaviors symptomatic of RAD.[11]

- Lack of eye contact
- Lack of ability to give and receive affection on parents' terms
- Inappropriately demanding and clingy
- Indiscriminately affectionate with strangers
- Superficially engaging and charming
- Phoniness, deceitfulness
- Poor peer relationships
- Abnormal speech patterns
- Learning problems—disabilities, delays
- Abnormal eating patterns
- Theft, pointless theft
- Destructive to self, others, and property
- Cruelty to animals
- Preoccupation with blood, gore, fire, weapons
- Difficulty learning from mistakes
- Poor impulse control
- Intense control battles
- Hypervigilance/Hyperactivity

* Chronic lying, lies about the obvious
* Lack of remorse

Lack of eye contact

Eye contact is excellent only when the child is manipulating or is extremely angry. Otherwise, contact is avoided by averting or rolling the eyes, or by rapid blinking.[12]

Lack of ability to give and receive affection

Affectionate touching and hugs are verbally and physically rejected. The child stiffens, pulls away, or turns the face away from a kiss on the cheek. Hugging a RAD baby can be like hugging a board.[13] Gifts are often rejected. Praise and affection do not build reciprocity; he does not unconditionally give affection or gifts to family members.

Inappropriately demanding and clingy

Although he resists parental affection *on the parents' terms*, he will, in his own timing, initiate ultra cuddly-sweet, even desperate, hugs.

Indiscriminately affectionate with strangers

A RAD child indiscriminately initiates overly intimate responses to relative strangers. He may initiate conversations with strangers or run to greet an acquaintance new to the family and interact delightfully, but he refuses reciprocal affection with family.[14]

Superficially engaging and charming

The child presents himself as mannerly, cute, sweet, bubbly, demure, cuddly, adoring, or helpless. He will laugh, hug intensely, rub his cheek on the adult's hand, and even cling to the new acquaintance with appealing possessiveness. Shy or bold, RAD children are shrewd analysts of others and calculate precisely how to get whatever response they want.[15]

Phoniness, deceitfulness

The unattached child diligently studies people and practices how to con others. He tells others what he thinks they want to hear. He becomes so skilled at an appearance of normalcy that it may be months before a person realizes he has been emotionally duped. The constant phoniness creates a sense of disconnect or remoteness in relationships.[16]

Poor peer relationships

The antisocial child is usually a loner even if he appears to be friends with everyone. He tends to play with younger children because peers avoid him and younger children are more easily manipulated. He lacks long-term childhood friends.

Abnormal speech patterns

The unattached child speaks not to communicate but to control. A favorite technique is mispronouncing a word so that the adult will correct him. Slurring, mumbling, and nearly inaudible speech keep adults asking "What?" Yet, enunciation is crystal clear during an angry outburst. Giving ambiguous, rather than direct, answers to questions keeps adults probing for information.[17] Other techniques include squeaks, screeches, forced laughter, incessant laughter, and incessant chatter. Nonsense questions, questions about the obvious, or questions that make others feel awkward are also utilized.

Learning problems (disabilities, delays)

RAD children have trouble learning, so they test out at a lower level than their age mates.

Abnormal eating patterns

Patterns include stealing and hiding food, hoarding and gorging, refusal to eat, and eating strange things.

Theft, pointless theft

Theft is chronic, brazen, cunning, and even nonsensical. A grade-schooler named Charles stole baking powder, something useless to him. Albert stole a bicycle when he already had one.[18] They enjoy being sneaky.

Destructive to self, others, property

A RAD child recklessly disregards safety and appears to have no fear of dangerous situations such as cliffs and fire. Tolerance for pain is unusually high.[19] For example, instead of crying in pain, five-year-old Jackie showed excited pleasure over a finger that was smashed in a car door to the point of bleeding.[20] Hurting oneself may be intentional.

Hurting others is sport. The RAD child will deliberately be a nuisance, and bully, terrorize, and humiliate others.[21] He underhandedly stirs trouble with others in a way that they are blamed. He may throw his younger siblings down the stairs or be sexually aggressive by age five.[22] Boys, especially, may escalate into abuse and rape in adolescence. Ken Magid and Carole McKelvey, authors of *High Risk: Children Without a Conscience*, record an incident related by one parent: "One day, the other children came running into the house, screaming that Danny was trying to drown a visiting girl." When confronted, Danny said that in holding her under water he had just been joking.[23]

Vandalism may include anything from adorning the wall with mucous, to punching holes in walls, to arson. Young Danny "took food and rubbed it on the walls. He threw food at people. He broke 'anything and everything.'"He "went to the neighbor's house, broke in and did $6,000 worth of damage while they were out of town."[24]

Cruelty to animals

Animal cruelty is common. For example, parents find that the pet turtle or fish has been boiled.[25] Because the child is so cunning, violent acts are seldom seen or appear to be accidents. If the child is accused, blame is effectively shifted to someone else.

Preoccupation with blood, gore, fire, weapons

Depending upon the severity of disorder, the child will be more or less obsessed with those things associated with evil. Drawings go beyond those of dragons and demons to incorporate blood and gore, and can be frightening.[26] Girls and boys may be overly fascinated with uncouthness, sensuality, and promiscuity at an unusually young age.

Difficulty learning from mistakes

No matter the consequences given by parents and society, the child will continue the behavior. He does not learn from positive or negative reinforcements.

Poor impulse control

A RAD child may speak kindly one moment, viciously the next. He may steal one moment, be generous in the next.

Intense control battles

The antisocial child works persistently to wrest control of the household away from the parent. He behaves well when he wants something. Otherwise, testing, bossiness, arguments, baiting others, and pushing the limits continue unendingly. Every conversation is a manipulation opportunity. He pretends to not hear, not understand, or to misunderstand. A simple morning greeting might be delayed, dramatized, normal, a deliberate snub, a contemptuous grunt, a glare, a burst of laughter, or an antagonistic "What do you want?" A minute incident may start a control battle that continues unresolved for hours or days. He is as likely to sabotage a fun game as he is to participate.

Hypervigilance/Hyperactivity

Hyperactivity, hypervigilance, and anger are common.

Chronic lying, lies about the obvious

Lying is highly skilled, chronic, blatant, and sometimes so ridiculous that the child seems unaware of reality. With his hand in the cookie jar, the child will answer, "What jar?" Lying is not reserved only for escape from trouble. It is a lifestyle. The child may lie about the color of the shirt he is wearing or who was at the birthday party, lying when it gains him nothing and when telling the truth would require less effort.[27]

Lack of remorse

When confronted with misbehavior, the child rationalizes, minimizes the harm he caused, shows total indifference, offers excuses, or blames the victim. Remorse is shown only to reduce or prevent punishment. He becomes insolent or furious if an authority expects him to admit wrongdoing. His actions are justified. The expectations of the victim and/or the authority are unreasonable.

In summary, from babyhood RAD children develop a pervasive emotional self-sufficiency. Key characteristics include drive for control, hypervigilance, and lack of conscience. Most criminals or rebellious people usually maintain a loyalty to someone, friend or family. RAD children retain no loyalties and exercise a disregard for, and violation of, other people.

What is Generally the Prognosis?

According to most experts, "No effective treatments for RAD have yet been developed."[28] Rates of success for treatment centers are hard to find. When asked what success looks like, Chaddock staff's first response was a young adult who gets arrested for burglary instead of murder. The second response was a youth who can stay in the home long enough to graduate from school, or a decrease in the intensity, duration, and frequency of the old behaviors.[29] Koplewicz states that RAD is "by far the most difficult disorder to treat in all of child and adolescent psychiatry," so psychiatrists look for other disorders that they can treat and try to improve the child by treating them first.[30] RAD behavioral patterns continue into adulthood and many RAD children become criminals.[31]

Are All Cases the Same?

This chapter attempts to color a detailed picture of the RAD child. The danger with extensive detail is that it may suggest that a RAD child is a super-monster. Magid and McKelvey begin their book, *High*

Risk, with with a shocking example of a nine-year-old boy in Florida who, in 1986, deliberately pushed a three-year-old into the deep end of a pool to watch him drown.[32] They also call them psychopaths in recognition of the similarities between Reactive Attachment Disorder and Antisocial Personality Disorder (APD), what used to be called psychopathology.[33] ("Psychopathology" is mental illness. "Psychopathy" is the disorder characterized by lack of empathy.) The difference between APD and RAD is in age; the *DSM-IV* allows for no one under the age of eighteen to be diagnosed with APD.

However, a degree of caution is needed. Any one child with RAD fits on a continuum of antisocial behavior from mild to criminal. While all children exhibit these characteristics sometimes, RAD children exhibit them with multiplied frequency, intensity, and duration. Not every RAD child becomes violent; some become master swindlers, thieves, or just emotional con artists within their social circle. Males will usually be more extreme than females. A child with a high IQ will be more cunning and creative than one with a low IQ.[34] Just because a parent sees signs in a very young child does not mean that he is destined to have a criminal on his hands.

God Knows and Cares

 Psalm 139 shows that God is not surprised by any person's problems. God formed each person and He knows every person's movements, thoughts, sleep, location, everything about him. Every day is ordained by God. Your RAD child is not a mistake. Somehow, God is incorporating him and your family into His great, wise, and loving plan. He is good; for His lovingkindness is everlasting" (Ps. 118:1).

Footnotes

1. Steve Friess, *USA Today*, 14 Sept 2005, 8D.
2. Ibid.
3. Stanton E. Samenow, *Before It's Too Late: Why Some Kids Get Into Trouble—and What Parents Can Do About It* (New York: Three Rivers Press, 2001), 168.
4. Ibid., 168.
5. American Psychiatric Association, *Diagnostic and Statistical Manual of Mental Disorders*, 4th ed. (Washington, DC: American Psychiatric Association, 1994), 116.
6. Ibid., 116-118.
7. Karen Buckwalter, Associate Director of Clinical Services, and Michelle Robison, Therapist, interview by author, notes, Chaddock, Quincy, Ill., 27 Sept. 2004.

8. Buckwalter, interview.

9. Samenow, *Before It's Too Late*, 122.

10. Sara Elizabeth Kay Hall and Glenn Geher. "Behavioral and Personality Characteristics of Children With Reactive Attachment Disorder." *Journal of Psychology* 137, no. 2 (2003): 151.

11. Association for Treatment and Training in the Attachment of Children, "Signs and Symptoms of Attachment Problems," Lake Villa, IL: Association for Treatment and Training in the Attachment of Children, 2004, http://www.attach.org/signssymp.htm (13 Jan. 2005); Ken Magid and Carole A. McKelvey, *High Risk: Children Without a Conscience* (Golden, Colo.: M & M Publishing, 1987; reprint, New York: Bantam Books, 1988), 13-14; Amy Baker, "Reactive Attachment Disorder," National Association of Nouthetic Counselors Annual Conference, 2005 [CD N0507], (Chesterton, Ind.: Sound Word) (5 Nov. 2005).

12. Ken Magid and Carole A. McKelvey, *High Risk: Children Without a Conscience* (Golden, Colo.: M & M Publishing, 1987; reprint, New York: Bantam Books, 1988), 91.

13. Ibid., 81.

14. Ibid., 53.

15. Ibid., 95-96.

16. Ibid., 84-85.

17. Ibid., 86-88.

18. Robert Karen, *Becoming Attached: Unfolding the Mystery of the Infant-Mother Bond and Its Impact on Later Life* (New York: Warner Books, Inc., 1994), 56.

19. Magid and McKelvey, *High Risk*, 82.

20. The name is changed.

21. Magid and McKelvey, *High Risk*, 83.

22. Harold S. Koplewicz, *It's Nobody's Fault: New Hope and Help for Difficult Children and Their Parents*, (New York: Random House, Inc., 1996), 234.

23. Magid and McKelvey, *High Risk*, 54.

24. Ibid., 53-54.

25. Koplewicz, *Nobody's Fault*, 234.

26. Magid and McKelvey, *High Risk*, 93-94.

27. Ibid., 98.

28. Hall and Geher, "Behavioral and Personality Characteristics," 159.

29. Buckwalter, interview.

30. Koplewicz, *Nobody's Fault*, 237.

31. Hall and Geher, "Behavioral and Personality Characteristics," 159.

32. Magid and McKelvey, *High Risk*, 1.

33. Ibid., 2.

34. Koplewicz, *Nobody's Fault*, 235.

Chapter 2

Look at the Symptoms Through a Biblical Lens

Romans 15:4 says that what "was written in earlier times was written for our instruction." The Bible has much to say about a child that fits the RAD description. In chapter 1, I used psychologists' description and the concise analysis in the *DSM-IV* to identify our subject. Now, we will look at how the Bible views those same characteristics.

Jesus taught an important principle, that what you value bears fruit in what you do. He said

> For there is no good tree which produces bad fruit, nor, on the other hand, a bad tree which produces good fruit. For each tree is known by its own fruit. For men do not gather figs from thorns, nor do they pick grapes from a briar bush. The good man out of the good treasure of his heart brings forth what is good; and the evil *man* out of the evil *treasure* brings forth what is evil; for his mouth speaks from that which fills his heart. (Luke 6:43-45, italics original)

As a tree is known by the fruit it bears, so a man's values (root) are known by his words and actions (fruit). Behaviors are indicators of the state of the heart.

While use of this principle can be productive, caution must be exercised. A kiss may be given for greeting, for love, out of duty, or even for identifying a target, as Judas did to Jesus (Luke 22:47-48). The only way we can know what is in another's heart is if he tells us or Scripture explains what underlies the words and behaviors we observe. For example, Proverbs 6:6-11 and 26:13-16 show that someone who, with no justifiable reason, stays in bed a lot, is not being productive in season, and makes excuses is lazy, loves comfort, and may be cultivating fearful thoughts. Proverbs 28:22 and 11:28 indicate that a miser is greedy and a greedy person is trying to find security in money and materialism. When counseling someone who is causing a lot of trouble, we should probably investigate whether he is habitually angry and broods on anger-producing thoughts (Prov. 29:23; Ps. 37:1-8). The fruit and root principle can steer us in the direction of understanding while we correct or confirm that understanding based upon the person's own testimony or what the Scriptures say about the observed behaviors.

So then, characteristics that psychologists have observed, like shame, defensiveness, lack of trust, and pursuit of control,[1] are important indicators about what the child wants. For example, Buckwalter's summary of RAD child motivations is, "They live in a state of fight or flight.... For the child, it is survival. I have got to win this argument in order to survive."[2] This sounds like James 4:1-3, where James asks his readers why they fight and tells them that it is because they want things and when they cannot obtain those things they fight to get them. For the RAD child it is, "I will fight to get the survival that I want and must have." The child habituates to living more according to emotions than to truth. A sense of fear constantly lurks in the background. Anger covers it and is an effective manipulative tool. These are logical reactions for a child who has suffered neglect and abuse.

Looking at RAD behaviors, it appears that the most dominant underlying motivation may be self-preservation. That is the fulcrum for fear and anger, and generates his pursuit of control. A sense of justice, expressed in revenge, and autonomy also seem to be dominant desires. While there may be other motivations, these appear to be those most fundamental and compelling. This is a general disposition; in any given situation, you may not know the precise motive for a given behavior. The following review briefly examines symptoms through the lens of Scripture.[3]

Lack of eye contact

Averting the eyes can be a fear reaction (Exod. 3:6), a sign of guilt feelings (Ezra 9:6-7), a way to hide desires that the eyes might reveal (Prov. 6:13; 16:30), or a method of manipulation (Prov. 6:25). Perhaps there is an abiding shame from guilt over infractions never rectified. Eye contact communicates awareness of the other person, so lack of eye contact can be a method of alienation, revenge, hurting the other, or conveying disrespect (Ps. 27:9; Prov. 30:17; Isa. 1:15).

Resists affection on parents' terms

Risk of pain from loss of relationship may be avoided by rejecting present relationships. Refusing to be affectionate can also be a method of revenge or a rejection of authority (Luke 15:28-30; Matt. 23:37; Luke 7:32).

Inappropriately demanding and clingy

A child's rebellious behavior can induce guilt feelings or at least reap negative consequences. By showing extremely affectionate behaviors, the child can persuade himself that he is not so bad after all, even if the affection is all show and no heart (Luke 6:46). Shows of affection can manipulate attention from others. Demanding love on his terms puts him in control. If authorities do not cooperate, their seeming unkindness becomes the brush for painting them as mean (Luke 7:32). Then he can justify defiance and his demand that giving and receiving affection be on his terms.

Indiscriminately affectionate with strangers

A fearful child will want a defender (Ezek. 16:28-29). The child has learned that if he can win a new person, he has an ally when disciplined. Or he can use that new relationship to hurt the parent, like saying, "See how Teacher Mary lets me hug her? You don't love me like Teacher Mary does!" In the stranger's presence, he is nonverbally acting out what he will boldly state in private to his parent (Ezek. 16:26).

Superficially engaging and charming

Charm can be a deceitful way of getting something without showing one's true thoughts or desires (Prov. 2:16; 12:2; 29:5; 31:30). Attention received can temporarily dull the ache of loneliness. Fleecing another person can spark a thrill (Prov. 9:17). It can also inspire a sense of achievement[4] and/or control.

One motivation that is likely not at the base of attention-oriented behaviors (clinging, affection toward strangers, charm) is desire for approval. This child is the card shark, not the circus clown. He wants control, the fleece, the ally, or validation of how mean and inept his authorities are.

Phoniness, Relational deceitfulness

This characteristic is similar to that above. Hypocritical love (Rom. 12:9) fakes relationship without commitment; it keeps the other at arm's length. It keeps up appearances while the person also covertly pursues his own agenda. Jesus addressed the phoniness of people's supposed close relationship with God when He said, "Why do you call me Lord, Lord, and do not do what I say?" (Luke 6:46).

Poor peer relationships

Any child who is centered on protecting himself, his rights, and his possessions, and on trying to control others, is going to have problems keeping friends (Prov. 13:10; 16:28). A loner is selfish (Prov. 18:1).

Abnormal speech patterns

Speech and language abnormalities, like persistent nonsense questions and incessant chatter (Prov. 10:8, 19), are an easy and effective control method. The book of Proverbs is packed with verses on foolish and manipulative speech.

Learning problems (disabilities, delays)

While some RAD children truly have learning problems, the learning problem of many is simply that they refuse to learn. Quickness to learn what they want belies test results indicative of retardation or learning disabilities.

There may be several reasons for the refusal to learn. A child obsessed with safety is too distracted to learn and avoids risk of failure (Matt. 25:24-25). Learning is hard work. An appearance of being stupid can dupe others, possibly inducing teachers and parents to reduce the work load and expect less (Prov. 12:20). Learning situations are opportunities to play control games (Prov. 9:17; 10:23; 26:18-19). Some people take delight in showing contempt for knowledge (Prov. 1:22, 25).

Whatever the reasons, learning time is wasted and education lost. Then, it can appear that the child is less intelligent when the real problem is a refusal to learn (Prov. 1:7; 22).

Abnormal eating patterns

Fear and revenge can motivate stealing and hoarding (Luke 12:18). Eating odd things may stir a sense of control over natural reactions, produce a thrill, or gain attention.

Theft, pointless theft

Many desires motivate theft, including anger. Possession of a forbidden object gives a sense of power over the object and over those from whom it was stolen (Prov. 9:17; 20:17). This is true regarding possession of pets and, in adults, kidnapped people.

Destructive to self, others, property, cruel to animals

Anger commonly leads to destructive behaviors. Revenge motivated Esau to plot to kill Jacob (Gen. 27:41). Fear could be a motive when there is a desire to avoid discovery of a crime. The Pharisees plotted Jesus' death to avoid facing the truth about Him. Cruelty to animals can excite a sense of power (control) or be a convenient and "safe" outlet for anger.

Preoccupied with fire, blood, weapons, and gore

The child who is afraid will think about what he can use to protect himself (Matt. 12:14; 26:4-5, 59; 27:1-2). The child who is angry plans how to get revenge.

Difficulty learning from mistakes

Proverbs 27:22 describes the RAD child when it says, "Though you pound a fool in a mortar with a pestle along with crushed grain, yet his foolishness will not depart from him." The foolish accounts that what he wants is worth suffering the same consequences repeatedly. Habits are hard to change.

Poor impulse control

Often, when people are feeling afraid or furious, they do not think logically. They react impulsively (Prov. 12:16, 18; 17:14). Lack of self-control becomes a habit.

Intense control battles

For the child who is afraid, control of others produces a sense of power and invulnerability. For the child who is angry, provocations can achieve revenge.

Besides, contests can be fun. That is why people play games and sports. Some people enjoy wrangling over words (2 Tim. 2:14, 16, 23), so Paul warned Timothy to not get caught up in it. Like a coal to fire is a RAD child to strife (Prov. 26:21; 17:19); he is constantly hot to spark a fight for control.

Hypervigilance/Hyperactivity

Someone who feels constantly threatened, who feels driven to maintain control, must be always on the alert. Hypervigilance keeps him attuned to people. For example, feeling threatened, the Pharisees watched Jesus, spied on Him, and tried to trap Him (Matt. 20:19-20). Like a boxer, the hypervigilant person studies others to find weaknesses and stays ready to seize opportunities.

Chronic lying, lying about the obvious

Lies ward off punishment and guilt and keep others baffled. The Pharisees lied to themselves, and lied to others by refusing to answer when they did not want to admit to the obvious (Luke 20:1-8). Lying may arise from an abiding sense of guilt. "The wicked flee when no one is pursuing" (Prov. 28:1). Tricking others can also be a thrilling challenge. Whatever the reason, lying becomes an automatic reflex (Hosea 11:12-12:1).

Shows no remorse, seeming lack of conscience

Feelings of remorse are unpleasant, so people avoid them. A feeling of guilt implies a fault or weakness, which produces fear. Some people get angry at the idea of being wrong. The child becomes all the more desperate to rid himself of remorse feelings by justifying his actions.

To the person who considers his own survival to be the ultimate value, it seems logical that self-defensive behaviors must be rightful and good. With this view, the survivalist determines that he deserves what he steals or that he deserves the right of retaliation. People who love control will not care who they hurt to get the things they want (James 4:2-3). They will care more about keeping everyone under their control than about the basic needs of others (Matt. 9:9-13; 15:1-9; Luke 13:14). Examples of hardheartedness and shamelessness are throughout Scripture—Sodom, Esau, Pharaoh, Israel's child sacrifices, the Pharisees. In these examples, people demanded to do what they wanted without responsibility to any authority for it.

Refusal to request help

This characteristic is not listed in RAD literature. I have added it based upon my own observations only because I think it is an indicator of an underlying attitude essential to the child's alienation. The observation is, an antisocial child obtains what he wants by his own way (through power or manipulation) or else not at all. Just like the angry people described in James 4:2-3, he will suffer loss or pain rather than ask for help, or even for simple wants like a toy or an outing.

This trait is easily missed, probably because absence of something is harder to spot than its presence. It takes time for parents to realize how often they think, "I would love to have given him that. If only he would tell me what he would like to have. If only he would ask." It is an important piece of the puzzle because it silently shouts, "I don't need you!" A RAD child appears determined to trust in only himself (Prov. 3:5; 16:25; 28:26).

Checking the Wide Angle

Our psychological labels are manmade categorizations. Even though the Bible speaks to every human condition, it would be impertinent to demand that it fit our categories. We must find our solutions in the Bible's categories, not vice versa.

What people do and say expresses something about their heart desires. Major themes for a RAD child include self-preservation (selfishness), control, fear and anger, bitterness and brooding, and making emotional rather than rational decisions. Over all, the characteristics fit what the Bible calls an "angry man" (Prov. 29:22). Another pertinent big-picture label that accompanies and facilitates anger might be "he who separates himself" (Prov. 18:1), which we might abbreviate to "alienated."

The charts on the following pages provides a sampling of possible biblical evaluations of the RAD child's characteristics. You can use the accompanying verses to gain a clearer understanding of your child and as a starting point for probing what might be your child's particular motivation in the moment.

Possible Biblical Evaluations of RAD Behaviors

Rad Characteristic	Behavioral Expression	Possible Motivation/Heart Issue	Scripture
Lack of Eye Contact	• Looking down	• Fear reaction • Guilt • Hiding Intent	Exod. 3:6 Ezra 9:6-7 Prov. 6:13; 16:30
	• Averting face or eyes • Hiding the face	• Rejection	Ps. 13:1; 27:9 Isa. 1:15
	• Mocking parents with eyes	• Arrogance, • Disrespect	Prov. 30:11-13, 17

Resists affection on parents' terms	• Accusing instead of receiving affection
	• Despises parents
		• Fear of rejection or harm
		• Jealousy
		• Revenge
		• Control
		• Rejecting Authority
			Prov. 15:20
			1 Sam. 13:6-8
			  - *People fled*
			Luke 15:28-30
			  - *Older son*

	• Stubborn resistance of physical affection	• Rebellion	Matt. 23:37 - *Jerusalem*
	• Flute and dirge (happy face, sad face)	• Control	Luke 7:32 - *Pharisees*

Inappropriately demanding and clingy	• Demands affection on own terms
	• Show of affection, but disobedient
		• Fear of rejection
		• Desire/demand for attention or security
		• Love of control
		• Hiding and distracting
			Prov. 9:17; 23:7;
			  29:5; 30:20
			Gen. 27 - *Jacob*
			Lev. 10 - *Nadab and Abihu*
			Judg. 3:15-23
			  - *Ehud*
			Luke 6:46;
			  15:28-30
			  - *Older son*

	• Seizing and hugging	• Luring for a selfish purpose	Prov. 7:13; 23:6-8 Judg. 16 - *Delilah* Ezek. 16:15, 25, 32-33

Rad Characteristic	Behavioral Expression	Possible Motivation/Heart Issue	Scripture
Indiscriminately affectionate with strangers	• Seizing and hugging	• Luring for a selfish purpose	Prov. 7:13; 23:6-8 Judg. 16 - *Delilah* Ezek. 16:15, 25, 32-33
	• Flirting • Seducing	• Demand for affection on own terms • Desire for control	Ezek. 16:15, 25, 32-33
	• Seducing strangers while rejecting family	• Revenge • To make parents angry • Sense of intimacy without responsibility • Disloyalty • Fear of rejection or broken trust (trust in man)	Ezek. 16:26 Prov. 25:19 Jer. 17:5-8 John 9:18-22 - *Blind man's parents*
	• Winning a friend	• Obtaining a defender	Ezek. 16:28-29
Superficially engaging and charming	• Empty words • Bribery • Flattery	• Cover disobedience • Control • Obtain underhandedly • Entrap	Ezek. 16:33 Prov. 2:16; 29:5; 31:30 Luke 6:46
	• Charming words	• Deceit	Matt. 15:8-9
	• Veneer of respectability	• To spy • To manipulate	Matt. 20:20
Poor peer relationships	• Conflicts • Frequent broken friendships • Few friends	• Sowing and reaping consequences • Pride and autonomy • Thrill of the hunt for winning new loyalties • Fear of rejection	Exod. 10:11 Prov. 13:10; 16:28; 1:10-14; 2:16-17; 7:12-13; 18:1

Rad Characteristic	Behavioral Expression	Possible Motivation/Heart Issue	Scripture
Abnormal speech patterns	• Chattering • Outbursts • Rash speech • Dissension	• Fear • Control • Anger • Revenge • Lack of self-control	Prov. 10:8, 19 12:16, 18 Gal. 5:19
	• Perverted in language	• Crooked heart	Prov. 17:20
	• Calling to strangers	• To lure	Prov. 9:14-15
	• Not eloquent	• Fear	Exod. 4:10
Learning problems	• Refusal to try • Careless	• Fear • Anger • Control • Laziness	Matt. 25:24-25 Prov. 12:20; 9:13-17; 10:23; 26:18-19
	• Despises being instructed	• Rebellion • Wise in his own eyes	Prov. 1:7, 22, 25; 3:7; 18:2
Abnormal eating patterns	• Eating too much; • Hoarding	• Fear • Safety • Gluttony • Greed • Lack of self-control	Prov. 23:20; 25:27; Luke 12:18
	• Odd (out of carcass)		Judg. 14:8-9
Theft, pointless theft	• Theft	• Coveting • Love of possessing things • Control • Craving	Josh. 7:20-21 *- Achan* 2 Pet. 2:14
	• Theft	• Fear of loss • Treasured object	Gen. 31:19, 34
Destructive to self, others, property	• Attacks on another • Cruel • To cause injustice	• Fear • Enjoyment of cruelty • Revenge • Hatred	Prov. 12:10; Matt. 20:19; Jer. 6:23 *- Assyrians* Matt. 27:20 *- Chief Priests*
Cruelty to animals	• Cruelty to animals	• Animal won't cooperate • Retaliation • Convenient target for anger	Prov. 12:10; Num. 22:27-29 *- Balaam*

Rad Characteristic	Behavioral Expression	Possible Motivation/Heart Issue	Scripture
Preoccupied with fire, blood, weapons, gore	• Starts fires • Draws and reads about weapons and gore • Acts and words demonstrate fascination with fire, blood, gore, weapons	• Fear • Loves the thrill • Loves evil; hates to leave it • Unforeseen consequences of foolishness • Does not care what it costs him	Prov. 13:19; 1:18-19 Judg. 14; 16:4-21 - Sampson
	• Plotting to kill • Lying in wait for blood	• Fear • Response to threat • Coveting • Greed • Love of evil	Prov. 1:11-16; 13:19 Hosea 4:2 Matt. 12:14 Luke 22:2 - Counseled how to seize and destroy Jesus John 7:32 - Tried sending officers to seize, stoning John 10:31-33 - Stoning Matt. 26:59; 27:1-2 - Weapon of false testimony Matt. 27:1-2 - Pilate as weapon
Difficulty learning from mistakes	• Learns nothing from consequences	• Enjoys mischief • Loves evil	Prov. 10:23; 13:19 26:11; 27:22
	• Responds poorly to discipline • Hardens against reproof	• Fear • Anger • Stubborn • Rebellion	Prov. 17:10; 29:11 1 Sam. 15:23
Poor impulse control	• Impulsive behaviors • Behaves according to feelings	• Feeling-oriented • Habit • Escape the situation or feelings	Prov. 12:16, 18; 17:14; 5:22-23; 25:28

Rad Characteristic	Behavioral Expression	Possible Motivation/Heart Issue	Scripture
Intense control battles	• Various verbal and behavioral manipulations • Stubbornness	• Fear of loss • Anger • Bitterness • Selfish love of winning • Simple pride	2 Tim. 2:14, 16, 23 Hosea 7:4-7 Heb. 12:15 James 4:1-3 Prov. 26:21; 17:19
Hypervigilance	• Watching • Spying	• Fear loss of control • To spy, control an authority	Matt. 20:19-20 Prov. 7:13-14
	• Watching	• To betray for gain	Luke 22:3-4 *- Judas* Prov. 1:11, 13
Chronic lying, Lying about the obvious	• About the obvious • Multiplied lying	• Fear • Rebellion • Unruly (restless straying)	Matt. 20:1-8 *- Pharisees* Hosea 11:12-12:1
Lack of remorse, conscience	• Repeated cruelty • Hates to turn from wrong-doing	• Rebellion against authority • Demand for control • Demand to possess • Exchange truth for lie	Luke 20:9-15; *- Cain; Pharaoh (Exodus); Esau* Ezek. 16:49 Prov. 30:12; 16:2 James 4:2-3 Rom. 1:18-32
Lack of compassion (complement to lack of remorse)	• Cruel • No compassion	• Pride • Love of self • Fear (Self-preservation)	Prov. 12:10, 15 Ezek. 16:49 Luke 10:30-32 *- Priest and Levite*
	• Scolding • Demeaning	• Pride (Haughty)	Luke 13:10-14 *- Synagogue official* Prov. 20:20; 30:11,17
Refusal to request help	• Suffers loss and even deprivation rather than ask for something	• Desire for what is forbidden • Pride and autonomy	James 4:2 Prov. 18:1; 3:7; 28:26 *- Eve with Satan, David with Bathsheba*

⊢ Footnotes ⊣

1. Kelly Wilson, "Helping Kids Help Themselves," *Quincy Herald-Whig* (Quincy, Ill.) 22 Aug. 2004, 6A.
2. Buckwalter, interview.
3. These descriptions were compiled from personal experiences and from Baker, "Reactive Attachment Disorder."
4. Alan Harrington, *Psychopaths* (New York: Simon and Schuster, 1972), 225.

Chapter 3
Human Nature 101

It has been said that anyone who behaves so illogically as a child labeled Reactive Attachment Disordered must be mentally ill or disordered. The aberrant infant and child behaviors are so strange and extreme that society labels the child "pathological."[1]

Actually, behavioral problems need not be so mystifying. For example, when David ran in fear from Saul, he first ran right into the nest of his enemies, the Philistines (1 Sam. 21:10-15). How crazy is that?! Solving one problem created another because the Philistines had a propensity to skewer enemies. So to avoid becoming shish kebob, he pretended to be insane. It worked. They excused him for his mental illness. What appeared irrational to the Philistines actually had a totally rational explanation.

So does the behavior of a RAD child. This chapter and the next establish, from a biblical perspective, a foundation for understanding children's behavior in general and what factors make any child vulnerable to RAD symptomatology. This chapter discusses the nature of a child, the source of motivations, and the influence of nurture.

Nature of Babies

Since the mid-1900s, psychologists have tried to understand the essence of an infant's attachment to his mother. Behavioral researcher Harry Harlow asked, "What is an infant's love for its mother?" and used rhesus monkey research to answer the question. He found that rhesus monkey babies "raised" by surrogate wire moms with food and cloth moms without food went to the wire moms only for food. Otherwise, they cuddled the cloth moms, especially when frightened. He concluded that love during babyhood is vital.[2] He said that it is "love" that drives a frightened toddler to run to its mother for comfort.[3] John Bowlby, the founder of attachment theory, states that "for babies to love mothers and mothers to love babies is taken for granted as intrinsic to human nature." One example of infant love that he cites is thirteen-month-old Bob, a subject in a study of several mother-child dyads. Bob constantly watched his mother. When his mother became too absorbed in other activities, he whined and expressed frustration.[4] Bowlby espoused that love begins at birth and that the best lover of all is a child.[5]

Is it true that babies naturally love mothers? Do the behaviors of Harlow's frightened toddler and Bowlby's Bob demonstrate love? According to 1 Corinthians 13, love is patient, kind, and not jealous. That is not Bob. Love "does not seek its own, is not provoked." How many thirteen-month-olds fit this description? Love is self-sacrifice for the welfare of another, hardly a trademark of children. So, whatever this attraction is of a baby to its mother, it is not love.

A child may learn to love others, but a baby is not born inclined to love anyone but himself. He is not inclined to love because he is not inherently good, nor even neutral. Psalm 58:3 says, "The wicked are estranged from the womb; these who speak lies go astray from birth." Babies, like all people, are inherently sinful, harboring selfish intentions from the day of birth (Gen. 8:21; Eph. 2:1-3). Precious as babies are, foolishness is inseparably woven into their hearts (Prov. 22:15). The sin nature permeates every aspect of every person, but that does not mean that every person is as bad as he could be. People have some vestiges of the image of God. They have intellectual, moral, and social capacities to do some good things, as people count good. But because of sin, every aspect is stained so that no person bears the image of God in purity and completeness. We are born preprogrammed for selfishness. The constant tendency of little children is to go their own way (Isa. 53:6; Jer 17:9). "I," "me," "my," "mine" is their constant theme. In AD 397-398, Augustine wrote of his observation that moral innocence in a baby is an illusion:

> What then was my sin? Was it that I hung upon the breast and cried? For should I now so do for food suitable to my age, justly should I be laughed at and reproved. What I then did was worthy reproof; but since I could not understand reproof, custom and reason forbade me to be reproved.... Was it then good, even for a while, to cry for what, if given, would hurt? Bitterly to resent that persons free, and its own elders, yea, the very authors of its birth, served it not? That many besides, wiser than it, obeyed not the nod of its good pleasure? To do its best to strike and hurt, because commands were not obeyed, which had been obeyed to its hurt? The weakness then of infant limbs, not its will, is its innocence.... Though tolerated now, the very same tempers are utterly intolerable when found in riper years.[6]

As Augustine realized, inability, not choice, is what makes infants seem sinless. This is not to say that all crying from pain or hunger is sin. The point is that all people are, from the womb, contrary at heart (Gen. 6:5; Col. 3:5-8). Puddn'head Wilson illustrated man's basic nature in irony: "Adam was but human—this explains it all. He did not want that apple for the apple's sake, he wanted it only because it was forbidden. The mistake was in not forbidding the serpent: then he would have eaten the serpent." [7]

Desires and Choices

Desire and choice are key elements of human behavior. For illustration purposes, imagine the hypothetical Donnie as a normal small child playing in the park near "Mama" (Mrs. DeSpare) in a typical situation similar to Harlow's frightened child and Bowlby's Bob. While Mama gazes at the pond, Donnie examines a bug in the grass. When he hears feet pounding and the jangle of tags on a collar, Donnie looks up and sees a big dog running at him. Maybe he dashes toward Mama who, seeing his face and actions, determines fairly accurately why Donnie is running toward her (probably fear) and what he most wants (safety). Donnie is looking to Mama to deliver what he wants.

Wants is the operative word. Scripture portrays man as motivated by desire. James told his readers that "each one is tempted when he is carried away and enticed by his own lust" (James 1:14). He asked, "Isn't the reason you fight because you lust [want, desire] and do not have, so you fight to get what you want?" (4:1-3, *paraphrased*). According to the Bible, desires are generated in the "heart." The immaterial heart thinks (Ezek. 11:5), generates desires (Mark 7:20-23), perceives, doubts, and believes (Mark 11:23), and plans and intends (Luke 12:45; Acts 5:4; Heb. 4:12).

Desires can be good. Joseph fled from Potiphar's wife because he wanted a good desire, to please God (Gen. 39:7-9). James teaches that whether we do good or sin, the reason we do it is because we want something.

Even babies desire and make choices. Newborns in research studies choose human faces above other visual patterns. Newborns given electronically-wired pacifiers choose, by the rate of sucking, which music they hear. They choose human voices over music, and their mother's voice rather than the voices of others. [8]

Babies take action on their choices, like by changing the rate of sucking. Babies just out of the hospital may refuse to breast feed if they take a liking to the ease of bottle-feeding in the hospital nursery.

Babies who do not want to be held will squirm or arch their backs, or even pull themselves out of their mothers' arms. Babies fuss if they do not get the attention they want and show delight when they do get it. Precious as they are, babies can and do deliberately apply behaviors to obtain what they want or gain relief from what they do not want.

So then, choice is not driven by circumstances but by wants. Circumstances just provide the framework for the wants. Therefore, although nurture is influential, good or bad parenting is not the determinative factor for how a child develops. For example, Ezekiel 18 describes a righteous man whose son turned violent (18:10-13). The violent man raised a son who turned to righteousness (18:14-18). King Asa is an example. Although he had a wicked father, he chose to do what was right (1 Kings 15:1, 3, 9, 11). In these cases, the sons chose lifestyles contradictory to what an environment-determinative model predicts. Right parenting does not guarantee a good parent-child relationship as though the child is automated to respond rightly if the parents train rightly. Nor can children blame the past for their continued selfish choices in the present. Parents are influential, but not determinative.[9]

Psychologists debate whether nature or nurture dominates the development of children. Science uses the word "nature" to indicate the physiological makeup of a person, his genetics and brain structure. Scripture uses the word "nature" to indicate the character and moral bent of the person, the inner man, the immaterial aspect, including his mind, perceptions, values, desires, intents, and will. According to Scripture, it is not nurture and it is not nature (genetics and brain), but it is nature (immaterial inner man/heart) that dominates choices and development.

 Desire-driven choice of the sinful heart/nature is a vital key to the RAD problem.

Moses appealed to choice when he said, "I am setting before you today a blessing and a curse" (Deut. 11:26). Joshua said, "Choose today whom you will serve" (Josh. 24:15). Jesus frequently informed people that loving Him would require a choice, one that countered both human nature and cultural training (Luke 14:26-27). Volition, exercised in the immaterial nature of man, can override both physiological construction and social influences. Therefore, and wonderfully, an abused child is not consigned to a criminal lifestyle like the attachment model predicts.

Truth in Compassion

But an infant doesn't know right and wrong. Isn't it harsh to blame him for his choices? This question reveals a lack of biblical thinking and misdirection from the goal.

First, obviously ignorance calls for age-appropriate instruction. It should be carefully seasoned with grace and discipline to reshape habits.

Second, ignorance about right and wrong does not cancel guilt. Leviticus 5:17 says, "Now if a person sins and does any of the things which the Lord has commanded not to be done, *though he was unaware*, still he is guilty and shall bear his punishment" (emphasis added). For example, I have lived in several states. When a new resident, if I broke a traffic law of which I was ignorant, that ignorance of laws would not excuse me from a ticket. The solution to ignorance is instruction.

Third, the issue is not blame but a right understanding toward a good end. A doctor diagnoses cancer not to be harsh, but because the truth will guide him to the right cure and save the life. The goal for using biblical terms to identify the child's sinful response to abuse is so that the biblical solution can be accurately determined. Non-biblical, morally neutral terms, though they sound non-confrontative, can actually be unkind. By veiling the problem in vagueness they distract from or conceal the solution. Exactly what does one do with "dissociative behavior," "problematic stress regulation," or "collapse of attachment system organization"? A descriptive like "negative aggressive affect" blurs the distinctions of the anger, lying, hitting, sassing, and stealing that Donnie is doing in Mr. and Mrs. DeSpare's house.

Condemnation is not the goal of any theorist or counselor. But shifting responsibility to parents, genetics, neural disorganization, lack of attachment, inability to trust, and unmet needs is not compassionate because it shifts the responsibility away from the one person who can choose to change–the child. Moral neutrality squelches hope.

In contrast, when the sin is lovingly revealed, the angry child can, by God's grace, receive forgiveness, salvation from the power of sin, and empowerment to make right choices. If the problem is ignorance or misguided habituation, the child can receive instruction and support in practice. Truth, lovingly conveyed, offers the real compassion.

Responsibility of Parents

Placing responsibility on a child for his choices does not relieve parents of their responsibilities. Scripture acknowledges that parents influence children. It is evident in God's commands that parents instruct and in Proverbs' many exhortations that children listen to parents. Scripture says that children absorb parents' ideas, habits, and mannerisms and that what is absorbed includes sinful habits (Ps. 106:6; Jer. 9:14; 1 Pet. 1:18).

God takes very seriously the power of parents over these little people He has entrusted into their hands and proscribes against negative influence. Ephesians 6:4 tells fathers, "Do not provoke your children to anger." Violation of that verse is a sin like any other. Parents are responsible for how they parent.

Benefits of Nurture

How does a positive relationship with a mother influence the infant in his sin nature? It prevents provocation to sin; it teaches; and it woos.

Considering that a high percentage of children diagnosed with RAD are adoptees and foster children, psychologists are right that there is something happening with respect to relational continuity and type of caregiving. It is no psychological mystery. The Bible teaches that generally, people respond in kind. Harsh treatment most often provokes angry responses. Kindness and gentle treatment cools anger and encourages gentle responses (Prov. 15:1, 18; 21:14; Judg. 8:1-9). People like those who give gifts and show themselves friendly and may become loyal to them (Prov. 19:6). A man's gift makes room for him (Prov. 18:16), which is exactly what parents want in their children's hearts. A baby's reciprocity may begin as interaction and his possessiveness of his parents or the caregivers with whom he is familiar. It develops into affection and trust and, hopefully, grows into real love as the child learns from the parents what 1 Corinthians 13 love is.

A child who is fearful or angry due to maltreatment will not be teachable because any profitable lesson the parent tries to teach is drowned by the din of parental offense (Prov. 15:1; 10:12; 1 Kings 12:1-18). On the other hand, parental love facilitates learning because kindness quiets the already active sin nature of the child (Prov. 15:1) and "makes knowledge acceptable" (Prov. 15:2). This is how Timothy's mother shaped his thinking and conscience "from childhood" (2 Tim. 3:14-15). Kind shepherding quiets the clamor of the child's fear and pride so that he can hear the lesson being taught free of distracting concerns of self-defense. Love demonstrated provides a model by which the child learns what real love is (Phil. 2:5; 1 Pet. 2:21). It entices him to make right responses to instruction and correction and encourages him to exert the effort required for self-control.

Like sugar water entices hummingbirds, loving nurture woos the little child to reciprocate with love for others. And loving others, not feeling loved, is the essence of being sociable. By loving the child, parents are not filling some inner empty spot or bargaining, "If I love you, you must reciprocate." Rather, love attracts, invites, models, and persuades (Prov. 15:1a; 15:18b; 25:15a).

Footnotes

1. Magid and McKelvey, *High Risk*, 81, and John Bowlby, *Attachment and Loss*, 2d ed., vol. 1 (New York: Basic Books, 1982), 242

2. Deborah Blum, *Love at Goon Park: Harry Harlow and the Science of Affection* (Cambridge, Mass.: Perseus Publishing, 2002), 159, 178, 5.

3. Blum, *Goon Park*, 2-4.

4. John Bowlby, *Attachment and Loss*, 2d ed., vol. 1 (New York: Basic Books, 1982), 242, 254.

5. Blum, *Goon Park*, 170.

6. Saint Augustine, *The Confessions*, Book 1, Section 11, translated by Edward Bouverie Pusey. *Augustine*, vol. 18, The Great Books of the Western World, ed. Robert Maynard Hutchins (William Benton, Publisher. Chicago: Encyclopaedia Britannica, Inc. 1952), 3.

7. Mark Twain, *Puddn'head Wilson* (New York: Bantam Books, Mar. 1981), 6.

8. Karen, *Becoming Attached*, 347-348.

9. John Street, "A Biblical View of Child Development for Biblical Counselors," National Association of Nouthetic Counselors Annual Conference, 2005 [CD N0550], (Chesterton, Ind.: Sound Word) (5 Nov. 2005).

Chapter 4
Alienation:
How it Develops

What situations appear to instigate the symptoms collectively labeled Reactive Attachment Disorder? Consider the case of Lila, a war orphan from Bosnia, who was confined in a crib for her first two years and received attention only for feedings and diaper changes. Or there is the case of Donnie, whose drug-addicted mom was jailed when he was an infant and he was shifted through six homes in the foster care system before being adopted at age three. He had no time to become familiar with anyone. Maria was found abandoned on the street at age three, with scars showing abuse. She lived in an orphanage for two years vying for the attention of too few overworked caregivers, having no possessions of her own, fighting for emotional survival among peers as desperate and angry as she. Carter was in the hospital for his first three months and had several surgeries during infancy. His parents both worked and cared for their other children, so he was usually alone and without comfort in the hospital. His parents could do nothing to stop his worst pain. These are examples of the neglect, maltreatment, or painful experiences that are common to children labeled RAD.

How do these experiences lead to RAD behaviors? Tina's doctor told her that their inexplicable son "did not have the love he needed when he was born and you just need to love give him a loving home" (*sic*). A specialist told her, "Damage is done to the frontal lobe when in the first 6 months a child's needs are not met. A chemical is secreted in response to this stress, and it is a toxin that will never be reversed."[1] As is shown in Part 3 of this book, there is no scientific validation of this etiology. These professionals are counseling out of a psychology-driven philosophy, not medical science, and offer no real hope.

The Bible's explanation provides far more hope because it leads directly to solutions. In a biblical view, the hurt child reacts with fear and anger that grow into bitterness, rebellion, fanatical self-preservation, and obsessive demand for control. Five key factors in the process include the sin nature, desire, choice, self-trust, and habituation. Emotions complicate the mix. Simplified, the hurt child reacts out of a mind twisted by sin so that he misperceives, believes lies, and generates selfish desires. Initially craving a sense of security (not to rule out other desires), he trusts in himself to gain it. His erroneous perceptions, feeling orientation, and sinful attitudes and behaviors become magnified and implacable through habituation. The Bible speaks effectively to all of these factors.

Look Again at Hope

Does it seem hardhearted to say that an abused two-year-old has sinned by responding wrongly to maltreatment when he had neither the training nor the mental aptitude to respond any differently? That depends upon whether it is said to condemn or to aid. Maltreatment is a horrible wrong. But excusing present rebellion for the sake of his past only compounds the problem by crying over his battered limbs while his bones calcify misshapen. This is not mercy. Pity doesn't heal. What demonstrates true compassion is to show him his way out. Get those limbs reset, give him crutches, and get him moving.

To help him, you need a biblical assessment of his worldview. Then you can know how to reset his thinking and get him moving in the right direction. To that end, this chapter continues from the last, highlighting the effect of moral corruption on the mind, self-trust, and habituation.

Effects of Sin on the Mind

In most RAD cases, mistreatment and neglect have tempted the infant to fear and anger, yet the only person he knows who might help him is the one who is hurting him. What a tragic dilemma! As a child grapples with his plight, his thoughts are a key factor in his reactions, so it is important to examine sin's effects on the mind.

In Psalm 42:5, we find someone listening to and talking to himself. He says, "Why are you in despair, O my soul? ... Hope in God." People constantly listen to and talk to themselves in their thoughts. The trouble is that, because the mind is morally corrupted, we deceive ourselves (Ps. 14:1).

 "The heart is more deceitful than all else..." (Jer. 17:9).

Rather than see truth accurately, we view it from a selfish, inaccurate, and distorted orientation (Eph. 4:18). For example, right thoughts about justice for abuses can be perverted into thoughts of revenge which we are quick to justify (Prov. 16:2).

Little children have no experience or knowledge of God's Word as a foundation for making accurate judgments about reality. Their minds are susceptible to appealing ideas from others and their own imaginations (Eph. 4:14; 2 Cor. 10:5). What is a baby to think about a chilly bath when he prefers being dry and warm, or when he is picked up and given to Grandma just when he was pleasantly drifting to sleep? What is he to think of Mama when she feeds him nasty peas instead of those tasty cookies? With an inborn sin tendency and lack of discernment, little ones are especially prone to faulty conclusions and they generate erroneous perceptions, beliefs, and imaginations. Further experiences are filtered selectively through those erroneous perceptions. By this practice he may, e.g., deliberately deny the truth that another person might actually be faithfully loving him (Rom. 1:19-23).[2]

The fearful, angry child deludes himself like King Saul did. His digression is recorded in 1 Samuel. David was faithfully serving Saul in a variety of ways. But when Saul understood that he would lose his kingdom to David, fear caused suspicion of David. Brooding exaggerated his fear until he viewed David as a personal threat. He became aggressive and then exiled (alienated) David from him. He repeatedly plotted David's demise and became "David's enemy continually." When he kept failing to achieve his goal of securing his rule by David's death, an abiding anger took hold. He even turned on his own son. Others, such as the innocent priests at Nob, were also wrongly perceived as threats to be destroyed without compunction. Saul irrationally wasted years of his life obsessed with killing David. All the while, David would have gladly served him (18:6-9; 10-15; 20-29; 20:30-34; 22:8-13; 14-19; 24-27).

Fear of loss and desire for gain fit hand in hand. We can often discover a desire by identifying the fear of loss. If Saul feared loss of his kingship, then he wanted the kingdom and was determined to have it. When a child fears loss of something like security, he also has a driving desire for security and probably other related objectives such as comfort, control, or possessions.

How can RAD behavior become so extreme? Proverbs 18:14 says that people can endure physical discomfort, but "a broken spirit who can bear it?" Repeated emotional hurts from his caregiver are hard to bear when they are not properly resolved. Common responses include include anger, withdrawal, retaliation, efforts to prevent another occurrence, and other responses. As the situation continues, the little child goes to increasingly extreme lengths to control his environment so as to prevent discomforts and make the situation "right" as he perceives "right" to be. The anger, manipulations, and other behaviors are tools applied to gain that end.

Unresolved anger usually precipitates a rehearsing of the offense. Rehearsing, anticipating hurtful situations, planning preventive measures, and plotting revenge all require time in thought. This is brooding. Psalm 37:8 says, "Cease from anger and forsake wrath; do not fret [brood]; it leads only to evildoing." Brooding is closely tied to anger. Brooding habituates an attitude of anger and sprouts the seed of bitterness into a root (Heb. 12:15). A bitter root will bear bitter fruit.

Self-imposed alienation complicates the problem because there is no accountability; his brooding imagination can run wild (Prov. 18:1). As he cogitates on the record of wrongs and his own ever more distorted fears and demands, he grows more suspicious. His beliefs and behaviors become exaggerated. He is prone to erroneously conclude that others are mad at him or that his survival is at stake. He may attribute hostility to others even for kindnesses. As a result, he approaches others with hypervigilance and anger.[3]

A person who habitually thinks of others as opponents out to hurt him cannot sustain a concept of them as persons because if he is hating persons then there is guilt for his hatred, and guilt feelings are too heavy to bear. His worldview depersonalizes people into objects and allows for only two categories, enemies and victims, or threats and tools (Prov. 21:10). No way will he cooperate with anyone! What began with hurt and fear developed into stubborn anger and rebellion.

Subversive Trust in Self

Since neither enemies nor victims can be trusted to provide safety, the RAD-type child chooses self-sufficiency. Like Saul, he relies on his own understanding (Prov. 3:5) for how to gain the desires he craves and satisfy his sense of justice for the perceived wrongs. Jeremiah writes, "Cursed is the man who trusts in mankind," himself in this child's case, and "Blessed is the man who trusts in the Lord" (17:5, 7).

Trust in self is central to the problem of Reactive Attachment Disorder.

Can infants really practice emotional self-sufficiency? Emotional self-comfort is what thumb-sucking is. Later, infants comfort themselves with other objects (favorite blanket) and people (moms). Rejecting people, an alienated child has learned that he can comfort and counsel himself and, all by himself, survive deprivation.

James speaks to the self-sufficiency of his readers when he says, "You lust and do not have; so you commit murder.... You do not have because you do not ask" (James 4:2). Rather than ask God to grant their desires, his readers determined to obtain what they wanted by their their own means. Likewise, rather than run to God, Saul resorted to brooding, anger, aggression, false accusations, and murder. While David often reacted to fear in godly ways, one of his sinful responses was a play of schizophrenia. Self-sufficiency leads to extreme, even bizarre, behaviors.

Why would a supposedly needy child do such an irrational thing as to deliberately provoke loving parents to discipline, anger, or rejection? Each child will have his own reasons, but let me suggest a few possibilities. Perhaps their love tempts him to care for them and he fears being hurt if they fail him. Perhaps he considers them unjust to dare expect him to give up his independence. Perhaps the pain is worth getting evidence (the parental discipline) of parents' so-called rejection to justify his perception of parents as bad. Perhaps it validates both his right and ability to control them rather than love them. It justifies anger and rebellion.

Some would argue that he behaves badly and provokes rejection because he sees himself as bad. Identity is certainly a factor. It can become a beloved possession feeding the "us versus them" mentality that provides a sense of uniqueness and determinism (Prov 1:14). Many people excuse sin with, "That's just the way I am."

Desire for thrills can be habit-forming. People get a buzz out of flirting with danger. The daredevil biker or street racer are examples. Others enjoy the thrill of seeing if they can get by with theft or with tricking other people (Prov. 9:17; 26:18-19). They become risk-takers. So, for example, what if the strongest desire of the hypothetical Donnie in the park was not safety, but the adrenaline rush from overcoming danger? He might stand and face the dog rather than run to his mom. This act may seem strange to Mrs. DeSpare, who assumes that Donnie would be afraid. But Donnie likes the thrill. Besides, in antisocial thinking, Mama is not an option because she is an enemy or a victim. Handling danger by himself is presumed.

Self-sufficiency affirms selfishness. If the child doesn't depend on others, then neither should they expect anything from him. He is free from responsibility to love them.

Privacy is another self-sufficient reaction to fear. Adam tried it when he felt guilty and feared meeting God after eating the forbidden fruit. He tried to handle his problem himself by running, hiding, and covering (Gen. 3:8-10). Concealing thoughts, feelings, and actions provides freedom from accountability and reduces chances of receiving reproof. Maintaining emotional distance keeps the fearful or angry person "in the know" and his authorities blind-sided. Proverbs 18:1-2 says that the one who separates himself seeks his own way and viewpoint and resists any advice. Separation to oneself both expresses autonomy and prevents protective restraints on indulgence in false imaginations, so behaviors degenerate to the bizarre. As Adam, Saul, and David illustrate, alienation is a common form of trusting self to gain a sense of survival or other desired ends.

Directive Impact of Emotions

Emotions influence our decisions. Joseph's brothers let feelings of jealousy tempt them to sell Joseph as a slave (Gen. 37). Later, Joseph's care of his family in Egypt was evidence of his kind disposal toward them. Yet his brothers let feelings of guilt and fear influence them to believe less of Joseph and unnecessarily plead for his mercy (Gen. 42:21-33). We've already seen how Saul's anger made him impulsive and foolish.

 Proverbs 29:11 says, "A fool always loses his temper, but a wise man holds it back." Proverbs 5:6 describes a woman who "does not ponder the path of life; her ways are unstable, she does not know it." A person who gives decision-making control to his emotions makes rash, impulsive (unstable) choices because he does not control himself enough to rightly consider his situation, yet he "does not know it" and assumes he is in the right. A person without self-discipline lets his passions rule. He is like a city without walls, vulnerable to the influence of temptations and sinful thoughts, and their consequences (Prov. 25:28; 16:2, 32; 18:6-7).

Proverbs 5:21-23 says,
For the ways of a man are before the eyes of the Lord,
    And He watches all his paths.
His own iniquities will capture the wicked,
    And he will be held with the cords of his sin.
He will die for lack of instruction,
    And in the greatness of his folly he will go astray.

The words "go astray" can also be translated "exhilarated" as in 5:19, inferring intoxication. It describes feeling out of control, seemingly helpless to irresistible urges. The word "instruction" also means "discipline," which is the idea of self-control. What this passage conveys is that a person habituated to a sinful behavior has feelings so compelling that he grows convinced that he cannot stop himself. He does not believe God's Word, that he can be self-disciplined. Children wielding the behavioral tools listed as RAD live by their feelings.

Crucial Role of Habituation

So far, we've seen how a right understanding of the human heart and its bent toward sin accounts for the generation and exaggeration of RAD perceptions and behaviors.

 Habituation explains how the lifestyle becomes more extreme and fixed. Habit is "the capacity to learn to respond unconsciously, automatically, and comfortably." [4] Habit allows us to drive or to tie our shoes or to fix a cup of tea without much conscious thought. Habits are learned by training.

Through training, habituated thoughts and behaviors become second nature. Romans 7:14-23 teaches that the flesh habituated to evil does it automatically.

Desires can also be habituated. Peter describes someone who had "a heart trained in greed" (2 Pet. 2:14), which means a heart habituated to wanting more and more. Such a person does not think twice about wrongs that he does. [5]

Automatic behaviors seem to just happen, as if the person was born that way. This is one reason why people confuse their learned behaviors and attitudes with temperament or personality. [6] It also explains why it appears that a child thought to have RAD acts without thinking, cannot help himself, or has a mental illness.

Habituation is why parents must correct a child "while there is hope," lest his innate foolishness becomes habituated and resistant to change (Prov. 19:18; 22:15). Repetition scrapes a rut into the soil of daily responses so that, like wheels slip into ruts, people tend to revert to habitual ways.

Cravings help to explain how habits worsen and widen. A craving is a desire intensified. Psalm 106:14 says that Israel "craved intensely in the wilderness," meaning that her desires were insatiable. She incessantly demanded more water, food, safety, leadership, idols, and control (Ps. 106:6-31; Num. 11:4-9; 14:1-4) until, as Psalm 81:11 says, "They would have none of Me." Israel wanted what she wanted and refused to be satisfied with God's provisions or ways.

The people Peter describes, whose hearts were "trained in greed," also had "eyes full of adultery that never cease from sin" (2 Pet. 2:14), i.e., intense desires drove their behaviors. Practice increases the frequency, intensity, and duration of habituated desire. Because sin never completely satisfies, worse extremes are needed to get the same effect. Desire is addictive.

Robert Karen's story of a little boy driven to extremes illustrates some aspects of habituation. Karen tells about Patrick, a three-year-old in Hampstead, England, during World War II. His home had been bombed, so his mother left him to the care of a residential nursery while she lived in a shelter and worked in a munitions factory. Sometimes she visited; he cried at their partings. To prevent his crying, his mother threatened to not visit if he cried. So, Patrick replaced crying with a ritual. Whenever someone looked at him, he nodded his head and said that his mother was coming to dress him and take him home. He went through the motions of dressing. If the listener contradicted his story, he burst into tears. While the other children occupied themselves with toys, games, and making music, Patrick remained standing in a corner, moving his lips and his hands as if dressing.

> Within a few days the ritual became more monotonous and compulsive, Patrick constantly attempting to reassure himself with his story. As he continued, it became more elaborated: His mother would come for him, she would put on his coat and leggings, she would zip up the zipper, she would put on his pixie hat. When someone asked him whether he could stop repeating this again and again, he tried to be a good boy and cooperate. But now, instead of speaking the words, he mouthed them and simultaneously began enacting the ritual by putting on the imaginary clothes. Within a few days, this was further streamlined and reduced to something of a tic.[7]

This story offers salient similarities to an alienated child's case. The situation was one of abandonment and emotional hurt. Little Patrick wanted, craved, his mother's attention to the exclusion of all other interests. He practiced denial and vain imaginations. He separated himself and rejected counsel, which contributed to exaggeration of his reactions. The fact that his nursery mates, similarly abandoned, practiced social play while Patrick did not is evidence that the children were *choosing* their desires, thoughts, and behaviors. Patrick's choices were repeated until they became a habit. The habit was refined and ingrained to a compulsiveness beyond association with the original cause. If a stranger met him a couple of years later and did not know the history, he would notice a strange tic with no discernible cause, and Patrick also probably would not know how it came to be. In his heart, the concomitant emotions (fear, despair, loneliness, and anger) would also be habitual and unconscious. Patrick illustrates that chosen reactive behaviors, whether positive and "normal" or negative and "pathological," can become second nature.

The truth is that what psychologists distinguish as RAD behavior is really just an extension beyond the range of selfish behavior that society tolerates in what it deems "normal" people. The differences in evil deeds from one person to another are in degree, not in kind. Considering how resolutely bent toward selfish desires and thoughts every infant is, and considering how extensively and stubbornly that selfish bent pervades the child, teen, and adult heart, what is amazing is that we are not all RAD people. The root of all of us is?

Difficulty of Change

The stubbornness with which a RAD child pursues his folly in the face of painful consequences is mind boggling. Sometimes, he feels consequences or notices the pain that his behavior causes to others (Prov. 17:25), but those consequences do not deter him (Prov. 27:22). Because psychologists have seen minimal success in changing RAD children, these children are considered some of the hardest people to counsel.[8] What truths about change might help guide parents' attitudes, thoughts, words, and behaviors toward their antisocial child?

First, change is impossible if desires do not change (Mark 7:21-23; James 1:13-14; 4:1-3). Proverbs 26:11 says that the fool enjoys his folly and fully intends to repeat it. RAD children have to want to change their desires, not adapt a behavior just to get relief from present consequences. Otherwise, the same desire will find expression in another behavior.

Second, habituation makes sin a hard nut to crack. Jeremiah told Israel, "Can the Ethiopian change his skin or the leopard his spots? Then you also can do good who are accustomed to doing evil" (Jer. 13:23). "Accustomed to doing evil" literally means "learned in evil." Jeremiah was telling his listeners that they had so wrapped themselves in habits of disobedience as to make them a second skin. Only God's grace had the power to reverse them.[9] *Amen*

Third, change is difficult because it is uncomfortable and hard work. Familiar ways feel comfortable even if they are destructive (Exod. 16:1-3; Num. 11:1-6). Right behaviors, even though beneficial, feel risky because they are new. Risk itself irritates the child's hair-trigger sensitivity to fear and, if he does not thoughtfully, courageously, willfully decide to trust God instead of self, his habituation will knock his wheel back to the old self-preservation rut.

Glorious Hope of Redemption

There is hope for the child habituated to fear, anger, and control. Antisocial behaviors can become features of the past. According to Ephesians 5:8, the Ephesian believers "were formerly darkness, but now you are light in the Lord; walk as children of light." "Were" is an emphatic,[10] meaning that although they were, they are not now, nor are they to revert to darkened thinking. First Peter 1:14 says, "As obedient children, do not be conformed to the former lusts *which were* yours in your ignorance" (emphasis added). As rebellious ways become a habit, so righteous ones can also (Heb. 5:13-14).

How can that change be effected? It starts with salvation, and salvation requires accurate self-assessment. Take that term "bad." "Bad" is vague. What do you do with it? You cannot honestly tell the child that he is "good." He knows better, and it contradicts the Bible. So what hope is there for change? Correct his term "bad" to the biblically accurate term "sinful" and now there is hope. God promises that when someone agrees that he has sinned and deserves punishment, commits to the truth that Jesus is the Son of God, and repents from self to trust in Christ's redemptive work on the cross, God cleanses him from sin and gives a new heart that desires to please Him (Ezek. 36:25-26; 2 Cor. 5:9). The person wants God and His right ways more than self or safety (Matt. 22:37; Rom. 6:17-18). This salvation is available to RAD children by the power of Christ (John 15:4-5).

Salvation ushers the child into a new identity. He becomes a child of God. He trusts in Christ to have Christ's righteousness. Children of God want to purify themselves and walk worthy of their Father (1 John 3:1-3; Eph. 4:1).

With the new heart comes the ability to renew the mind (Eph. 4:22-24). Through God's Word, the child can learn and believe the truth about his world, himself, and God, and change his desires.

The Bible shows how to throw away old tools of controlling the situation and pick up God's tools for handling trouble effectively. He can decide that when fears arise, he will run to God rather than to his own coping strategies (Pss. 18:2; 56:3). When anger boils, he will put on self-control instead (Gal. 5:19-23).

Change of environment helps a great deal. Parents and counselors can influence him by modeling love and the joy of fellowship with God. They can teach truth and gently challenge or correct misperceptions by a calm, logical application of Scripture. They can patiently provide reward and disciplinary consequences. Prayer is essential. Loving parents can woo a child to choose to change.

The child's behaviors can change because in redemption, God frees from the power of sin, and the person becomes controlled by righteousness (Rom. 6:17-18). Galatians 5:16 says that walking by the Spirit prevents acting on fleshly desires. Victory over sinful habits is possible. By the Spirit's enablement, the RAD child's behaviors can change through willful practice of putting off old behaviors and putting on new behaviors (Eph. 4:22-24) until the term "RAD" is no longer descriptive of him (1 Cor. 6:9-11).

Footnotes

1. Bruns, "finally," 12 June 2006, personal correspondence.

2. Karen, *Becoming Attached*, 210.

3. Mark T. Greenberg, "Attachment and Psychopathology in Childhood," Jude Cassidy and Phillip R. Shaver, eds. *Handbook of Attachment, Theory, Research, and Clinical Applications* (New York: The Guildford Press, 1999), 482-483.

4. Jay Adams, *A Theology of Christian Counseling* (Grand Rapids: Zondervan, 1979), 161.

5. Jay Adams, *The Christian Counselor's Manual: The Practice of Nouthetic Counseling* (Grand Rapids: Zondervan, 1973), 182.

6. Ibid., 172.

7. Karen, *Becoming Attached*, 63-64.

8. Buckwalter, interview.

9. Adams, *Theology*, 163, 235.

10. Kenneth S. Wuest, "The Exegesis of Ephesians," *Ephesians and Colossians in the Greek New Testament*, Wuest's Word Studies from the Greek New Testament, vol. 1, (Grand Rapids: Wm. B. Eerdmans Publishing Co., 1952; reprint, Grand Rapids: Wm. B. Eerdmans Publishing Co., June 1988), 123.

Chapter 5
Needs, Trust and Conscience

Let's grant that, as much as I wish it were not true, my child who shows the symptoms grouped under the label Reactive Attachment Disorder has a baseline sin nature bending his desires toward selfishness and misleading his perceptions so that he views others as threats. Let's grant that my child has been emotionally hurt, so much that he has determined that he will not trust anyone, and that his beliefs, attitudes, and behaviors have become domineering habits in his life. I still think that it makes sense to think of him as emotionally needy. It seems obvious to me that he is completely unable to trust. He just can't help it. It sounds logical that his conscience has been destroyed. From the way he acts, he obviously does not have one.

I don't know if you are thinking like this, but I sure did. Surely Scripture would agree with psychologists on these topics. But if it didn't, how could I accept the implications? I had no desire to condemn my child or heap onto her responsibilities that she was not able to shoulder.

The compassion of God called me to trust His Word. Truth may hurt, but it frees. And what does it hurt but our pride? That is a small price to pay for freedom.

So, let's look at what Scripture says. It addresses these three major complicating misconceptions that attachment literature teaches parents about needs, trust, and conscience.

Needs; Meet My Needs

Parents of children labeled RAD commonly complain that it seems like their child cannot get enough love. Loving such a child is like hooking the water hose from the house to the storm sewer drain and leaving the water on full blast twenty-four hours a day. Nothing done in love is ever enough to turn the child's heart toward parents.

The functional premise is that if they love the child enough, he will have absorbed enough love that he can reciprocate. This idea comes from one of the most frequently-cited explanations for an adopted RAD child's misbehavior, that because he was not given enough love in infancy he has unmet emotional needs.

They say I have an empty love tank.

The emotional needs philosophy is rooted in Maslow's theory that people have a hierarchy of needs. Physical needs like food and water are basic. Once physical needs are met, then psychological needs of affirmation and significance must be met. Only then is a person self-actualized and able to think of others. Therefore, man's emotional and relational problems arise from unmet underlying needs.[1]

Applying needs theory to misbehavior, psychologist David Levy, in the 1930s, hypothesized that the cause of the dissociative behavior of children in orphanages was some emotional deficiency disease.[2] Deficient in love received, they could not relate positively to each other. Psychologists view emotional problems like physical deficiency diseases; if psychological needs are not met then a mental pathology develops.

Similarly, empty stomachs needing food typify empty emotional tanks needing love. Some even assert that overeating is an attempt to fill an inner emptiness. Magid and McKelvey write, "These children have a chronic emptiness inside. They have emotional wants that need to be sated. Some may try to fill this emptiness with food..."[3] Many Christians echo Maslow, not Christ, when they say, "If you don't love yourself, you won't be able to love others."

Christian psychologists Tim Clinton and Gary Sibcy agree that the most fundamental question of human existence is, "Am I loved?" In an interview with Sibcy, Clinton relates that in his experience in marital counseling, the most common need he encounters can be summarized in the statement, "All I've ever wanted is for someone to love me."[4] Sibcy responds,

> At the heart of what goes on with folks are what we call attachment beliefs... core beliefs about whether people can be there for you, whether you are lovable, whether or not you can get the love like [sic] you really feel like you need from other people. Most of the people that we work with... have some kind of deep question about these beliefs.[5]

In other words, at the base of people's problems is an attachment problem related to insecurity about whether they can get the amount of love they need. Supposedly, getting enough love is essential for successful functioning in society.

Needs are all about me.

Does a strong desire to obtain love (also described as significance, respect, self-worth, and acceptance) translate into a God-given need? To answer, consider the goal for the meeting of the need. Sibcy says,

> About themselves, they [infants] form two important beliefs about: Am I worthy? And am I competent? Am I worthy of love? ... and am I capable of getting the love that I need when I need it? About other people it's, are other people trustworthy? Can I count on them to be there for me? Are they reliable? Are they accessible?[6]

This person wants love in order to consider himself worthy of being loved and safe from being hurt by others. So the goal is not really love, but good perceptions and feelings about himself. *I* must be safe and others are to be accessible to *me*, giving *me* the love that *I* need. This person is selfish! If psychologists are right about what infants are seeking, then it says more about infants' sin nature than about infants' actual needs.

Underlying needs-based thinking is an unstated assumption that others are obligated to meet the need. Someone wondering "whether or not you can get the love like [*sic*] you really feel like you need from other people.... Can I count on them to be there for me?" places the responsibility for his happiness on others. Any emotional damage is the fault of others.

This person is a "lover[s] of self" (2 Tim. 3:2). In a clashing contrast, Jesus said that we can't have Him unless we deny self (Luke 9:23). Philippians 2:3-4 commands us to "regard one another as more important than yourselves."

The Bible teaches that people already love themselves more than they love anyone else. This is assumed in the command to "love your neighbor as yourself" (Matt. 22:39). Ephesians 5:29 states, "for no one ever hated his own flesh, but nourishes and cherishes it." People are, by nature, self-serving. Children need no training to demand attention, the biggest piece of cake, or the coolest toy. Loving self too much, not too little, is at the heart of misbehavior.

Is it wrong to want security, affirmation, love, or significance? The answer rests on degree and purpose. Paul says that the right ambition for a Christian is to be pleasing to God (2 Cor. 5:9). As long

as the desire for security, and so on, is small compared to the desire
to please God, and as long as it is for God's glory and not for selfish
pleasure, then it is not wrong.[7]

Therapists say that RAD children hate themselves. Consider the
self-scold, "I hate myself! I can't believe I did____!" Why not? Does
this child really think that he is above making mistakes or sinning?
This is pride. We are surprised at our sins only because we underestimate our sinfulness and think we are better than we are.

The truth is, RAD children love themselves. Self-hate is just an
upside-down self-exaltation. Words like, "I can't believe I did____!"
actually imply, "Surely I am better than that." The person considers
himself to be pretty good; he's just not living up to it at the moment.
He is giving himself benefit of the doubt, which fits the description of
love in 1 Corinthians 13:7—love "believes all things."

What about the feeling of self-hatred? These feelings are simply
physiological responses to evaluations. Think of the reverse. If the
person had behaved according to his ideal he would feel happy.
What we hate is, perhaps, the behaviors. But more than that, we hate
having the truth uncovered by the behaviors. Failure to perform to
our ideal is evidence that we are not what we would like to think, and
we don't like to face that fact.

In self-degradation, the topic of conversation is self. So-called
hating oneself keeps the attention on self, which is self-exaltation.

What about the feeling of emptiness? It can legitimately arise
from loss, but loss of what? Usually, felt needs are self-made (not
God-ordained) desires that are not satisfied.[8] "I *need* Jake to love
me or I'll feel empty inside." Isn't it curious that the girl who says
this doesn't feel empty when Jim, Jerry, John, and Joe don't love
her? The difference is in her particularly chosen desire, in her
expectations, not in some need for love.

Feelings must not rule. John 15:13 says that the greatest love is
that which dies for another, and a sacrificial death certainly goes
against one's feelings.

What about brain problems due to neglect? For the moment,
assume that the antisocial child has a pathology; his brain is sick,
damaged, or neurons are misconfigured. Assume even that it influences his thoughts. Nowhere in Scripture is illness an allowance for
selfishness.

What about Genesis 2:18? If it was not good for man to be alone
(Gen. 2:18), then he must need love, right? It is true that man is

created a social creature and one important purpose of marriage is companionship. We cannot reason from this that people are hollow statues dependent on others to fill us with love. After all, if the other person's love tank is full, does that mean I don't bother with loving him until his tank empties?

No, love moves outward, not inward. God loves because He is love. According to Genesis 1:26-27, man was created to be God's image-bearer. We are intended to need each other because no single person can self-sufficiently provide an accurate image of God (Eccles. 4:9-12). Imaging God means giving love irrespective of a perceived need in the other, giving because it is one's nature to love. The purpose of sociability and companionship is to give. Marriage is a place to practice loving. Ultimately, the purpose for man's existence, including his sociability, is to give worship to God by bearing His image.

Of course God's love is vital for us. (So are His holiness, righteousness, omniscience, etc.) If God did not love us we would not be the recipients of forgiveness, only justice. God's love counters doubts of His goodness and demonstrates that He is trustworthy. Taking hope in the love of God, we look for His compassion in our trials and failures. God's love attracts us to Him and motivates gratitude so that we exalt Him for it. Receiving of His love in salvation produces in His child a delight in the great privilege of being loved by Him. See more on this topic in the section on instruction on God's character in chapter 9.

For now, note that the biblical emphasis on God's love is directed at His glory. Using it to encourage some idea of self-worth in we who are unworthy of it is fraudulent. God loves because He is love. It is not contingent upon us. God's love toward us should motivate us to gratitude and to exalt Him for His amazing love of the unlovable.

We are never commanded to seek love, neither God's nor that of others. Love is given, not demanded, given before it is gained, and given without thought to gain (Matt. 22:37, 39; 1 Cor. 13:5).

Maslow is wrong. Jesus said that even food is secondary to God's Word (Matt. 4:4; John 4:34). Jesus died rather than meet His need for medical attention or His need for another breath. He loved when no one loved Him.

Children are not constructed with love tanks any more than they are constructed with joy tanks or peace tanks. Getting enough love does not guarantee the right result. Some children loved in childhood become criminals. Some not loved in childhood become Christians.

Multitudes are loved and become well-behaved adults, yet still reject He who is love. The problem of a child labeled with RAD is not an empty love tank but a refusal to believe (agree, stake one's life upon, and live accordingly) that God is loving and good.

I want more!

How does Scripture explain why the alienated child never gets enough love, so to speak? James 1:14 says that people are "carried away" and "enticed" by desires. The idea in the Greek is of being lured and caught by bait. He is caught in a web of desires that he wants so strongly that he demands satisfaction at any cost (James 4:1-3). Terms in attachment literature such as "chronic emptiness," "emotional wants," and "sated"admits to the insatiable "I want" that James describes. Self is never satisfied. It craves intensely (Ps. 106:14). It says, "I want more. More, more, more."[9]

Love from others is important.

Practically speaking, everyone "needs" the goods, services, intimacy, and counsel that others, like mailmen, grocers, family, and pastors provide. There are ways in which children need the love and companionship of others. For example, love from others is needed because love does not provoke the selfish nature of the child (Eph. 6:4). It helps to prevent the tragic survival habits that alienated children adopt.

God's love is supremely attractive. It appeals to our "I want that" bent and communicates His supreme trustworthiness. Parents need to love in order to image God so that children have opportunity to feel its attraction.

Children need the inducement that love provides. It can stir them to love others (Heb. 10:24). It can aid learning because truth spoken out of love and in a loving manner makes knowledge seem good and appealing (Eph 4:15; Prov. 15:1-2). A parent's call on the child to obedience should always be made in the context of parental love.

Children need love from others because it instructs in how to love God and others (Deut. 6:5-7). In a loving relationship, the child learns a more accurate perspective of the world than in an abusive relationship. He learns that while the world is a painful place, not every situation requires a panic button. While he can have confidence in legitimate God-given capabilities, self-sufficiency is not wise. While no human is totally reliable, some can be trusted to a measured extent. Also, being the recipient of love provides a model that shows him how to fulfill God's command to love others (Matt. 22:39). The focus is his worship and service. The call to obedience is always on the basis of love for God and others.

Real love, self-sacrifice for the welfare of others, given by both parties in a relationship creates the most fulfilling relationships. There is peace in mutual enjoyment, but each party must choose to love the other, not require that the other meet his needs.

Receiving of love does not fill some mystical love tank. We do not talk about getting enough forgiveness before we can forgive others. Rather, we forgive as He has forgiven us (Eph. 4:32). We do not fill mercy tanks before we show mercy. Rather, we must "be merciful as your heavenly Father is merciful," merciful even when oppressed and shown no mercy (Luke 6:36). Love from parents or caregivers entices and teaches the child to love. It proffers hope.

What are the essential needs?

So then, what does the RAD child need? His essential need is forgiveness. Jesus died to forgive. He died to forgive sin, not to fill love tanks. Love from others is important for reasons stated above, but without it, he can still have relationship with God. Without forgiveness, he *cannot* have relationship with God. He needs forgiveness in order to remove the debt of sin that bars him from God. He needs forgiveness in order to be freed from the penalty of sin (John 5:24; Rom. 6:23) and from the power of sin that is controlling him (Col. 1:13-14).

He needs and absolutely must have God's Word. How will he know about God's character, his own sin nature, Christ, forgiveness, eternal life, and sanctification without it (Matt. 4:4; Rom. 10:17)?

What the child needs is to believe God. God has given ample proof that He is good, full of compassion, and loves the child. The problem is not in getting enough love but in believing the love that God has already given. Do parents need to keep communicating God's love to him? Yes. But remember that his problem is not quantity; it is rejection. It is unbelief. Unbelief is a choice.

What the antisocial child needs is to deny himself and follow Christ (Luke 9:23). He needs to repent from self-sufficiently leaning on his own understanding of how to behave, and lean on God's way (Prov. 3:5).

What the alienated child needs is to love others (Matt. 22:39). Rather than seek significance, self-preservation, self-worth, or revenge, he must consider others more important than himself (Phil. 2:3-4).

Finally, and the foundation of all, rather than demand to be loved he needs to love God (Matt. 22:37). That is the foremost commandment. It is essential. Rather than seek his own he must seek for God to be glorified. This was Jesus' strongest desire (John 12:28).[10]

In the 1970s, culture's proposed fundamental question was "Who am I?" At the turn of the millennium it is "Am I loved (significant)?" Attachment theory adds, "Am I safe? Are others trustworthy?" In contrast, Scripture presents the ultimate fundamental question: "How can I glorify God?"[11]

To Trust or Not To Trust

As with emotional needs, beliefs about trust affect how parents and counselors think about and treat difficult children.

Can't or won't? That is a Question.

Dissociated children are renowned for not trusting anyone. Attachment therapists characterize it infrequently as a choice, and primarily as an inability. Magid and McKelvey state that the child decides "in his subconscious that he cannot trust anyone to care for him and so will not trust anyone." But then they state that RAD children have "psychological damage," the "disease of psychopathy," and are the child version of a "psychopath."[12] The terms "disease," "damage," and "–path" (from "pathology") imply incapacitation. He can't help it.

Victoria Kelly writes, "The fundamental problem in disorders of attachment is the child's profound inability to form that kind of trusting relationship."[13] So, lack of trust is usually viewed as an inability, a *profound* inability.

The idea of an inability to trust is based in psychological theory. Freud taught that a mind can be literally sick. Erikson taught that the first essential developmental stage is trust.[14] If the baby does not learn to trust in infancy, he may never do so and is vulnerable to adult psychopathology.[15] If trust for attachment does not occur, neither does optimal brain development.[16] Neurons become disorganized, and so the child has no capacity for intimate interpersonal relationships once he matures.[17] The child would comply if he could, but he cannot because of his disorganized brain development.[18] Antisocial children have a brain problem literally preventing trust.

Is the RAD child *unable* to trust? Theologically, this idea contains at least two enormous implications. First, it holds eternal consequences because to say that he *cannot* trust is to take away from the child the hope of salvation that God offers to all only on the basis of faith, which is trust (John 3:16). Second, it implies injustice, partiality, and maliciousness on God's part. If God promises salvation only through trust (Rom. 3:28; Eph. 2:8), then RAD children, physiologically unable to trust, are excluded through no fault of their own. The truth is, God is just and merciful, and His promise is available to all. Therefore, whatever the child's appearance may be regarding inability to trust, though he seems pathological about it, inability is not a legitimate conclusion to make.

By making trust and intimacy contingent upon neural organization, developmentalism wrongly identifies the trust organ as the brain. But the brain is a material organ. Scripture teaches that trust and distrust originate in the immaterial. Mark 11:23 says, "Whoever [tells] this mountain to move will succeed if he does not *doubt in his heart, but believes...*" (emphasis added). Experiences may influence neurons, but trust is ultimately a mind-moral-volitional issue.

Everyone trusts in something. The question is not whether RAD children are able to trust but in what they choose to trust.

Is it true that RAD children trust no one? No, they do trust someone. Proverbs 3:5 identifies who. It says, "Do not lean on [trust in] your own understanding, but in all your ways acknowledge Him." The antisocial child trusts himself. In infancy, he found that others failed him and hurt him. From his perspective, who was left to care besides himself? One of Nancy Verrier's counselees expresses that it was as if she figuratively sat up in her crib and decided, "I can't trust anyone. I will have to take care of myself." [19] The child who tries to control others to gain safety is leaning on his own understanding of how to live.

How trusting others is helpful

Isn't trust in others important? Certainly it is! Society cannot function without some degree of trust among people. People, even antisocial children, trust the teacher to teach, the grocer to stock eggs, Amazon.com to send ordered books, and pilots to fly safely. In Jesus' parable of the servants with talents, the master entrusted money to the servants (Matt. 25:14-30). Paul entrusted the Ephesian church to Timothy. Timothy trusted Paul's counsel. The benefit of a child trusting Christians parents' credibility and compassion is that it induces openness to receive the instruction that leads him to place his total trust in Christ.

The critical questions lie in to whom and to what degree trust is given. Trust in people must be limited; trust in God and His Word must be total (Acts 17:11).

To trust God or not to trust God? That is THE Question.

In the belief that attachment and trust are essential cures, psychologists, therapists, and parents devote much time, money, and energy to persuading the RAD child to trust therapists and parents. Some use holding therapy. Others try to build neural pathways for trust. The child must learn to trust a caregiver.

Trusting his caregiver is helpful, but as a primary emphasis it distracts from the real problem, which is that the child does not trust God. This is not to argue whether a toddler or infant can trust God (more on this in the note below). It is only to say that his problem is misplaced, not lack of, trust. Jeremiah 17:5-7 says, "Cursed is the man who trusts in mankind.... Blessed is the man who trusts in the Lord." Shifting the child's trust from self to therapist or parents keeps it misplaced onto mankind.

While the alienated child takes distrust to an idolatrous extreme, there is a valid point within his distortion. It is true that not one person in the world is worthy of his total trust. (Neither is he himself.) Everyone fails sometime. God is the only being who is perfectly faithful, never fails, and is worthy of total trust. The only hope for an eternal solution and abundant life on earth is to turn from trust in self to trust in Christ. The good news is that because obedience and trust are choices of the heart by the Holy Spirit's power, no abuse or broken bonding cycle or brain problem can prevent trust in and obedience to God.

Scripture does not emphasize a child's trust of his parents. Moses never commanded children to trust parents, but to honor them (Exod. 20:12). Paul did not command trust, but obedience and honor toward parents (Eph. 6:1, 2; Col. 3:20).

Obedience to parents, though aided by trust, is not contingent upon it. After all, Paul commanded obedience to Roman dictators with whom Christians certainly were not safe (Rom. 13:1). Slaves were to obey masters irrespective of treatment (Col. 3:22). Children's obedience to parents must be based on trust in God, not parents (Col. 3:20).

Ecclesiastes 3:11 relates that people are born with a sense of the eternal and a moral conscience. Men cannot necessarily determine whether a very young child can trust God in some infantile way. Some children do seem to have a firm confidence in the goodness of God by the time they can verbalize it and then continue to love and follow God for their whole lives.

When afraid, the child can and must trust in God (Phil. 4:6; Ps. 18:1-2). Psalm 56:11 says, "In God I have put my trust, I shall not be afraid. What can man do to me?" When angry, he is commanded to cease from his anger and trust God for justice (Ps. 37:7-10). It is trust in God that leads to peace of heart (Isa. 26:3).

Hand in hand with trust in God is being trustworthy among men. All of the focus on a RAD child's "inability" to trust relieves him of attention on the fact that he is failing in his responsibility to be trustworthy. He is disobeying God's many commands against deceit and unfaithfulness. Rather than point the finger at untrustworthy people who don't meet his emotional "needs," he needs to be cultivating trustworthiness in his own life, and parents need to be calling him to his responsibility (Ps. 37:3; Luke 16:11).

Proverbs 22:19 says, "So that your trust may be in the Lord, I have taught you today." Teaching and inducing trust in God is where the energy of counselors and parents should be directed.

Conscience, Conscience On the Wall

Cold-hearted lack of remorse in RAD children is so characteristic that Magid and McKelvey entitled their book, *High Risk: Children Without a Conscience.* Closely correlated is a lack of empathy, what one dissertation describes as "callous-unemotional."[20]

They say there is no mirror.

A conscience is like an internal moral mirror. It is "the God-given ability to evaluate one's own actions *(Romans 2:15)* and respond emotionally to that evaluation."[21] The person looks inside, evaluates, and either accuses or affirms himself. Proverbs 20:27 says that "the spirit of man ... [searches] all the innermost parts of his being," and Romans explains that this inner search leads to a judgment of motives in light of right and wrong (Rom. 1:32; 2:14-15). When the conscience affirms, the person feels good. When it accuses, bad physical feelings awaken the person to the need for change (2 Sam. 24:10; Acts 2:37). Therefore, conscience is a God-given restraint on evil, personally and societally (Rom. 1:32; 2:14-15).

When a person's conscience accuses him, he feels badly. Remorse is what we call the thought-feeling response to a negative self-evaluation by the conscience.

A variety of reasons are given for lack of a conscience. Bonding cycle theorists explain that "such children [of broken bonding cycles] cannot love or feel guilt.... they simply have no conscience."[22]

Some parents are told that their child was born without a conscience because fetal-alcohol syndrome destroyed the part of the brain where a conscience develops. Some are told that their child is developmentally delayed, that children develop a conscience at about age two and RAD children fail to do so because, due to soft neurological damage, they do not have neuropathways for expressing remorse.

As with the issue of trust, there are moral, behavioral, and societal implications to the question of whether one has a conscience. If someone has no conscience, he cannot make moral evaluations of his behavior. Then, there is no moral motive to turn from wrongdoing.

A society may be influenced toward indulging criminals. Serial rapist and murderer Ted Bundy was questioned about an author who described him as having no conscience and sinking into a compulsive state. He replied that she was doing him a favor. "As long as the contemporary impression is that I'm just a, uh, incapacitated, uh, uh, incoherent—unable to handle myself or am no longer an energetic, healthy young man—then they're always going to underestimate me." [14] He is right. If we believe that someone has no conscience, then we lower our expectations of right behavior and give unwarranted allowances for sins.

The implication for eternity is even greater. A person without a conscience would not be able to sense conviction, so he would not honestly confess sins (Prov. 30:20; Luke 18:11; 1 John 1:8-10). He would have no reason to seek salvation.

Everyone has a mirror.

Is it possible to have no conscience? Scripture teaches that everyone has a conscience. Romans 1:19-20 says, "That which is known about God is evident within [people]..., so that they are without excuse." Untaught people have an innate knowledge that God exists and that there is a moral standard to which they are accountable. About those unaware of God's written law, Romans 2:14-15 says, "... they show the work of the Law written in their hearts, their conscience bearing witness and their thoughts alternately accusing or else defending them." The fact that people who have not been instructed in the Law innately do some right and condemn some wrong shows that possession of a conscience is universal.

Developmental psychologists teach that a baby is born without a conscience but develops one at about age two. One situation used as evidence is that of a baby who sticks his finger in another's eye and feels no guilt, but is simply fascinated by the reaction. [23] But just

because infants do not know particular wrongs and do not demonstrate conscience in a way that adults can measure does not mean
that they do not have a conscience. Adam did not experience developmental stages and in his innocence did not give evidence that he
had a conscience. Yet, as soon as he sinned, he felt shame and hid,
demonstrating that he possessed a conscience. It had just not previously been activated to sound an alarm.[24] Every person is born with
an innate sense that some sort of right and wrong exists and possesses
the capacity for moral self-judgment.

Some propose that brain damage can destroy the conscience.
This idea is based on the belief that the mind is equivalent to, dependent upon, and originates in the physical brain. But man is more than
physical (2 Cor. 5:8). His mind, his intangible self, is expressed in
and influenced by his brain but is not dependent upon the brain.
Conscience is not just a brain function but a moral capacity. Therefore, even mentally handicapped people can know right and wrong,
can confess sins, and can trust Christ for salvation.[25]

Everyone has a conscience. The problem with a seeming lack of
conscience is not absence but to what direction it is trained.

Different types of conscience

The capacity for distinguishing right from wrong does not imply
that the person knows all the particulars of which behaviors are right
and which are wrong. The example of a baby poking another's eye
actually illustrates the need for a conscience to be trained to know
what is right and wrong. His internal mirror is warped. That is why
parents teach and discipline.

Hebrews 5:14 speaks of those "who because of practice have their
senses trained to discern good and evil" (emphasis added). Second
Peter 2:14 speaks of people "trained in greed" (emphasis added).
Whether we train the conscience to rightly discern good and
evil, or train it to affirm sin (like greed), instruction and training
determine the type of conscience, or the bent toward which that
conscience ripens.

Scripture describes several types of consciences. An uninstructed
conscience is one which has not been instructed in particular laws
(Rom. 2:12, 19). Therefore, it may not feel guilt over some sins, not
knowing they are wrong. It needs instruction. The baby needs to be
told that eye-poking is wrong.

The "weak" conscience has been misinstructed so that it
produces guilt feelings over behavior that is not wrong (Rom. 14:1, 2, 23;

1 Cor. 8:7-12). The weak conscience needs correct instruction in biblical standards.

The "good" conscience has been well-instructed and well-trained to be activated by biblical standards (1 Tim. 1:5). Instruction and practice in obedience have refined it to discern and heed right and wrong (Heb. 5:14).

The hardened conscience is described as seared "as with a branding iron" (1 Tim. 4:2). Cauterized past feeling, it is not moved by biblical standards. Ephesians 4:19 describes people who, "having become callous, have given themselves over to sensuality for the practice of every kind of impurity with greediness" (emphasis added). The sin becomes so automatic that the person feels little or no guilt over it and gives himself to indulge in it freely (2 Pet. 2:13-14). This is why certain awful conduct does not seem to bother those who do it.[26] This conscience needs retraining with instruction and discipline.

Wrong training hardens a conscience.

Whether a conscience becomes calloused or good depends upon the direction to which it is trained. Those "trained in greed" (2 Pet. 2:14) trained themselves to ignore or shut off the alarms of conscience when tempted with coveting. Training shapes the conscience.

The hardening process starts with a desire that the conscience warns is forbidden (Rom. 2:15). Rejecting that warning (Rom. 1:21, 25), the person sins. Then he feels guilt and perhaps fear of discovery and horror that he could do such a thing. Rather than repent, he dulls himself to the guilt feelings. When the desire returns, the sin is easier to commit again. With practice, the warning of the conscience sounds fainter. Ignoring his conscience becomes a habit. It happens thought by thought, choice by searing choice.

The Pharaoh of Exodus repeatedly and stubbornly hardened himself against doing what God said, even though he suffered for it through ten plagues. Rather than change, he impoverished his country, sent his army to annihilation, and even suffered the death of his own son. The more he stiffened against doing right, the more irrationally stubborn he became until resistance was worth any cost.[27] He seared his conscience by training himself to resist conviction.

A hardened conscience smothers compassion.

With a hardened conscience comes what psychologists label a lack of empathy. This evaluation fits the vernacular, in which "empathy" usually means that someone feels another's pain vicariously and in a manner favorable to the other person. RAD children have had enough of emotional pain. No wonder they refuse more, even vicariously.

I think, though, that "lack of empathy" leads away from the real issue of the heart. "Empathy" literally means "to feel with." *The American Heritage Dictionary* defines it as an "understanding so intimate that the feelings, thoughts, and motives of one are readily comprehended by another." While it is true that antisocial children dull themselves to the pain of others and to a wide range of emotions, they can also empathize quite well. That is why they know how to cause emotional pain.

What RAD children lack is the compassion often associated with the word "empathy." The term "compassion" in Colossians 3:12 includes an empathetic sympathy with the suffering of others along with an attitude of mercy, affection, and a feeling of pity.[28] RAD children are selfish. They understand the pain they cause, but they choose to take pleasure in it rather than exercise compassion.

People who study the criminal mind note that whereas the social person sees two classes in the world, people and objects, the antisocial person sees only objects.[29] (Though I appreciate their point, it seems to me that he still sees two classes, himself [the person] and objects.) For example, when transporting his victims, Ted Bundy deliberately steered conversations away from personal topics so as to convince himself that they were merely objects; otherwise his conscience hindered him. After the rape, they became people again in his mind, but only briefly. As soon as fear of discovery hit, they became "*prob-lems*—that's not the word either. Threats" (ital. original).[30] If survival is considered a basic human "need," a person has a right to destroy a threat to that survival. By this logic, murder is justified. Depersonalization and alienation smother compassion.

Young abused children are faced with tremendous temptations while being untaught in what to do about them. It is no wonder that some seek relief by steeling their hearts and minds against compassion and the warnings of a conscience. With practice, indulging self and rejecting remorse and compassion becomes a way of life.

Right training builds a good conscience.

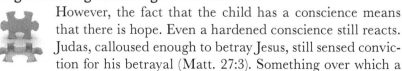 However, the fact that the child has a conscience means that there is hope. Even a hardened conscience still reacts. Judas, calloused enough to betray Jesus, still sensed conviction for his betrayal (Matt. 27:3). Something over which a child feels remorse provides an area of appeal to his conscience. It is like a chink in his armor which a parent can coax him to widen.

The commands of Scripture offer hope. They proclaim the ability to choose. Since Colossians 3:12 commands the putting on of compassion, then that is something that can willfully be done. The angry child's feelings will protest. No matter the feelings, acts of compassion can be chosen and practiced (Col. 3:12; 1 Cor. 13:4-8).

Rehabituation offers hope. Practicing right behaviors can increase sensitivity to moral rightness and compassion for others. Caution must be applied so that putting on good habits is not taught as behavior modification. That is, in addition to actions, habits of heart desires and thoughts are retrained (Heb. 5:14), and then bear fruit in actions.[31] God's glory is the goal. Through salvation, instruction, and discipline exercised with compassion, there is hope for a hardened child to choose to heed what the Bible says is right, practice compassion, and retrain his conscience.

Solutions to the RAD problem are hard to find because the vocabulary of psychologists is vague. What exactly is "conduct disorder," a "high maintenance" child, or "a dysfunctional family"? What exactly should the character-disordered child change? What should the child do with love hunger or low self-esteem? When solutions are ambiguous, then hope is lost. The chart below compares a few of the psychological terms used about RAD children with biblical terms. We can begin to see how, if RAD characteristics are labeled biblically, much of the mystery of RAD fades and biblical solutions become easier to identify.

Psychological Term	Biblical Term Options	Possible Biblical Solutions
Lack of self-regulation Dysregulation	• Impulsiveness (Prov. 16:32; 25:28; 2 Tim. 3:6)	• Put on self-control by the power of the Spirit (Gal. 5:22-23)
	• Lack of self-control (2 Tim. 3:3)	• Put on self-control by the power of the Spirit (Gal. 5:22-23)
	• Disobedient to parents (2 Tim. 3:2)	• Obey your parents so that it may be well with you (Eph. 6:1-3)
	• Stealing (a manifestation)	• Steal no longer, but labor and give to the needy (Eph. 4:28)
	• Contentiousness (Tit. 3:2) • Outbursts of anger, disputes, and dissensions (Gal. 5:20)	• Do all things without disputing (Phil. 2:14; Prov. 29:11)

Psychological Term	Biblical Term Options	Possible Biblical Solutions
Shyness	• Pride • Fearfulness • Untrained in how to relate to people • Disrespectful • Manipulating for attention (Prov. 29:25; Prov. 3:35)	• Consider others more important than self (Phil. 2:3-4) • Parents need to train the untrained (Eph. 6:1-3)
Low self-esteem	• Selfishness and conceit (Phil. 2:3-4) • Focuses on feeling good about self	• Put on an accurate view of self (Rom. 12:3) • Deny self and follow Christ (Luke 9:23) • Love God and others (Matt. 22:37, 39) • Consider others as more important than self (Phil. 2:3-4)
No conscience	• Hardened conscience (1 Tim. 4:2)	• Retrain the conscience (Heb. 5:14)
No conscience (will do whatever it takes to get what he wants)	• Lover of self • Lover of pleasure (2 Tim. 3:2, 4)	• Deny self and follow Christ (Luke 9:23) Love others (Matt. 22:39; Phil. 2:3-4)
No conscience (rationalizes so that he can do what he wants)	• Foolishness, Pride (The "fool" denies God's existence so that he can rationalize that he won't have to pay for his sins. –Psalm 10:4, 11, 13; 14:1)	• Fear God to learn knowledge and wisdom (Prov. 1:7) Trust in the Lord when threatened (Ps. 10:14-18; 14:4-6)
No conscience (Lack of empathy)	• Lack of compassion (Matt. 9:9-13)	• Put on a heart of compassion (Col. 3:12) • Go and learn this: "I desire compassion" (Matt. 9:13) • Good Samaritan (Luke 10:27-42)
Lack of trust	• Trust in self (Prov. 3:5; Jer. 17:5)	• Trust in God, not self (Prov. 3:6; Jer. 17:7)
Character disorder toward parents	• Not honoring parents (Eph. 6:2-3) • Attitude of disrespect	• Honor and obey parents that it may be well with you (Eph. 6:1-3; Prov. 30:17)
Character disorder	• Attitude of "rebellion" in which God's Word is rejected (1 Sam. 15:23)	• Obey His Word (1 Sam. 15:23; John 14:21)

Footnotes

1. Edward T. Welch, *When People Are Big and God is Small* (Phillipsburg, N.J.: P & R Publishing, 1997), 88.
2. Blum, *Goon Park*, 49.
3. Magid and McKelvey, *High Risk*, 85.
4. Clinton, *Counsel CDs: Attachments.*
5. Ibid.
6. Ibid.
7. Welch, *When People Are Big and God is Small*, 149.
8. Ibid., 151.
9. Edward T. Welch, *Addictions: A Banquet in the Grave.* (Phillipsburg, N.J.: P & R Publishing, 2001), 57.
10. Welch, *When People Are Big and God is Small*, 156.
11. Ibid., 165.
12. Magid and McKelvey, *High Risk*, 61, 6.
13. Victoria J. Kelly, "Theoretical Rationale for the Treatment of Disorders of Attachment," 2003 (Lake Villa, llinois: Association for Treatment & Training in the Attachment of Children–ATTACh), http://www.attach.org/theorationale.htm, (13 Jan. 2005).
14. Magid and McKelvey, *High Risk*, 193.
15. Martha Peace, *Attitudes of a Tranformed Heart*, (Bemidji, Minn.: Focus Publishing, Inc., 2002), 38.
16. Kelly Wilson, "Nurturing Love," *Quincy Herald-Whig* (Quincy, Ill.) 22 Aug. 2004, 5A.
17. Daniel J. Siegel, *The Developing Mind: Toward a Neurobiology of Interpersonal Experience* (New York: The Guilford Press, 1999), 16.
18. Buckwalter, interview.
19. Nancy Newton Verrier, *The Primal Wound: Understanding the Adopted Child* (Baltimore, Md.: Gateway Press, Inc., 1993), 31.
20. Deborah Mahan Phillips, "Developmental Pathways for Children with Disruptive Behavior Disorders," Ph.D. diss., University of New Orleans, December 2003. http://etd-db.uno.edu/theses/submitted/etd-12042003-33751/ unrestricted/2003_phd_phillips_deborah.pdf. (31 Jan. 2005).
21. Adams, *Christian Counselor's Manual*, 94.
22. Magid and McKelvey, *High Risk*, 76.
23. Stephen G. Michaud and Hugh Aynesworth, *Ted Bundy: Conversations with a Killer: The Death Row Interviews* (Irving, Tex.: Authorlink Press, 2000), 260.
24. Buckwalter, interview.
25. Adams, *Theology*, 198-199.

26. Edward T. Welch, *Blame It on the Brain?: Distinguishing Chemical Imbalances, Brain Disorders, and Disobedience.* (Phillipsburg, N.J.: P & R Publishing, 1998), 49.

27. Adams, *Theology*, 162-163.

28. Exod. 5:2-9; 7:13, 22; 8:15, 19, 32; 9:7, 12, 34-35.

29. Adam Clarke, "1832 Adam Clarke's Commentary," *Online Bible*, 2.5.3. CD-ROM (Oakhurst, N.J.: Ken Hamel, 1996).

30. Harrington, *Psychopaths* (New York: Simon and Schuster, 1972), 224.

31. Michaud and Aynesworth, *Ted Bundy*, 83, 115.

Part 2: Parenting the Alienated Child and Siblings

Reactive Attachment Disorder is a manmade label for a constellation of behaviors. For each of those behaviors, we can find Scriptures that counsel how to respond in a way that pleases the Lord and leads the child with grace to God's transforming solutions. Part 1 built the foundation for dealing with RAD children by using Scriptures to describe the problem biblically. Part 2 further develops biblical labels from which to build practical biblical applications.

When considering how to parent the angry, alienated, rebellious child God's way, what better role model could there be than God Himself? We can learn from how He related to His people, Israel.

While Old Testament Israel practiced behaviors characteristic of a variety of so-called disorders and cannot be reduced to a diagnosis of RAD, she definitely displayed the same behaviors. Especially pertinent summaries may be found in Ezekiel 16 and 23:11-21, Hosea 11:1-7, and Psalms 78 and 106. Scripture relates that Israel was abandoned and abused. Though adopted by God, she was committed to autonomy and absolutely determined to reject God's love from infancy through adulthood (2 Kings 21:15). Often driven by fear and anger, she digressed into reckless and manipulative behavior. Discomfort and fear of attack were triggers to rebel. She wanted safety, but only on her terms. Judges, Kings, and Jeremiah record how she was indiscriminately affectionate to the strange nations around her, hugging them in political alliances. She grew calloused, even to practicing child sacrifice and bizarre behavior (Ezek. 16:27). If God dared to discipline her, she retaliated. She hardened herself by deliberately thinking wrong thoughts (Ps. 78:11) and denying God's kindness (Ps. 78:32). She lied, charmed, tried manipulation, dared God (Ps. 78:19-20), and back-stabbed Him (Ps. 78:56-58). She resorted to violence rather than hear a rebuke (Matt. 23:37). She murdered the prophets, and then God Himself, Jesus the Messiah (Acts 7:51-52).

As recorded in the gospels, the Pharisees also demonstrated RAD-type attitudes and behaviors. They were afraid—afraid that Jesus was going to draw people to abandon them. They were defensive and aggressive. They wanted no relationship with God and would not trust Him. They maintained an entitlement to control and authority over others and were angry at Jesus' authority. They were manipulative, conniving, self-sufficient, remorseless, and hardened against compassion, even to torture and murder. Much of the following counsel on guiding alienated children is based on lessons from God's parenting of Israel and Jesus' responses to the Pharisees.

Chapter 6
Establish Right Priorities as Parents

Recall Mrs. DeSpare's appeal to Pastor Helpin. She felt hurt, angry, confused, and exhausted, and her focus was on what she needed to do to make Donnie a well-behaved child. It is common that the stubborn insubordination of a RAD-type child challenges parental assumptions about what parenting and family life should be. When expectations are not met, parents often grow anxious and angry, maybe even depressed. They have a mix of desires and concerns.

When trouble with children arises, the tendency is to make a beeline for improving the child's behavior. If the child would just behave, the family would be happier. Rather, parents are the starting point for change because they are the foundation of the family. They must first be established in right views, attitudes, reactions, and habits, or any discussion of parenting will be futile. So we will start with you.

What Could be More Important than My Child's Improvement?

How would you answer these foundational questions?

* What is God's first priority for parents?

* Do you see yourself primarily as the key to your child's rescue?

* Is your primary goal to fix your child? How would you take it if your child never changes?

* Between you and your child, what is and is not your responsibility?

Answers to these questions begin in Deuteronomy 6:4-9, where God commissions parents. It says:

> Hear, O Israel! The Lord is our God, the Lord is one! You shall love the Lord your God with all your heart and with all your soul and with all your might. These words, which I

am commanding you today, shall be on your heart. You shall teach them diligently to your sons and shall talk of them when you sit in your house and when you walk by the way and when you lie down and when you rise up. You shall bind them as a sign on your hand and they shall be as frontals on your forehead. You shall write them on the doorposts of your house and on your gates.

Note that this passage sets parenting within a much broader context. Before any specifics about human relations can be decided, we must be clear about God. Why? Theology produces function. Our view of God affects how we live and how we parent.

It begins, "The Lord is our God, the Lord is one!" God exists. He alone is God and deserves glory and primacy in our lives. God rules. He has the right to set the rules of family life and priorities. This means that parents are accountable to Him, must parent His way, and must adopt His priorities.

So if theology produces function, then we must conclude from this passage that glorifying God must be our primary goal for what we do as parents. Is improving your child's behavior important? Is leading him to salvation important? Yes, but if God is primary, then those other goals must not constitute your strongest motivations.

Parent to glorify God, not to get your child to behave. *God's sovereignty is the foundation of parenting and His glory its highest purpose.*

What is the next requirement? "Love the Lord your God." We're right back to God again. The Lord sets our relationship with Himself as top priority. We were made to love and adore our great God who rules. This is called worship.

People are, by nature, worshipers, which is to also say that we are lovers. Everyone loves something; the only question is what. As Jesus said, "No one can serve two masters; for either he will hate the one and love the other, or he will hold to one and despise the other. You cannot serve God and mammon" (Matt 6:24). He was speaking of worship and identifying only two options: God or something other than God. We might love God, but often we have more love for sports, comfort foods, respect from our children, reputation as parents, peace in the household, having the last word, or our image of an ideal family, to name a few. Your greatest love must be God.

Again, since theology produces function, and God commands that we love Him above all, while we love our children greatly, everything that we parents do will be done more for love of God than for love of the child, more for God's glory than for the behavior of the child. This by no means precludes the motive of love for our children. Rather, parental love should be all the stronger and wiser because it is in submission to love for God.

How do we demonstrate love for God? We do so by obeying Him in our families and speaking of Him with our children when sitting and walking, in the evening and the morning (all times), and in what is done with hands and thoughts (all actions), at home and in the neighborhood (all places). Parenting is a worship issue. Communication and discipline are worship issues. Bedtimes, allowances, clothing, music, movies, toys, camping, party attendance, friends, time spent as a family—all are worship issues. At the heart of every decision is the worship question: Am I loving God?

Love for and obedience to God were commanded prior to the commission to parent. God Himself sets relationship with Him in priority over relationship with your child. You must be God-centered.

The demands of an angry, controlling child can quickly suck well-meaning Christian parents into a child-centered vortex. That is, they parent in whatever way produces a desired outcome in the child. Does he fidget easily? They avoid locations and situations where he is likely to do so. Does he cry easily or whimper? They give him more attention and comfort than he needs. When spouse and child's demands compete, they give attention to the child. Rather than risk upsetting the child by requiring patience, they allow him to interrupt when they are on the phone or talking to other adults. They entertain the child out of bad moods. They don't push his limits, let him do without, or let him struggle, but step in to relieve his discomfort. They resort to a behavioral system of rewarding good behavior and punishing bad behavior. The widow refuses to remarry until the children are grown so that they do not have any more upset in addition to their father's death. All of these actions are child-centered. While parenting requires sacrifices for the good of children, being child-focused violates the mandate in Deuteronomy 6:4-5.

So what happens when he refuses to cooperate? If our primary desire is to get the child to behave, we are likely to respond with manipulation, frustration, anger, withdrawal, guilt, or despair. When I noticed these responses in myself, I realized that my heart was set more upon obtaining a well-behaved child than upon the goal of glorifying God. I needed to repent and make God's glory my priority.

At one point, Moses, the proxy parent of Israel, fell into this kind of leadership. By God's direction, Moses led the people out of Egypt into the desert. For two years, Israel grumbled about their discomforts, especially over food and water. Numbers 11:11 relates that when they would not stop complaining, Moses accused God. "Why have You been so hard on Your servant? And why have I not found favor in Your sight, that You have laid the burden of all this people on me?" He was mad because they would not behave, and he was tired of it.

What about you? When your child refuses to cooperate, how are you responding? What do your responses demonstrate that you most want in that moment? The goal you choose will make the difference between joy and despair, contentment and anger.

Who Comes First: Spouse or Child?

In our sample case study, Mrs. DeSpare came alone for counsel. Mr. DeSpare's absence raises the question, how is their marriage?

With a difficult child, there are factors that pressure couples beyond the usual marital differences. The mother may be exhausted by addressing problems with the child's school while the father is in denial. Or because the child behaves well around him, the dad thinks the mom is overreacting.[1] Perhaps every evening the wife dumps on her husband an epic of the day's conflicts so that talking about the child dominates their conversation. Often, a RAD child tries to divide and conquer. He may privately accuse one parent to another. "Mom is wicked. She did _____ to me." He may play the confidentiality card. "Dad, you didn't tell Mom that I got arrested for shoplifting, did you?" (This dad rightly informed his child that he would not keep such secrets from his wife.) Tina Bruns writes, "Our experience with parents [sic] groups is that these kids rip apart marriages."[2]

If we follow the first lesson of Deuteronomy 6:4, then we take God's priorities as our own. In God's economy, marriage takes priority over child-rearing. Genesis 2:24 says, "For this reason a man shall leave his father and his mother, and be joined to his wife, and they shall become one flesh." God ordained marriage to be an exclusive relationship between one man and one woman. Adam and Eve comprised a family before there were children. Children are the fruit of a marriage union and, though part of the family for a while, they are not essential to it. They are temporary; they leave father and mother to form a new family of their own.

Because God makes marriage the priority relationship, you need to make each other your first priority, guarding and nurturing your relationship. For example, though for years our children swarmed my husband upon his arrival home each evening, he always refused to hug them until he first greeted me. That was one of several ways he chose to intentionally demonstrate to all that under God his marriage took first place.

What about you? Are you actively demonstrating that your spouse is a priority over your child?

What is My Role as a Steward?

Deuteronomy 6:4-9 is a commission to a stewardship. Children belong to the Lord. He gives them temporarily to parents to train for His kingdom (Ps. 127:3). This stewardship is a great privilege. You and I, sinful people, are granted participation with God the perfect Creator in the wonderful work of shaping another little sinful person to love Him.

As stewards, we have responsibilities. Very simply, we parents are responsible to love God and teach His Word diligently to our children (Deut. 6:7-9). Loving God means obeying all of the commands that any non-parent must obey. Additionally, we train our children. We must command their obedience and discipline their disobedience (Prov. 6:20; 13:24; 19:18; 23:13-14). We are responsible to "not provoke [our] children to anger" (Eph. 6:4). After all, it is sin to tempt others to sin (Mark 9:42; 1 Cor. 10:31-32). Parents are to live in a way that does not influence children to sin and that does teach and guide them to love God. These are a parent's Deuteronomy 6 responsibilities.

For what are parents *not* responsible? They are not responsible for a child's response. The Deuteronomy 6 commission says nothing about children's responses, only about parents' obedience. The command to honor and obey parents is given to *children*, not to parents (Deut. 5:16; Eph. 6:1). They are not responsible to *make* their children obey from the heart.

Doesn't a child's outcome depend on parents? Many Christians base hope for their children on a misinterpretation of Proverbs 22:6, "Train up a child in the way he should go, even when he is old he will not depart from it." The idea is that if they parent well, the child will eventually behave well. Coin in, candy out. This is pragmatism, not stewardship.

This view sets parents up for control, pride, and guilt. Wanting the best for our children and thinking that their outcome depends upon us, we insist on cooperation. The child must behave. This takes on the responsibilities of owner, not steward. If the child behaves, we take bragging rights. If the child consistently gets into trouble, we feel the guilt of failure.

An alienated child comes along and helps! With him, parents' limitations become inescapably obvious. Nothing we do works. We are confronted, more obviously than are parents with compliant children, with the question of what our responsibility is and what it is not.

Proverbs 22:6 is not a promise from God that right parenting produces cooperative kids, or that the rebellious child of good parents will one day come to his senses. Proverbs state general principles, not promises. Verse 22:6 applies the fact of habituation to inform us that early training builds habits that continue into adulthood. It urges parents to be proactive about training the child in good habits. However, by the same maxim, if a child practices rebellion despite godly parenting, he will most likely develop a habit of rebellion. Take Proverbs 22:6 as an exhortation to parent diligently, not as a guarantee in which you place your hope.

Ezekiel 18 teaches that each party is responsible for his own choices. Parents are responsible for how they influence, children for how they respond. Verse 2 sets the background of the passage with a proverb of the day, "The fathers eat the sour grapes, but the children's teeth are set on edge." By quoting this proverb, the people of Israel were complaining that they were having to suffer for their parents' sins. In essence, they were blaming their parents.

God answered, "The soul who sins will die" (Ezek. 18:4). The righteous man will live because of his own righteousness (18:5-9). If he has a violent son, the son's "blood will be on his own head" (18:10-13). If the wicked son has a son who turns to righteousness, that righteous son will not die for his father's sins (18:14-18). Ezekiel 18:19-20 continues:

> Yet you say, "Why should the son not bear the punishment for the father's iniquity?" When the son has practiced justice and righteousness and has observed all My statutes and done them, he shall surely live. The person who sins will die. The son will not bear the punishment for the father's iniquity, nor will the father bear the punishment for the son's iniquity; the righteousness of the righteous will be upon himself, and the wickedness of the wicked will be upon himself.

Esau's father played favorites and indulged Esau's pleasures. One day, Esau sold his birthright for a bowl of soup. Later, he lost his first-born blessing (that goes with the birthright) when his father was tricked into giving it to his brother, Jacob. Although Jacob sinned, Esau had no right to blame him or his father. Esau was the one who sold his own birthright (Gen. 26:19-34; 27:1-40). King Asa had a terrible father, yet he chose to follow God (1 Kings 14:21-24; 15:1, 3, 9, 11). The blessing he received for obedience was his, not his father's.

Children are accountable for what God has delegated to them just as parents are for being a right influence. Parents can take credit for neither the child's sin nor his godly choices. Before God, each has individual responsibility. So then, parents are responsible for their influence, not for the child's sinful choices.

An understanding of the child's responsibility does not imply that parents should not discipline. Delivering negative consequences for disobedience is part of parental training responsibility. It does not imply that parents can be overbearing. Both indifference and harshness provoke children to anger and are sins (Eph. 6:4; Mark 9:42; 1 Cor. 10:31-32). The difference is that parents are accountable for disciplining, not for forcing compliance in the heart of the child.

It does not imply that parents do not grieve over their child's foolish choices. God grieved deeply over Israel's rejection. He cried out, "Oh that My people would listen to Me, that Israel would walk in My ways!" (Ps. 81:13). Jesus wept over rebellious Jerusalem (Luke 19:41).

This is not to say that gaining a child's love or trust is wrong. It is to say that those who wrap their time and emotions around a child's response are making their happiness contingent upon something outside of their control and, therefore, are taking on a responsibility that is not theirs. Moses' anger over Israel's continued grumbling demonstrated that instead of focusing on pleasing God in *his* responsibilities, he wanted to make *them* behave. If your heart is set on your child reciprocating love to you, you set yourself up like Moses for disappointment, anger, and bitterness. Besides that, such a heart-set is idolatrous.

Clarifying the limits of our responsibility takes pressure off. We don't have to do the impossible, which is change the child's heart. We only have to obey God in our own heart, words, and behavior (which is no small job in itself).

Clarifying responsibilities helps us keep ourselves from interfering in the loving Owner's work. We lead the child to the Lord by His Word and do not step between them. The parent who views himself as steward will heed God's limits on his authority. He accepts that he cannot control the child's heart and is responsible for his own parenting, not for the child's responses to God. So, he will teach God's Word God's way with kindness and discipline, and trust his loving, sovereign Father for the results.

Clarifying responsibilities zeroes our focus on God's goal. We set a higher priority on the child's heart than on his behavior. Behavior takes its right role as the tool or the barometer, not the goal.

Clarifying responsibilities comforts. We parents sin. Our failures influence our children and make it harder for them to obey. We must repent and then press on in faithful teaching. We can do this because we have a God who is able to use even our failures for the good of both we and our children (Rom. 8:28-29). God is responsible for your child whom He created and is fully able to accomplish His purposes in your child even when you fail to parent perfectly.

Clarifying responsibilities promotes joy. Because you are responsible only for your own obedience, your joy is not dependent upon the behavior of your child. When you obey, you receive the joy that follows obedience. You are able to love God irrespective of your child's behavior.

Parenting is not about bonding, gaining the RAD child's trust, filling the child's love cup, forcing compliance, or gaining relief from trials that the child causes. Parenting is about glorifying God and loving the child (1 Cor. 10:31; Matt. 22:39). Parents are stewards demonstrating His love to children by obeying Deuteronomy 6:4-9, trusting God with the child's heart. Your child may never change. If you seek God's glory first and still see no change in your child's behavior, you may grieve over your dear child, but you can also experience the joy of knowing that you obeyed God by not contributing to the child's problem and by persistently holding before him the central issue expressed in the book of Deuteronomy, "Do you love God?"

Footnotes

1. Samenow, *Before It's Too Late*, 165-166.
2. Bruns, "finally," 12 June 2006, personal correspondence.

Chapter 7
Prepare Your Own Heart

The situational teaching commanded in Deuteronomy 6:7-9 requires that parents discipline themselves to live what they teach. You must model love for God before you expect it of your children.

Build Your Relationship with God

If you enjoy God as he intends, you will glorify Him. Your pleasure in God will be a delight and comfort to you and, secondarily, present to your child the attractiveness of a relationship with God. The Lord may use your right responses to help him see his wrongs, be convicted, and change (1 Pet. 3:15-17). Even if not, right living keeps your heart free from sin and guilt so that you will have more accurate sight of the truth and be less vulnerable to self-doubt.[1]

Practice Intimacy with God.

Deuteronomy 6:6 says, "Love the Lord your God." Psalm 27:8 says, "When You said, 'Seek My face,' my heart said to You, 'Your face, O Lord, I shall seek.'" Walking with God is not a life of rule-keeping or task quotas. God wants personal communion with you. Relationship with God involves daily conversation with Him (in Bible reading and prayer), studying Him (in regular personal Bible study), and application of what is learned in order to love Him in action.

Study God's Word.

The battlefield of personal growth is the heart, with its desires and thoughts. God's Word renews the mind with truth, revealing false beliefs and selfish desires. This confronts us with the opportunity to desire what God desires and think the way God thinks (Eph. 4:23). Knowledge of God's Word will increase your love for Him because it builds understanding of how great and wonderful He is.

It is rightly said that if we would teach Scripture to our children, we must first understand and apply it to ourselves. May I suggest that we change our emphasis? Let's give primacy to the view that *if we would please the Lord,* we must understand His Word and apply it to ourselves.

Understanding is gained through regular study. Search out verses that best apply to situations and trials in your life. Study to understand how they apply, memorize them for ease of use as situations arise, and be diligent in applying them.

Then use the same process to find and apply verses pertinent to situations in the family and in the child's life. There are books that can help with Bible study for parenting. For example, *Teach Them Diligently*, by Lou Priolo, has an appendix that lists Scriptures that apply to anger, arguing, complaining, fear, and more. Scripture will teach and correct you in your own life (Ps. 119:11; 2 Tim. 3:16). When your life is ruled by Scripture, then you will be able to convey love for and understanding of God's Word heart to heart because it will be life to life. Scripture will become lodged in the child's heart, not just his memory bank.[2]

Pray faithfully.

In prayer we enjoy intimacy with God and express dependence on Him. The believer's prayer delights God (Prov. 15:8b). Besides other times, pray before, during, and after interactions with your child. Seek the Holy Spirit's control and ask God to transform your child's heart and your own.

Practice gratitude.

A person has nothing except what has been given to him, so gratitude is fitting (John 3:27). Gratitude is also an essential because it humbles us and reminds us of our dependence upon the Lord Jesus and of His sovereignty and goodness. Even trials warrant gratitude because they provide opportunities to grow in Christlikeness (Rom. 8:28-29). We are often unaware of our misconceptions and sinful attitudes. Trials uncover sin problems in us that might otherwise have remained hidden. Perhaps we have a temper, dislike for a child, desire for relief at any cost, or envy of other "normal" families. When we identify a problem, then we can deal with it. Romans 5:3-5 tells us to exult in tribulations because tribulations produce perseverance, character, and hope in God's love.

Seek fellowship.

Hebrews 10:24-25 says, "Let us consider how to stimulate one another to love and good deeds, not forsaking our own assembling together as is that habit of some, but encouraging one another; and all the more as you see the day drawing near." God commands believers to fellowship. Lone ranger Christians are presuming self-sufficiency. Believers encourage, correct, and build one another in Christ (Col. 3:16). Parents need to be in regular church attendance and fellowship with other believers.

Evaluate Yourself

Matthew 7:1-5 says that before removing the speck from someone else's eye, we must remove the log from our own. It means that before we correct others, we need to be correcting ourselves. With this in mind, recall Ephesians 6:4. "Fathers, do not provoke your children to anger." In many cases of angry children, parents are provoking the child to fear and anger. They may not even realize that they are doing so. Below are a few questions that you can use to examine yourself:

* Are you loving God so much that you are turning from sin in your own life? Do you demonstrate what trusting God looks like? If you are not loving God, you cannot expect your child to be attracted to love Him.

* Are you consistently obeying God's Word? Are you in submission to your church leaders? Parents who live by their own rules instead of God's are modeling the same autonomy and self-sufficiency that the alienated child practices.

* Husband, are you loving and leading your wife? Are you a learner, studying her so as to love and lead her most effectively? Wife, are you truly submitting with a gentle and quiet spirit or do you resist or manipulate? (Eph. 5:22-33)

* Are you modeling sinful anger? Do you argue, manipulate others, or lose control with them? Do you discipline your child while angry?

* Are you modeling faithfulness? Do you do what you say you will do? Do you live by the same standards you expect of your child?

* Do you listen to your child? Do you spend time just being with him? Do you hear him out when he has a complaint or disagrees with you? Do you interrupt him?

* Are your expectations above his ability? Do your expectations for your child change from day to day? Are rules too restrictive? Are there too few limits? Is he allowed to sin without restraint or correction? Is he allowed to do things that are beyond his ability to handle responsibly?

* Are you instructing your child about rules or do you discipline him for things before telling him the rules?

* Do you discipline consistently? Do you discipline your child for something one day, but not another? Do you apply different consequences to the same misbehavior? Do you discipline impulsively, before getting all of the facts and thinking it out?

* Do you correct him in private or where others can see or hear?

* Do you examine your own heart before confronting the child? Do you ever ask for forgiveness from your child when you have sinned against him?

* Are you demonstrating selfishness, weakness, or self-pity? Do you withdraw when your child is intractable or angry? Do you complain about him, cry, or whine, "Why can't you just..."?

* Do you yell at him? Nag? Scold and lecture? Constantly find fault? Mimic or mock? Call him names? Accuse? Threaten? Belittle or frequently override his decisions? Withhold affection when he does not cooperate? What do your facial expressions and body language communicate?

* Are you frequently affirming him? Do you stay silent except when he needs correction, or do you encourage him?

* Do you show favoritism among the children? Do you compare them?

Please refer to the resources in the appendix, "Resources for Parents," for additional topics on which to evaluate your parenting. If you have provoked your child, you need to confess and begin to change. Here is how you can repent from provoking your child to anger:

1. Identify what you have done to provoke your child.

2. Confess these sins to God (1 John 1:9). Be specific, not vague.

3. Confess sins to your child (Matt. 5:23-24). State clearly and specifically what you did and ask, "Will you forgive me?"

4. Plan how you can change. You have identified what you need to stop. With what will you replace those behaviors? What can you do to provoke your children to love (Heb. 10:24)?

5. Carry out your plan.

Attitudes to Put On

Attitudes provide the atmosphere in which parental responsibilities are exercised. Attitudes of particular importance for the parents of angry, alienated children are watchfulness, compassion, hope, patience, and perseverance.

Watchfulness

Proverbs 4:23 says to "watch over your heart with all diligence, for from it flow the springs of life." Because an alienated child constantly ignites firestorms, parents must examine their motives frequently. Are you burning with passion for God or for self? Are you fervently seeking to love with Christ's love or seeking that the child love you back? Is there a persistent longing to lure the child toward Christ or to get relief from him? Keep watch on your own actions, thoughts, and intentions.

Compassion

Colossians 3:8-13 says to lay aside anger, malice, and the like. In their place, "put on a heart of compassion, kindness, humility, gentleness and patience." Compassion is an essential ingredient to mix into the parenting recipe.

The word "compassion" in Colossians 3:12 is a translation of *splanchnon*, which means "bowels." The bowels refer to emotions because emotions are visceral feelings.[3] Figuratively, it refers to inward affection, a feeling of pity, sympathy, or compassion. There is a spirit of sympathizing with the suffering of the other person.[4] Compassion mixes an attitude of mercy into an act of kindness.

Compassion does not demand to have love reciprocated. It imitates Christ's demeanor toward those caught in sin. Jesus did not condemn the woman caught in adultery (John 8:11). He "felt a love for" the rich young ruler, even as that man rejected Him (Mark 10:21). He loved us enough to die to pay for our sins (John 3:16). Parents must remember that if Jesus so loved them in their sin and rejection of Him, then they also must put on compassion for their child in his sinful state.

Compassion prevents a hardening of heart. After thousands of futile efforts to connect with the child, a calloused indifference may develop. Look at the compassionate father of Luke 15. Though his son prolongedly rejected the family, he maintained a heart eager to forgive so that when the son returned in repentance the father hurried to receive him. Compassion feeds a desire to forgive. According to Ephesians 2:4, it is out of God's compassionate mercy that He forgives. Compassion will leaven your heart to be willing to forgive and to reject anger and calloused withdrawal.

Compassion is something that alienated children need to receive, not to fill an emptiness but because it builds hope and makes parental guidance easier to receive. Someone who approaches with humility, kindness, and patience is not provoking fear and anger (Eph. 6:4), but is encouraging a sense of safety. Compassion is a friend prying open the heart's door for the entrance of truth. Compassion encourages hope.

Compassion is not permissiveness or blindness. It does not excuse or ignore sin, but truthfully identifies it for correction. The compassionate father of Luke 15 did not make a daily Meals-on-Wheels run to his homeless boy. Because compassion values character more than the child's comfort, it does not withhold or save the child from earned punishment.

Compassion drives discipline. It remembers that the child is at risk. Since God is opposed to the proud, if your child violates the commands to honor and obey parents then God is opposed to him. Should he continue in his way, the chastisement that will come from God will be far worse than parental chastisement. The way of the transgressor is hard (Prov 13:15). In compassion for your child, do what you can now to prevent hardships later. Be immovable about consistent discipline because you love that child too much not to be.

You can develop compassion by remembering your own past emotional pains so as to then sympathize with the child's past hurts. Many people experience serious losses of loved ones or of relationships. Many carry anger or wear self-protective masks to hide emotional pain. If you are a Christian, remember that at one time you, like your child, were enslaved to selfishness and needed God's merciful compassion in salvation.

Develop compassion by watching Christ. Read the Gospels and watch Jesus teach the ignorant, reason with the stubborn, forgive the repentant, and warn the unrepentant.

Dependence

We were made to be dependent on God. This is seen in Adam and Eve, who were perfect but still needed counsel. When they chose an independent decision to follow the counsel of Satan, they fell. They were never intended to live independently from God.

You will be tempted many times a day to react with sinful desires, thoughts, and words. Only the Holy Spirit has enough power to enable you to respond in a godly way. Even if you could manage to always generate in yourself love in response to provocations, it would be burned as the straw of man's work rather than God's (1 Cor. 3:12-15). God's love is the fruit of the Spirit (Gal. 5:22-23). Cultivate an attitude of constant dependence upon the Spirit for the parental qualities you need in the moment (Gal. 5:16).

Hope

Take heart, dear parent. There *is* hope! With God, all things are possible (Luke 18:27). God has more than enough power to draw this child to Himself. Cling to that truth. It will energize you to persevere and it will convey hope to your child.

However, hope is not naive presumption. There are hopes that we can count on because Scripture's promises are certain (Num. 23:19; Rom. 15:4). For example, a believer can count on heaven. God guarantees it. But God does not guarantee wealth, health, the ideal family, or even saved children. Proverbs 22:6 is not a promise. To set your hope on a changed or well-behaved child is idolatry. Your happiness or despair must not depend on the child's behavior. God must be your greatest satisfaction no matter what the child does (Exod. 20:3-5). Uncertain hope must be held with an open hand, seeking God's will above its own.

How does this look? Be content with God's sovereign choice. While is it certain that the child can change (joyful thanksgiving be to God for making it possible!), it is not certain that the child *will* change, even "when he is old." Prudent hope knows that the child can change, longs for it, works for it, and allows that the child might not change.

 Rejoice in the knowledge that your obedience pleases God. No matter what response your child makes, whether he gives you cause for happiness or sadness, if you in love obey the Lord you will bring glory to the Lord.

Willfully trust in God's sovereignty, wisdom, and goodness. The composition of your family is not an accident. This child is a gift from God for the spiritual welfare of the whole family, that you all might be drawn to Him. Your trials also are a gift that God intends for your good (James 1:2-3).

Maintaining a balanced hope means that you rest on God's sovereign and loving will while you invite the child to change. The invitation should be as if painted on a billboard, constantly advertising "Abundant Life Possible." Teach God's character, promises, and commands in a way that demonstrates the hope that your child can have something better (Jesus). Holding him accountable for his sinful behavior and calling upon him to change proclaim the hope that he can be free of enslavement. Godly hope pursues truth and compassion and trusts God with the results.

Patience

While the billboard advertises that change is possible, truth in advertising takes into account that change is hard. Therefore, practice patience. In Colossians 3:12, the word "patience" means long-suffering and refers to patience with people (as opposed to circumstances or physical ailments).[5]

Patience is important because the task that you will ask of your alienated child is daunting. For the child to turn *to* God he must turn *from* the only thing he trusts—himself. He has to come out of hiding and abandon his refuge, the habits that make him feel safe. Self-preservation is hard to give up. Letting others be in control is frightening. The moment he tries, he feels vulnerable, confused, even terrified. The old ways entice him back because they are easier.

Because changing habits is so difficult, you need to view change as a baby-step by baby-step process, strewn with failures. As Mark Twain put it, "Habit is habit, and not to be flung out of the window by any man, but coaxed down-stairs [*sic*] a step at a time."[6] Keeping expectations to only one step at a time will help you maintain patience. Patience incorporates practice in trusting God in regard to the other person's choices and practice in compassion as it allows for the difficulty of change.

Perseverance

Perseverance is needed when seeming failures and futility strike. You may do everything right, yet your child is implacable. Gentleness and loving discipline may even escalate the child's anger. For example, Christ's perseverance in pleasing God by loving people and speaking truth intensified the fiery gale of anger and hatred against Him. Anger escalates because love that cannot be manipulated by earning it or schmoozing it nor be pushed away by retaliation is out of the child's control. It shines light on the fact that he is not sovereign, which may frighten and anger him. You must press on.

What a challenge parenting is! No wonder God says, "You shall teach them *diligently*" (Deut. 6:7, emphasis added). God calls parents to persistence. Galatians 6:9 says, "Let us not lose heart in doing good, for in due time we will reap if we do not grow weary." Perseverance requires self-discipline. Be consistent; be persistent.

Persevere in discipline even when it seems futile. Those who do not discipline do not love their children (Prov. 13:24). Do it primarily because it is your obedience to God and, secondarily, your love to the child.

At times, you may think that you have no more love to give. Do not believe your feelings. Love is not a feeling, but an action; a matter not of having but of doing (1 Cor. 13:4-8). Love is a fruit of God's Spirit, so if He is in you then you will practice love (Gal. 5:22). Galatians 5:16 says that if you are led by (dependent upon) the Spirit, you can be kind and/or provide the needed discipline regardless of feelings.

Two ways that you can encourage yourself to endure are to remember Christ and remember your responsibility. It is your job to love God and the child. It is not your job to do what you cannot do, which is to change your child's heart. "Consider Him who has endured such hostility by sinners against Himself, so that you will not grow weary and lose heart" (Heb. 12:3). No matter how the child responds, by obedience you can succeed at loving and glorifying God.

─────────────── **Implement the Principles** ───────────────

* Consult the appendix for books on parenting.

* Use the questions in this chapter to evaluate whether you might be provoking your child to fear and/or anger. Afterward, ask your spouse to evaluate you. Use this information to work together to help each other overcome bad habits in how you relate to each other and your children.

* Read Deuteronomy 6:4-9 and Ephesians 6:4.
  Compare with Ephesians 4:1-5:18.

  – What am I doing that would/could/does provoke my child to anger?

  – For what am I responsible? For what am I not responsible?

    ⸭ What must I do in order to fulfill my responsibility?

    ⸭ What do I need to stop doing in order to trust God with my child's responses?

* Read James 4:1-10.

  – When do I respond in anger?

  – What does this say about what I believe about God? About myself? About my situation?

  – For what am I responsible? For what is my child responsible? With what must I trust God?

* Read these passages at least three times this week: Psalm 127:3; Romans 12:9-21; 1 Corinthians 13:4-8. Answer these questions.

  – How would God have me view my difficult child?

  – For what am I responsible? For what is my child responsible and I am not? With what must I trust God?

  – What do I need to do to fulfill my responsibility?

  – What words in these passages can I tell myself when I feel like giving up or getting angry?

* Seek counsel from your pastor.

Footnotes

1. Welch, *Addictions*, 104-105.
2. Lou Priolo, *Teach Them Diligently* (Woodruff, South Carolina: Timeless Texts, 2000), 11-13.
3. John F. MacArthur, *The MacArthur Study Bible* (Nashville: Thomas Nelson, Inc., 1997), 1838.
4. Clarke, "Clarke's Commentary."
5. Adams, *Theology*, 256.
6. Twain, *Puddn'head Wilson*, 31.

Chapter 8

Structure Your Home

Communication between parents and children is carried out within a context of household and relational assumptions about the way life is supposed to happen. What is the authority structure? Who does what when? How is the what to be done? Before considering what to teach an alienated child and how to handle confrontations, be sure that the environment is in order.

Understand What Discipline Is

Ephesians 6:4 commands parents to "bring [children] up in the discipline and instruction of the Lord." The word "discipline" *(paideia)* means to instruct, train, or educate.[1] It is the shaping of the child's faculties and habit patterns.[2] It enables him to skillfully utilize the knowledge gained from instruction.

First Timothy 4:7 says to "discipline yourself for the purpose of godliness." Here, the word "discipline" is a translation of the Greek word *gumnazo*, which means to train or exercise.[3] It describes the kind of training an athlete like a gymnast does, performing a vault over and over to perfect the skill and make correct execution habitual. Wrong moves are corrected, and right behaviors are practiced to replace the old wrong ones.[4]

Training takes time, patience, thought, consistency, and self-discipline. It requires the trainer to give up his/her own comfort and convenience in order to coach and supervise a less-skilled person. In a family, the process is generally not over for at least eighteen years per child. Because it is a demanding process, parents must discipline themselves.

While behaviors need to be changed, training in good habits is not to be behavior modification. By that I mean that the focus is not external, on a particular behavior. Instead, realize that behaviors express the heart, and a heart desire is likely to be expressed in a number of particular behaviors, so the target is heart change. A behavioral approach thinks of the present event while biblical training views that behavior in the context of a whole growth process. Biblical training incorporates God's character into every situation. The standard is not "Because I said so," but "My dear child, God is truth and so we must be truthful. It is He who commands that we not lie but speak truth." God wants the child's beliefs and desires trained in righteousness and his conscience trained to discern good and evil so that righteousness of both heart and behavior in everyday life are habitual[5] and based upon a right response to God from the heart (1 Tim. 4:7; Heb. 5:14; 12:11).

Discipline includes teaching and training through the day, not just consequences for infractions. Besides verbal teaching, it is carried out in orderliness, the regulation of time and activities, setting of limits, and practice of good deeds.

Structure Your Home

Establish relational priorities.

Parenting an angry, alienated child can easily absorb all of your time, energy, and money. You also have responsibilities regarding marriage, children, relatives, church, friends, and work. Refuse to pour all resources into the angry child at the expense of your spouse or the other children.

Someone might say, "But wouldn't we put a disproportional amount of resources into a child sick with cancer?" First, the alienated child has a moral problem, not a physical disease. Sad and enslaved though he may be, he does not have to live the way that he has chosen. Second, you risk provoking the other children to anger by injustice. Proverbs 18:5 teaches that wicked people can be skilled manipulators. Do not give in and show partiality to them. Amounts for each child will differ. Be wise and just. Third, if you neglect other God-given responsibilities for the sake of one, it is idolatry. A beggar will sometimes do anything to get a piece of bread. Do not accept the bribe of better behavior in your angry child so that you divert the major portion of your time, energy, and resources from the others (Prov. 28:21; Deut. 16:19).

Involve the church.

God does not intend that we forge through life alone (Heb. 10:24-25). When we refuse to attend church regularly and refuse to seek help, we are behaving as self-sufficiently as the child. Secular sources lead to man's ways of managing. In the church is where wisdom from

God's Word is shared. God ordained the church as a primary place to receive His counsel, and gives to the church people gifted to comfort, encourage, teach, and help each other (Eph. 4:11-16; Rom. 15:14). Members cannot help one another if they do not know what the problems are, so you should ask your spiritual friends and leaders for counsel (Gal. 6:1-10).

At church, others will reinforce the concepts that you most want your child to learn. Believers there will confirm to the child your authority in the home. They may even reinforce it. Jesus said that when someone is in sin, such as this child, and will not heed private counsel, the problem is to be taken to the church (Matt. 18:15-20). Church leaders can evaluate you to be certain that you are parenting in a godly manner that does not provoke the child. They may also have further wisdom for dealing with situations that arise.

Prepare your biblical toolbox.

The label "Reactive Attachment Disorder" indicates a constellation of habituated behaviors. You can help yourself to feel less overwhelmed and arm yourself with effective tools if you break the constellation into parts. Start a notebook or chart. For each behavior typical of your child, find Scripture passages that put God's label on it, offer an example of it, or show the solution to it. Chapters 9–13 will explain how to use the information you collect.

Although you must work to change the behaviors, remember that they are just symptoms, not the core problem. The philosophy of RAD as a "disorder" appears to explain the child without having to address the heart. Looking at the heart leads to topics of motive and sin, which hint loudly about God, so it is safer to stay away from the heart. In contrast, you want to go for the heart because that is what needs to be reconciled to God and what generates the behaviors. These habituated behaviors are expressing habituated desires of the heart. So start a list or chart on the heart desires that could generate the troublesome habitual behaviors that your child is demonstrating. As with behaviors, find passages that put God's label on said desire, illustrate it, or show the solution that God wants the child to put on.

These charts can be highly useful. Instead of trying to do something about RAD, you will have readily at hand Scripture that applies to stealing or rolling the eyes or inappropriate affection toward strangers. The exercise of compiling verses related to behaviors and heart desires will require time and hard work at study. The charts and verses in this book should give you a huge jump-start.

Structure your lifestyle.

An organized home and consistent schedules provide protective limits and guidelines for everyone. Reliability provides a sense of safety, which is especially important for alienated children. Consistency helps children to learn self-discipline and helps parents to keep tabs on what needs to be done next or what has not been done as it should be. Some protective measures may have to be extreme. One parent expressed, "We never used to have to have motion detectors in the hall. We never used to sleep with our bed in front of the door so they couldn't get out at night and set fire to something." [6] When you fulfill your own responsibilities and make the environment orderly, you are both modeling and enforcing self-discipline.

Visit the doctor.

Have the child evaluated for physical and neurological problems. If there are any, you can make adjustments accordingly.

Assign daily work.

Man was made to work (Gen. 1:28). Work counters laziness, teaches cause and effect (Gal. 6:7), teaches responsibility and industry, and requires the practice of self-discipline (1 Cor. 9:27). It opposes the pride of entitlement and superiority, and instills an unstated sense of belonging and teamwork within the family, all of which directly relate to RAD characteristics. Work teaches skills that will benefit the child in the future (Prov. 19:15; Eccles. 10:18). Completed work yields a non-parent-controlled, non-threatening satisfaction for the child.

Children should have age-appropriate daily chores and be held to doing them well. Sloppiness must not be allowed (Eccles. 9:10). The result does not have to be perfect, but if the job is age-appropriate, you can rightly require them to do their jobs well. They need to be held responsible and need the training that work provides.

Clarify rules.

God is careful to give clear commands. He specified exactly what Adam could and could not do and what the consequence of disobedience was (Gen. 1:28-30; 2:16-17). The Ten Commandments are well-defined. The laws and principles in passages like Romans 14, Ephesians 4, and Colossians 3 are specific and clear. Make your rules clear.

Base rules on God's commands and principles. For example, a rule like "Thou shalt be in bed by 9:00 p.m." might be based on a principle of stewardship of the body (1 Cor. 6:19).

God's will is explained in two ways, by outright commands and by principles for living. Commands are unchangeable. Principles guide decisions that might change. Commands like "honor parents" and "do not lie" are unchangeable. The 9:00 p.m. bedtime rule, which is based on a principle, can change to 10:00 p.m. on weekends or for a special event. *Rules without reason lead to rebellion,* so have a biblical reason for the rules you make and be sure to show your child the verse on which you base your reason.

Affirm often.

Words of affirmation demonstrate love, respect, and a kind intent in correction (Prov. 16:23). There will be many corrections. The practice of affirming helps to guard your attitudes by keeping you on the lookout for good and by offering peace (1 Cor. 13:8; Rom. 12:18). Affirmation is not for buying good behavior or building self-esteem. For a confused child, it confirms when he is getting something right, like when Jesus affirmed the lawyer for his correct answer on how to inherit eternal life (Luke 10:28). Your affirmation conveys to your child the hope that he can do right.

Have fun.

Proverbs 15:13 says, "A joyful heart makes a cheerful face, but when the heart is sad, the spirit is broken." Angry, alienated children have usually been given much cause for sadness. Like advertisements to consumers, play may entice the child with glimpses of something good that he might then want enough to try letting go of his selfish ways and participate in relationship.

Life with a contentious child can grow heavy and humorless. Paul says to rejoice (Phil. 4:4). Standing in the grace of Christ, Christian parents have many reasons to rejoice. So smile. Give an unexpected hug. Laugh. Be crazy. Do the unexpected. It injects grace and lightens the household atmosphere. Sometimes, a sudden hug or a lighthearted response can defuse a situation and prevent one more disciplinary episode. The intent is not to evade an issue but to add grace that dilutes negative emotions and tension so that everyone has a moment to pause and think.

The child might respond to fun with anger or sullenness. Others having fun around him demonstrates that they are not dominated by his manipulations. Whatever his view, humor and rejoicing winsomely invite him to participate.

Practice empathy.

Hebrews 4:15-16 says:

> We do not have a high priest who cannot sympathize with
> our weaknesses, but One who has been tempted in all things
> as we are, yet without sin. Let us therefore draw near with
> confidence to the throne of grace, that we may receive mercy
> and may find grace to help in time of need.

God is transcendent beyond our imagination and we are but clay,
yet Jesus sat down on the floor with us, so to speak. He descended
from heaven and stepped into human flesh. He joined in our work
and play and pains. He immersed Himself in empathy by coming to
be God *with us*. Seeing His great love, we know that we can draw near
to Him, and we want to.

Every parent is made of dust just as his child is. When hurt, have
you not withdrawn or wanted revenge? Do you not react with anger,
fear, and attempts to control others? Have you not been cold or hardhearted toward someone, and most certainly toward God?

Humble yourself and step into your child's world. Put on compassion, gentleness, patience, and forbearance (Eph. 4:1-3). Demonstrate
a desire to walk alongside, not to drive from behind or drag from in
front. Play games together. Do fun activities together. Join in activities that he thinks are fun. Do family with him, not to him. Jesus did
not cling to His superiority, but laid it aside to become human. Make
this an abiding attitude that permeates your parenting (Phil. 2:5-8).

─────── Implement the Principles ───────

The suggestions below are intended to help you improve as a parent
through three means: Increase your understanding of how God
parented His child, Israel. Study your child and his ways. Gain counsel about yourself from others..

* Study Numbers 11, Numbers 14:10-27, Ezekiel 16,
  Psalm 106, and Psalm 78 to see God's heart and actions
  as a parent.

  ("Study" means more than reading. List the attitudes
  and actions of God toward His child. Compare and
  contrast the two. Ask questions of the text.
  What does God desire? When does He teach, rebuke,
  correct, wait, discipline, or comfort? What precipitates

the difference? In what ways does He mix grace with His discipline? Etc.)

* Study what true repentance is. Compare the lives of Esau (Gen. 25 and 27; Heb. 12:16-17) and David (2 Sam. 11:1-12:23). Study 2 Corinthians 7:9-11.

* Journal the child's behaviors to get to know him better. It is easy to magnify a situation so that it appears worse than it is. It is also possible to overlook incidents that might indicate a pattern. Perhaps a child does not bring home a school notice of an assessment test day and, when asked, claims he never received it. The incident is soon forgotten. But if you see in a journal that the child has an overall pattern of lying about his irresponsibility, you might perceive that action is needed. Journaling can assuage fears, refresh the memory, and increase clarity, which all helps the parent in dealing with the child.

* Identify one right behavior that your child should develop and find one Bible verse that teaches it. Identify a godly desire that would motivate such a behavior and a Bible verse that teaches it. Plan ways to teach what God says to your child.

* Together with your spouse, read *Shepherding a Child's Heart*, by Tedd Tripp. The person on the right reads the right page, the person on the left the left page. Allow time for discussion, or for each chapter set a date night to discuss the main points and how you as a couple might implement them with your children..

Footnotes

1. W. E. Vine, *Vine's Expository Dictionary of Old and New Testament Words* (Old Tappan, N.J.: Fleming H. Revell Company, 1981), 1:183.
2. Lou Priolo, *The Heart of Anger* (New York: Calvary Press Publishing, 1997), 61.
3. Ibid., 62-63.
4. Priolo, *Teach Them Diligently*, 74.
5. Ibid.
6. Amy Baker, "Reactive Attachment Disorder."

Chapter 9

Instruction Particular to the Alienated Child

Part 1

In the last chapter, we began to examine Ephesians 6:4, "bring them up in the discipline and instruction of the Lord." We partially fleshed out the word "discipline" in the way of training by use of a disciplined structure. Now we will relate the word "instruction" to alienated children. The word "instruction" *(nouthesia)* means "admonition, exhortation."[1] It refers to teaching verbally. Admonishment assumes that there is a problem that needs correction. Because children start with sinful hearts and are influenced by a world of discomforts and sinful people, they wrongly interpret their discomforts and both generate and absorb false ideas.[2] Following the pattern of 2 Timothy 3:16, parents instruct, reprove, correct, and exhort their children to do better the next time, training them in righteousness.

Antisocial children have convinced themselves of many lies which fuel angry attacks and keep them barricaded away from people. Instruction will help to align their thinking with truth. For example, one problem a RAD-type child may have is ignorance of how to behave. If tantrums worked in the orphanage or foster care, he may not know respectful request methods. He needs instruction.

Teaching informs the conscience, thereby sensitizing it. Jesus many times taught to inform the conscience. For example, He taught the Pharisees about marriage, correcting their misinterpretation of Scripture, and then held them to account for it (Matt. 19:1-11). By feeding the multitudes, He taught his disciples about Himself and expected them to act on their knowledge by applying faith (Mark 6:45-52; 8:1-21).

Instruction of alienated children needs to emphasize the particular desires and erroneous perceptions driving their behaviors. In the moment, an alienated child may steal because he wants the toy, but he also has underlying habituated motives of fear, anger, and control. Fear drives the desire to control in order to feel safe. Anger drives the desire to control in order to force justice, gain revenge, or manipulate to get his way. Some important topics of instruction include God's character, love for Him, the gospel, authority, sowing and reaping, the relationship between love and obedience, the power of habituation, anger, fear, and the choice of who he will trust. Perhaps you will discover other underlying desires that drive your child's behavior.

While improved behavior is part of the solution, the most important goal in biblical instruction is not a well-behaved child. It is that your child will learn to live in the fullness of a right relationship with God. In all, your child needs to understand that he was made to worship God and doing so will be his highest joy.

Are you a new Christian or inexperienced with using the Bible? Lean on this book and those listed in the appendix as a start. Make time to study the Bible to gain a solid understanding of one passage at a time. Right application of one passage is more important than knowledge of many passages. Parenting provides an opportunity for you to grow in your Bible knowledge and understanding.

The implementation ideas offered in this chapter are only suggestions to get you started thinking of how you can implement truths into your child's life. They are not fix-its. The child may often be uncooperative. Choose the time when the lessons will be best received. No matter the timing, an alienated child is likely to sabotage many of your attempts. To persevere, you must be grounded in the determination to please the Lord above all and to love your child as God commanded in Ephesians 6:4, Luke 6:27-49, 1 Corinthians 13, and Philippians 2:3-4.

Teach God's Character

The chronically fearful and angry child interprets God through his circumstances. From his perspective, God never did anything for him. God is not even relevant. The child has survived on his own. Why be interested in trusting some entity who apparently has no power to protect him or who does not care? Why should he want to love God? These are valid questions. It would be foolish to trust and obey such a being.

The child may never verbalize such questions, but his life is functioning by his answers to them. Parents need to raise the issues and give him legitimate reasons. The child needs to know about God's sovereignty, wisdom, and love, and be taught to interpret his circumstances through God's character.

Make an effort to look at the Lord through the lens your child is using, to see what he perceives. Then raise related questions for him to ponder awhile before you answer them. For example, to an antisocial child, compassion and love may appear to be signs of weakness. How could a God who dies rather than fight back be worthy of respect? You can ask which he finds easier, retaliation or returning good for evil? Teach about the great strength it requires to do good (Prov. 16:32).

Why should he (an angry child) fear/reverence God like Proverbs 1:7 says? He needs to hear of God's holiness and justice as well as His love. Make teaching well-rounded.

God's love is attractive. By it, God offers us forgiveness and reconciliation. His love communicates His absolute trustworthiness and the possibility of joyful relationship. The writer of Lamentations felt alienated from God (Lam 3:1-20). Recalling God's love and faithfulness inspired hope (Lam 3:21-23). Knowledge of God's love combats doubts of His goodness; we are more likely to interpret our circumstances through it. Then, instead of fighting against trials, we submit to them as God's good work of discipline for our character development. His love motivates gratitude and praise.

God's character should be taught as it applies to present situations in the child's life and in relation to upcoming events that could provoke fears. It should also be incorporated into rethinking any past maltreatment. Teach truths and thoughts to put on, like the fact that God cares about those who suffer. He is a reliable shelter who defends the oppressed (Ps. 10:18), executes justice for them, and meets their needs (Ps. 146:7). In this child's past painful experiences, God was in some way preserving him and was there all along as a refuge to which he could have gone and found comfort (Prov. 15:3; Ps. 27:1). Even now, God has some great purpose, and if the child will love God then that purpose includes good in the child's life (Rom. 8:28).

Why did God allow someone to hurt this child? This is an excellent question when it is directed at learning more of God's character so as to trust Him. We cannot presume to know with certainty God's reasons for this particular case because this exact case is not recorded in His Word, but we do know that God has foreseen the question. He graciously informs us that He uses evil for His glory and the good of those who love Him (Rom. 8:28-29). "Will you, my dear child, be one who loves Him?"

Some people choose to hurt others. Joseph's brothers threw young Joseph into a pit and sold him as a slave. Joseph was, like the alienated child might have been, rejected by his own family. He was helpless, mistreated, insulted, made a slave, and put into prison when he was innocent. His dad did not come and save him. Everyone who had any power wanted to use or hurt him. There was absolutely no person in his life who would help him. It seemed that even God did not save him. It was a real them-against-me catastrophe. So he was alone in his helplessness, right? He had to fight for his life because if he didn't take care of himself, no one else would, right? No, this is how man mistakenly thinks.

Despite appearances, God was there all along loving him. Later, Joseph could look back and see that even in the beatings and deprivations God was protecting him from worse. God overruled the brothers' original intent to murder him. God overruled the captain of the king's bodyguard to save him from execution and bring him out of prison. God providentially turned the king himself to exalt Joseph at the right time. Rather than grow angry at the injustices done him, Joseph chose to trust God and use the trials to learn godliness. He learned compassion and wisdom. Then he was able to save thousands from starvation, including the very brothers who had sold him. It turned out that God had a good and wise purpose for all of the suffering (Gen. 37-50).

The story of Jesus is the acme of God's sovereignty, wisdom, and love in suffering. As they can with Joseph, fearful, angry children can identify to a degree with Jesus' rejection and mistreatment. Your child needs to see that Jesus knew that the mockings, insults, beatings, and death he endured were part of God's wise plan and see that He trusted God in it (John 19:8-11). Jesus' case was different in that He had the power to take control. Yet, He did not. He submitted to God's will because He wanted to please God more than He wanted safety, respect, or relief from pain. He loved God more than He loved comfort. As a result, God delighted in His Son and resurrected Him.

If the question of why God allowed past pain is used as an excuse for anger or depression, then the answer is, does today's obedience depend on knowing why the past happened? What is necessary is to trust and obey God. The Lord has given plenty of foundation for trusting Him.

The following are ideas to aid in implementation of the truth of God's love and sovereignty. Adapt them for the age and ability of your child. Use them to brainstorm ideas of your own.

———————————————┤ **Implement the Principles** ├———————————————

- Memorize and teach the passages listed in this section.

- Together as parents, pray with your child. Praise God for His attributes. Thank Him for His grace, mercy, love, and faithful protection. Make requests for present situations.

- Together as parents with your family, read or tell the story of Joseph (Gen. 37-50). Where was God when Joseph was attacked? When Joseph was thrown in prison? When Joseph was ignored in prison for three years? What did God do that was powerful? Wise? Loving? Just? What difference did belief in God's holiness and justice make in Joseph's thoughts and behaviors? How about belief in His goodness? Ask the child where God was when he was abandoned (or other past bad experience). Did he feel like Joseph probably did? What difference would belief in God's goodness make in his thoughts or actions? What difference would belief in God's holiness and justice make? What false ideas might he put off and what truths might he think from now on?

- Read John 18-20. Especially note Jesus' response to Pilate in 19:8-11. Who really had power? How much strength did it take to not exercise His power? Note other evidence that Jesus loved and trusted God so much that He willingly submitted to the trials that God ordained for Him. This horrible experience was what God used to make it possible for people, like this child, to have forgiveness. How are God's holiness and justice evident?

- With your child, read and discuss Psalm 139. What do you learn about God? What is God's view of you? What has He done for you?

- With your child, read and discuss John 4, 5, 8, and 9. What do you see Jesus doing and saying? What do His words and actions tell you about His compassion? Ask the child, "How might this relate to you?"

- With your child, read and discuss John 10. Also study about sheep and shepherding. Draw comparisons with people and Jesus. Of what benefit is it to think of Jesus as the Good Shepherd? Perhaps, tie in Psalm 23.

* With your child, memorize Isaiah 38:17. Teach this verse together with the story of Hezekiah. Observe in Hezekiah's story what happens to those who do not love God. God is just and those who reject Him suffer punishment. God is merciful and does not give to those who love Him the punishment they really deserve. He lovingly uses suffering for their benefit.

* With your child, read Lamentations 3:32-33. God has unfailing love and compassion. Discuss how, although God uses trials for the good of those who love Him, He is not glad to bring grief to His own. See also Lamentations 3:22-25.

* Together with the child list the good things that have come from his/her past. List what more good God might use it for if the child decides to trust God so as to become one of "those who love God" (Rom. 8:28).

Teach about Loving God

The greatest commandment is to love the Lord your God with all of your being (Deut. 6:5; Matt. 22:37). Mankind was made to love and worship God. We have a very practical way to demonstrate that love. Jesus told his disciples, "If you love me, you will keep my commandments" (John 14:15). It is a simple equivalence:

Obedience = Love

Obedience to God's Word demonstrates love for God; disobedience (obedience to self) expresses love for self. The problem of an antisocial child is who he loves. He says, "I love me and will do anything it takes to please me." As an equation, it might look like:

Obedience to Me = Love of Me

How can he repent and begin to love God? He must put off love of self and put on love for God (Luke 9:23). As Jesus said, he does it through obedience. He can put on the desire to please God so that his actions say, "I love God and will do what He says to please Him" (2 Cor. 5:9).

Obedience to God = Love for God

Love does not produce empty words. Jesus asked the Pharisees, "Why do you call me Lord, Lord, and do not do what I say?" (Luke 6:46).

Nor is love shown by a shell of good behaviors performed to portray an appearance of obedience or to avoid punishment (Matt. 23:27-28). David said that it is not offerings that please God but a heart of repentance over sins (Ps. 51:16-17).

First Samuel 15 is a good passage for teaching the love-obedience connection. When God sent King Saul against the Amalekites, He ordered Saul to destroy all of the Amalekites and their livestock. Instead, Saul kept King Agag and some livestock alive. When the prophet Samuel arrived, he asked about the bleating he was hearing. Saul answered that he had kept the animals to make sacrifices to God. Saul made it look like he was loving God. But Samuel saw that it was not love because Saul was doing what he wanted, not what God wanted. He declared Saul rebellious. God wants obedience, not fake sacrifices (1 Sam. 15:22-23).

The choice is simple—love God or love self. Since God's paradigm does not fit the antisocial child's victor/victim, win/lose model, it surprises with the hope of a whole new way of seeing relationships. It invites your child out of emotions and self-love and into love for God. This new choice fades your child's supposed antagonists and victims into the background and aims the spotlight on the God of compassion who sees all of his hurts and will also punish his continued rebellion.

This shift in focus needs to be taught with gentleness because it may feel threatening to him. It disorganizes his worldview matrix. It disarms him by taking away confusion, a manipulation tool. It shoots through the defenses he has built around his heart. It directly opposes his chosen religion and proposes to take his most cherished love from him. It pricks his conscience, which can produce fear or anger. As the Lord's ambassador to your child, gently, persistently, lovingly call your child back to his simple options by injecting the love question— love God or love self.

─────────────── **Implement the Principles** ───────────────

* Parent, spend time adoring and enjoying God for yourself. If you do not worship and adore Jesus, why would your child find Him appealing?

* Pray with your child. Adore God with praise and thanksgiving. Do not be general. Use truths from passages that you are reading.

- Memorize verses from this section. Discuss how they apply.

- Ask, "What purpose for living does God's Word teach?" "How does Matthew 22:37 relate?"

- Teach what obedience to God's Word communicates (love for God). Use 1 Samuel 13, 15; John 14:15, and others.

- Based on Luke 6:43-46, ask, "What did you do in _____ (situation)? What does that say about who you love?"

- Teach what repentance is. Use 2 Samuel 11:1-12:23; Genesis 25:29-34; Hebrew 12:17; 2 Corinthians 7:9-10, Psalm 51.

- Teach about fake fruit from Matthew 23:27-28. Illustrate with plastic fruit or fruit that looks good but is rotten on the inside.

Teach the Gospel

Obviously, this child needs the gospel, but how is it to be presented to him? "God loves you." What is love to a RAD-type child? "Jesus died for you." So Jesus is a weak victim. Tell him the sinner's prayer and he will parrot it back. By cooperating he, e.g., dupes his camp counselor and earns a chance to throw his stick in the fire and wow the other kids with a testimony. He will say all the right words and get "saved" for various people.

Do not be quick to lead this child in a prayer and profession. Can God save him in an instant? To be sure. But he is a talented, compulsive deceiver. What good is a false conversion? It provides more practice at deception by allowing him to play the "I'm a Christian" card to win others' trust fraudulently. It further hardens his heart by providing an escape from conviction. Worse, he takes God's name in vain when he swears falsely to salvation in Christ.

This precaution is needful for all of your children. Teaching gospel truths should be ongoing, but there is too much at stake to rush a child into a profession or prayer of salvation. Quickness to lead him in a profession of faith or to reassure him that he is saved is to do a disservice to him, to the church, and to God. What if he is not truly saved? Would you want him blind to his peril so that he would not know to take action? (Matt. 7:16; 13:3-23; John 6:60-66; 1 Cor. 11:19; 2 Cor. 7:9-10; 13:5; 1 John 2:4-6, 18-19).

The sixth chapter of John records that Jesus was not quick to accept as genuine the loyalty of the multitudes that followed. In addition, He put people off and continued to teach salvation truths difficult to accept. He did so knowing that many would then reject Him, but those whom the Father called would come. If your child shows an inclination to go through your church's motions identified with being "saved," perhaps have him wait, pray, and talk more with you. Like Jesus did, emphasize the obedience that will be required of him as a child of God. With grace and without compromise, build your child's understanding so that his eventual commitment will be well-informed. If waiting concerns you, remember that the Holy Spirit, by the power of God's Word, can save your child without you (Rom. 1:16; 1 Cor. 1:18, 24; 2 Tim. 3:14-15). If God is truly drawing your child to follow Him, your child will continue to pursue commitment to Christ. All whom the Father calls will come (John 6:37).

Jesus was not quick to assume saving faith. Matthew 9:10-13 records a time when the Pharisees saw Jesus eating with irreligious people and took issue with it. Jesus answered that it is the sick who need a physician. He said, "Go and learn what this means, 'I desire compassion, and not sacrifice,' for I did not come to call the righteous, but sinners." Jesus' point was that the Pharisees obviously saw themselves as in no need of spiritual help. They saw themselves as righteous, not as having hearts full of sin. So Jesus gave them an assignment focused on a glaring sin, their lack of compassion. The one who tried it might begin to realize that his heart did, indeed, lack compassion and fall far short of pleasing God. Only then would he see himself in need of God and His deliverance.

This child is just like those Pharisees. He holds a high view of self and low view of God. He is neither sick nor sinner, so what need does he have for forgiveness, salvation, or a savior? Salvation through Christ is a moot point, irrelevant, nonsensical.

"The fear of the Lord is the beginning of wisdom, and the knowledge of the Holy One is understanding" (Prov. 9:10). The antisocial child is not impressed by God because He has no fear of (respect for) God's holiness, justice, and power. So he has no understanding that would make any sense of salvation. How is God any different from all of the other authorities to be duped or ignored? Therefore, before any move toward a profession of faith, he needs much instruction on God's holiness, power, and justice, and that his sins make him guilty before God and in danger of eternal punishment.

Teach him who the wicked are. They are not just very badly-behaved people. The wicked include all who do not honor and obey or trust in God (Ps. 37; Eccles. 8:13; Jer. 17:5). The wicked put Christ to death (Acts 2:23), and since it was for sins that He died and we have all sinned, then we all (presalvation) can be classified as wicked, and that includes him.[3] All who do not repent of anger, bitterness, vengeance, and rebellion have broken the law. Before the Judge, they are guilty and the penalty is eternal hell. His only hope is repentance.

God, in His goodness and power, returned good for evil. He sent Jesus Christ to offer a way that the child could have his penalty paid for him. Jesus is not a weak victim; He is most powerful because He rose from the dead. If the child turns from his way to follow Jesus' way, he will be forgiven and receive a new heart in place of his uncontrollable one, rest in place of turmoil (Rom. 6:23; 2 Cor. 5:17; Tit. 3:5).

This must not be a shallow "invite Jesus into your heart" presentation. To this child, if that is all that this Jesus guy wants, "Sure, I'll add him to my cast of manipulable authorities."

Don't set the bar low. What good is it to run from hell but not find your full satisfaction and total delight in Jesus?

An alienaed child already feels victimized. Do not bait and switch with the gospel, presenting salvation from hell but not the obedience and self-denial that God requires of His children. That is false advertising. Lay the cost clearly before him. Following God brings the greatest satisfaction in the world, but it demands obedience and turning from self (Luke 9:23; John 14:21). He needs to know that it will cost him everything (Luke 14:26-27).

Be complete with the truth about heaven and hell, but do not utilize emotional appeals or heavy-handed threats of hell. Manipulation expresses distrust of God. We are to instruct the mind, not manipulate the emotions or the will.

What if he gives appearance of repentance? In consideration of his extreme habituation, take at least two measures. One, be sure to instruct him about how to change habits so that lack of know-how is not preventing him from changing his sinful habits. Two, wait and watch him for a long time. People are known by their fruits (Luke 6:43-46). Jesus gave the Pharisees an assignment that would reveal their hearts. I am not suggesting that you invent tests. Daily situations in a family will present many tests of his obedience to authority or compassion toward others. Waiting also allows time for him to gradually fail less and less in real changes to his habits. If he has been redeemed, your insistence on evidence is not going to damage him (1 Pet. 1:5). True repentance produces discernible and lasting change.

Teach about Authority

The alienated child has convinced himself that authorities are enemies. According to Ephesians 6:1-3, this view is false. It says,

> Children, obey your parents in the Lord, for this is right. Honor your father and mother (which is the first commandment with a promise), that it may be well with you, and that you may live long on the earth.

God loves children and places them under authority for their benefit. He includes a promise that life will go well with children who submit to His plan by obeying and honoring their parents.

Teach your child how the Lord uses authority structure to protect and bless people, including him. It could be that past caregivers were not a place of safety to this child. God loved him, and delivered him into the care of those who would protect him and teach him in love. You parents are also under the authority of this powerful, loving God. Your parental authority is not yours just because you say so. God placed you in authority and holds you accountable for how you treat your child. It is true that some authorities misuse power; they will receive justice from God. The Lord commands that we all obey our authorities and trust Him. Good examples of those who obeyed despite mistreatment include Joseph, David, Daniel, Jesus, and Paul.

Explain your intentions. The rules you set are for the welfare of him and the family. You would be delighted to see him blessed and happy and that will come only as he obeys God's command in Ephesians 6:1-3.

Teach about motive and attitude. Respect for parents shows submission to God's authority. We submit out of gratitude for God's great love for us. Gratitude is demonstrated by obedience done cheerfully and immediately, at the first command. You can say things like, "God says that being under the authority of parents is a good thing. It is God's will for you and He promises that if you obey you will be blessed. If you love God, you will obey Him by honoring me."

Make expectations clear. "Obedience for the glory of God does not dawdle. When I tell you to do something that you are able to do, I expect you to obey the first time I say it." "God says that you are to honor your parents. If you want something, you may ask me respectfully. You may not command me."

Do we always feel like cheerfully or contentedly submitting? Of course not. Teach how that can be done, that God gives the strength to do it, and that he must put off feelings and put on love.

Implement the Principles

- With your child, memorize Ephesians 6:1-3. Look at the original commandment. Discuss what each phrase means.

- Flesh out the promise in Ephesians 6:1-3. List all of the blessings that are included in it. Read through Proverbs 1-4 with your child and add to your list. How were people described in the Bible blessed by honoring their parents? What happened to those who did not, like Samson? How is God loving when He commands that children respect and obey their parents? How is your child blessed when he honors you?

- Parents, together with your child, read and discuss 1 Samuel 15. How was Saul disobedient to God? What was the result? Study and discuss others who disobeyed God or dishonored their parents: Adam, Esau, and Jonah. How would respect and obedience have provided safety and blessing? Relate this to a time when your child's respect and obedience worked for his/her safety and blessing.

- Read in Genesis about Joseph and his brothers. How did they honor and dishonor their father? What did God do in opposition to the disrespectful? How did Joseph show respect for each authority in his life? Was life always easy as a result? How did God give grace to the one who respected authorities? How does Joseph illustrate Ephesians 6:2-3? How did honoring of authorities provide security and blessing? You can do the same exercise with other young men like Daniel and his friends, David in his boyhood, and Timothy. Relate these truths to your child's life.

- Discuss the benefits that a child receives by being under parental authority. In what ways is it a blessing to him/her? With your child, pray and thank God for any benefits evident now.

- Where there is resistance, ask: "What does Ephesians 6:1 say?" "Now what should you do?"

Teach Sowing and Reaping

Proverbs says, "Like a dog that returns to its vomit is a fool who repeats his folly" (Prov. 26:11). "Though you pound a fool in a mortar with a pestle along with crushed grain, yet his folly will not depart from him" (Prov. 27:22). Since the angry child keeps returning to lap up his old folly, his lifestyle fits the biblical label "fool." If you study the word "fool" in Proverbs you will learn more about your alienated child and how to train him. Despite the determination to repeat folly, the principle of reaping what you sow can teach a child to be careful of his sowing (Gal. 6:7-10). God uses this principle to turn us from our foolishness.

In a way, an antisocial child knows the sowing and reaping principle. His problem is that he attaches value to the wrong crop, his immediate pleasure. He is shortsighted. When the later unpleasant harvest comes, he rages against it as unjust. So he does not learn to value godliness "though you pound [him]." Vision correction may help.

Extend your child's vision by highlighting future consequences. In the present, misbehavior can feel great, but it reaps a later harvest that is painful. In the present, godly behavior can feel unpleasant, but it reaps a later harvest of peace and joy (Heb. 12:11).

Teach your child about the kinds of consequences we reap in our relationships. We either build or destroy relationship with God as God is opposed to the proud or gives grace to the humble (John 14:21; James 4:6). We either build relationships with others or cause strife and division that destroys relationships (James 4:1-3; Prov. 14:11).

We reap consequences for ourselves physically, emotionally, attitudinally, intellectually, and in the joy/sorrow of living. Sin has a boomerang effect; the sinner's deeds come back on him (Prov. 26:27). Those who look for evil receive it (Prov. 11:3, 27). Sin heaps on him a load of guilt feelings, anxiety, anger, bitterness, fear, and the like. Life will be full of hindrances, "thorns and snares" (Prov. 22:5). There will be misery and even death (Prov. 1:32; 19:16; 21:16). "But he who listens to me shall live securely and will be at ease from the dread of evil" (Prov. 1:33). Wise behavior prevents dread and troubles, and leads to health, satisfaction, peace of mind, and honor (Prov. 22:4-5; 3:7-8).

Actions shape reputation, which impacts opportunities and relationships. A good reputation builds trust and opens opportunities. Irresponsibility or dishonesty discourages respect and earns a reputation of untrustworthiness (Prov. 20:11; 12:8; 25:19). Others won't trust him with jobs that could bring him rewards that he would like.

We reap in habituation. Our actions cultivate habits. Those habits create a lifestyle, a path of living that reaps benefits or sorrows depending on the course we choose (Prov. 16:17).

The principle of sowing and reaping is not intended just for behavior modification. Consequences should uncover our hard-heartedness toward God so that we see our offenses as personal to Him. They are to draw us into the fullness of a loving relationship with Him and then rich relationships with others.

Here are some questions to guide instruction.

1. What was going on when you had the problem?
2. How did you respond?
3. What was the result?
4. What might result if you had responded in a godly manner?

Identify the circumstances. What was going on when you had the problem? This question observes the situation. It slows the child's thinking and trains him to be more aware of events.

* I was gazing out the window instead of doing my homework.

* Sissy went to play.

* I started to leave to go play.

* You stopped me.

Identify the responses. How did you respond? This question observes the child's responses. His behaviors and words need to be listed exactly.

* I yelled, "You're mean!" (*False accusation* – Matt. 19:18)

* I slammed my book on the table.
  (*Lack of self-control* – Prov. 16:32; Gal. 5:23)

* I sat and glared at you. (*Angry countenance* – Gen. 4:6)

Identify the consequences. What was the result? If the child wants to focus only on his immediate pleasure or the difficulty of being obedient, parents can use this question to draw attention to conse-quences that the child may not be willing to admit. Since "every man's way is right in his own eyes" (Prov. 21:2), his role in the results need to be made very clear. For example, to allow an excuse like the homework being too hard would not be acceptable (Prov. 26:13-14).

After all, he could have applied effort or asked for help. Accurate statements might be:

* Because I did not do my homework, I did not get to play.

* Because I yelled at you and falsely accused you, I had to go to my room and think of a godly response.

Identify benefits of godliness. What might be the result if you had responded in a godly manner? There is a reward to obeying God. The angry, foolish child receives so many hard consequences that he may need help seeing what he could have. Here are some ideas. A parent could say:

* If you had done your homework, you would have pleased God and honored your parents.

* If you had done your homework, you would have learned something and had the satisfaction that hard work brings. You would also be building a habit of industry that will help you keep a job and pay for a car when you want one in a few years.

* If you had responded to my correction submissively, you would have peace inside and freedom from strife and guilt.

Or the child might say:

* If I had done my homework, I would have been able to play when Sissy did or even sooner.

* If I had responded to your correction submissively, I would not be having this exercise now.

The highest motive for obedience is love for God. However, disciplinary consequences are inherent in life and encouraged by Scripture as a motive for change. Learning the principle of cause and effect will build wisdom and motivate for change.

Implement the Principles

* Spouses, together, pray with your child about sowing and reaping. Ask that God cause you and your child to become more aware of the consequences that you reap, blessings for obedience, and chastisement for sin. Ask that it motivate you to love God by obeying Him.

- Read the story of Joseph, looking for what the various people sowed and reaped (Gen. 37-50). Find other good biblical examples, like Pharaoh in Exodus, Israel in Numbers 14, Rahab turning to God in faith (Josh. 6). There are many stories in the Bible that could be used.

- With your child, memorize Galatians 6:7-10, especially verse 7. Illustrate the principle of sowing and reaping by planting a small garden, or beans (which grow quickly) indoors, or observe someone else's garden or a farmer's field. Teach the need for perseverance in godliness before the reaping comes (James 5:7-11).

- With your child, read Proverbs 1:17-19; 11:3, 5, 6, 19, 24. Talk about how sinning people get caught by their own sin. Read about boomerangs. Sin has a boomerang effect. What Bible characters released sin in their lives only to have it fly back on them? Read about an animal trap. What Bible characters fell into a trap of their own making? How has this worked in your child's life?

- With your child, review a few past situations to uncover how he/she suffered for his/her own sinful behaviors and reaped reward for good behaviors.

- With your child, memorize Proverbs 3:9-10 and Hebrews 12:11. Teach the passages in their contexts. Teach your child how discipline from a parent demonstrates love. Find ways to illustrate it, such as in the restraining of a pet on a leash or the pruning of certain plants. Show and discuss the results of the neglect of diligent training. Discuss the purposes and benefits of discipline and training, and especially the loving intent of the one who disciplines his child.

- Read Psalm 37. Compare what happens to the righteous and the wicked. List the benefits of godliness. There are benefits to living God's way. Define the wicked and the penalties of wickedness. Be sure to emphasize several of the verses that reveal God's relationship with His own, the tenderness of His love toward them, and the love in their response to Him.

Footnotes

1. Vine, *Expository Dictionary*, 1:30.
2. Priolo, *Teach Them Diligently*, 51.
3. Baker, "Reactive Attachment Disorder."

Chapter 10

Instruction Particular to the Alienated Child

Part 2

Chapter 9 discusses instructing the child regarding God's character, loving God, the gospel, authority, and sowing and reaping. This chapter continues on the topics of compassion, fear, anger, forgiveness, and relational behaviors.

Teach Compassion

The second great commandment is to love others (Matt. 22:39). A hardhearted person who seemingly has no conscience loves himself in the extreme (2 Tim. 3:4). His conscience needs to be retrained toward compassion and love for others by overt instruction, modeling, and application. Highlight it often. Chapter 13 on manipulation works toward that end, so this section will be short.

⊢ Implement the Principles ⊢

* When reading Bible stories, highlight the compassion of God. The Gospels are a good place to start.

* Memorize and teach 1 Corinthians 13, which describes love for others. Help your child compare his/her behaviors to this description.

* Utilize questions like, "How did _____ (his/her words or behavior) show love?"

* Contrast the hardhearted with the compassionate. This is especially obvious in the Pharisees (Matt. 9:9-13; 15:1-4; Luke 10:25-37; John 8:1-9; 9; and many more). Observe the Pharisee in Luke 18:9-14. Observe the crowd's response to Zaccheus, a despised man (Luke 19:1-10). Notice that when he was demeaned by others Zaccheus did not retaliate but agreed that he was guilty (humility). He responded to God's mercy with joyful generosity to the poor, while the hardhearted people had no joy.

- Do service projects. Serving others gets the eyes off of self and onto others and their needs.

  - Bake cookies and take some to a new neighbor or Dad's office.

  - Make a dish to take to a sick neighbor or a mom with a new baby.

  - Make a card. Write a note of thanks. Do this for a relative, church worker (pastor, teacher, musician, janitor, sound man, etc.), or someone else in the community.

  - Thank you notes for birthday gifts ought to be a habit.

  - Find a place of weekly or regular service for the child (or family together) at church (like greeting, helping straighten the room after Sunday school, serving refreshments, folding bulletins).

  - Participate once a month in a service at a nursing home or as a family, clean a pregnancy center.

- Talk about the needs of those less fortunate and how it impacts them.

Teach to Put Off Fear

The alienated child has correctly assessed that people hurt each other. Where he errs is in trusting himself to gain safety. Parents can use the child's fear to direct him to God.[1] Jeremiah 17:5-8 is useful for identifying the problem and solution. It says,

Cursed is the man who trusts in mankind
And makes flesh his strength,
And whose heart turns away from the Lord.
For he will be like a bush in the desert
And will not see when prosperity comes,
But will live in stony wastes in the wilderness,
A land of salt without inhabitant.
Blessed is the man who trusts in the Lord
And whose trust is the Lord.
For he will be like a tree planted by water,
That extends its roots by a stream
And will not fear when the heat comes;
But its leaves will be green,
And it will not be anxious in a year of drought
Nor cease to yield fruit.

Your child needs to be taught that when he demands control, he is turning away from the Lord and is trusting in himself to control the situation to gain a feeling of safety. God says that this will be cursed with more want and he will never feel completely safe. God cares deeply for him and wants to give him things that satisfy forever. If he would trust God, though it would be hard at first, he would find that he will gain a sense of safety and happiness.

Show him the consequences of trust in self. Of his past or the present ask, "What were the results (of the attempt to control)?" Then use those results to show how trusting in his own ways made his situation worse and did not permanently satisfy. Like a bush in a desert, he cannot drink of God's love and joy or enjoy relationships. In the moment he thinks he has fun, but being alienated is a barren, lonely waste and troubles come back on him (Jer. 17:5-6). "The way of the transgressor is hard" (Prov. 13:15b).

Show him that trust in himself has him believing the lie, "I can keep me safe." The reality is that he can never rest but feels that he has to keep plotting and working to keep his parents, siblings, friends, teachers, feelings—his whole world—under his control. It is an impossible task. His days become a barren waste of useless struggle.

His lie has him valuing the wrong treasure. It is natural to want to feel safe. But although God provides spiritual safety, the goal of life is not to stay physically or emotionally safe. God's goal for the fearful child is to glorify God (1 Cor. 10:31). This truth calls him to turn from self to the highest and most satisfying purpose he could ever have.

Show him the solution. First John 4:18 says, "There is no fear in love, but perfect love casts out fear." Self-protection thinks only of self. Love thinks of others. The opposite of fear is love. To overcome fear, he must love God and others by doing what is right. Since his feelings will protest, it will require that he trust God.

Some fears are good because they warn of legitimate danger. Prudence avoids trouble (Prov. 22:3). As long as it rests on trust in God, fear that leads to wise precautions is holy.[2]

Warn him that there is something worse than suffering. Psalm 146:7 says that God will execute justice for the oppressed. That means that He will punish those who hurt others. This is true of the child, too. Therefore, "It is better to be the oppressed than the oppressor." Warn him that there is something worse than suffering and that is sin. Sin earns punishment from God. Psalm 146:7 says that God will execute justice for the oppressed. That means that He will punish those who hurt others. That includes not only those who hurt the child, but also the child if he hurts others. Therefore, it is better to suffer innocently than to suffer under judgment. "It is better to be the oppressed than the oppressor." [3]

Teach truths about fear and suffering that comfort. Jesus knows what it is like to be hurt by others. Yet He did not protect Himself, retaliate, or fight back with threats and fists. He did what was right even when it hurt because He loved His Father and others. He trusted God through it all (1 Pet. 2:18-24). The child can choose to identify with Jesus and be like Him.

Suffering has benefits. For example, oppression rightly used can help us become godly (Rom. 5:3-5). Suffering is a part of life. The child who chooses submission in difficult situations will become more like Jesus and please God (1 Pet. 2:18-23). Jeremiah 17:7-8 promises that his fear will lessen and he will enjoy fruitfulness.

Teach him that life on earth is temporary and eternity is forever. Therefore, his heart is more important than his body. [4] He will have pain on earth. There is no choice about that. His choice is whether he will trust himself to handle and avoid the pain and suffer forever in hell or will trust God and one day be free of those hurts in heaven (2 Cor. 4:16-18).

Many Psalms teach us to trust in God for safety. Psalm 18:2 calls God a rock and a shelter. Explain this verse and ask your child where he runs for safety when he feels scared. For example, he probably runs to anger and control. In Psalm 56, David is honest about fear, dangers, and the pain people cause. He models turning away from fear to trust God saying, "When I am afraid, I will put my trust in You...I shall not be afraid. What can mere man do to me?" He admits to fear and then puts it off to put on trust in God. Bring these verses to life with details. Where was David when he prayed out of fear? He was in imminent, mortal danger in the hands of cruel enemies. Read in 1 Samuel and Psalms 59 and 56 about the dangers he faced and how he handled them. For Psalm 18, describe the position behind a rock. Talk about the view that the child can have looking out from the safe shelter God gives him. [5] Remind him, "Remember 'When I am afraid, I will put my trust in You.' You can put your trust in God."

Psalm 42 begins, "As the deer pants for the water brooks, so my soul pants for Thee, O God." When does a deer pant? It pants when it has been running. When does it run long enough to cause panting? When it is being hunted. Like the psalmist is being hunted, so the child is hunted by his fears and anger. He cries and despairs (vv. 3, 5). God can be his cool stream of relief. You can help him apply this truth. For example, when Donnie is mad over some conflict with his brother, Alvin, Mom may say something like, "So Alvin rejected you and that hurts. You can run to God like the hunted deer we talked about. You can tell God how badly you want to control, and then choose to trust Him. He will stay with you even when you feel rejected."

Most times, the child is not likely to admit to fears. You will need to initiate the discussion.

———————— Implement the Principles ————————

* Memorize Jeremiah 17:5-8. To make it more vivid, try looking at healthy and dying trees, or pictures thereof.

* Memorize Psalm 56:4. Discuss it. What can man do to us? Is there something worse than that? Set the psalm in its context by reading the background in 1 Samuel 21:10-15. What was being done to the David (Ps. 56:1-7)? How did he feel about it? Where did he find his comfort? He'd been on a run for his life for days or weeks (1 Sam. 18:10-21:15; Ps. 59). Do you think his fear grew to panic? How did that work and what did he change to stop it?

* With your child, draw pictures of verses, like of a rock as a refuge (Ps. 18:1) or a deer in the stream (Ps. 42:1). Stick figures are fine. Make a family activity of it. Talk about the passages that the pictures are depicting. Pray, thanking God for His protection and provision. Post the pictures somewhere in plain view.

* Do service projects. Serving others puts 1 John 4:18 and other verses on love into practice. It also counters greed and hoarding, which can be fear-motivated.

* Read Psalm 63 to your child periodically. Your child believes lies. Psalm 63 confronts some of those lies with truth. Print out this psalm. Underline verses that impress your child. Discuss them. Pray with him using this psalm. Do the same with Psalm 139 and other psalms. Show your child from the psalms that God takes hurt ones into His arms and tenderly cares for them. Those who trust Him need not fear because He stays faithful and cannot lose His own.

* Use verbal images at the appropriate time to winsomely alert your child to the issue of who he is trusting. "Trusting in self is like trusting in a security blanket. It may make you feel good, but it won't resolve your problems." [6] "Loving to have your own way is like hugging a python; it hugs you back (and kills you)." "That crazy deer is running *away* from the stream!" Think of verbal imagery that fits your child's interests.

* Draw or build a fort of palisades. In the center, set a signboard, "Fort Self-Trust." On each rickety or weak palisade write a lie that he believes or has believed. "Others will hurt me." "Everybody hates me." "My parents are out to get me." "Mom is mean." "I deserve to be safe." "No one can be allowed to have the power to hurt me." "I can't let anyone see inside." "They mustn't know I care." "They are threats, so I have the right to defend myself." "I deserve to have (object) because it makes me feel better." "I should not have to be responsible." "I deserve to have no pain." "That's not fair!" "I'll show you!" "I'll get you for this!" By blockading others out, he is blockading himself into solitude and fear. When true love and joy come along, he sees only threats. He kills relationships and lives alone in a life of fear (1 John 4:18).

* Construct a thought chart listing your child's wrong thoughts countered by the appropriate biblical thought. This can be called a Put Off/Put On (POPO) Chart. It should be kept handy, such as on the refrigerator. It may be in words or picture combinations, tailored to the child's needs and preferences. The child can read them or have them read to him. A variation is a picture/illustration book of 4" x 6" cards on a single ring.[7] A chart may look something like this:

Fear POPO Chart

Self-Focused Thought or Action	Biblical Thought
Everybody hates me.	This is a lie and it is all about me. Even if everyone hates me, God cares about me. I will trust Him as my Rock and pray good things for my family. (Ps. 18:2; Phil. 2:3-4)
My parents are out to get me.	This thought is not loving (1 Cor. 13:7). I'm mad because I didn't get my way. I don't understand how my situation is good, but I will trust God that He does and honor my parents like He says to do. (Eph 6:1-3)
I am afraid. I need to defend myself.	I really do not know what might happen next. I am uncertain even about whether I will have food tomorrow. But instead of taking care of myself, I will let God supply my needs. (Matt. 6:26; Phil. 4:19; Ps. 56:4)
I must have control. Things must turn out a certain way. (Control battle)	God is in control, not me. He has planned this for my good and His glory. He says to obey authorities, so unless they tell me to sin, I need to do what they say. (Jer. 17:5, 7; Eph. 6:1-3)
Hypervigilance, or child not concentrating on school work: His unspoken question is, "What is going on around me? Am I safe?"	You might hurt me. But the Bible says, "When I am afraid, I will put my trust in Thee" (Ps. 56:3). I will trust God right now and pay attention to what I am supposed to be doing. (1 John 4:18)
Child does not want to meet the eyes of the other person.	Because God loves me, I will obey Him by respecting you. To show respect to you, I will look at you when you speak to me. (1 Cor. 13:5)
Child indiscriminately affectionate with a stranger.	I am trying to manipulate this person to like me. I will stop being selfish and will respect the other person by greeting him like Dad taught me to do. (Phil. 2:3-4)

Teach to Put Off Anger

Psalm 37:8 says to "cease from anger, and forsake wrath; do not fret, it leads only to evildoing." "Fret" means to "be kindled with anger." The angry person frets, or broods, or kindles anger into an attitude of offense, which is bitterness (1 Cor. 13:5; Heb. 12:15). If he does not turn from his bitterness, he grows stubborn ("I refuse to go your way") and rebellious ("I will go my own way").

Hosea described the anger of God's rebellious Israel like this:

> For their hearts are like an oven
>> As they approach their plotting;
>> Their anger smolders all night,
>> In the morning it burns like a flaming fire.
> All of them are hot like an oven
>> And they consume their rulers… (Hosea 7:6-7)

An abiding anger smolders hot enough to flame up at any time. When it breaks out in angry words and behaviors we call it blowing up or ventilating. When it is locked inside we call it clamming up or internalizing. Both responses are anger-perpetuating. Ventilation stokes the fire further by exercising the anger. Clamming up stokes more subtly by exercising the anger internally, like through withdrawal, brooding, and a critical spirit. Neither resolves anger because they do not resolve the problem.

Hosea said that angry people consume their rulers. They reject (and destroy) authorities, sometimes physically and many times in their thoughts and by their words. This rejection demonstrates allegiance to something other than God, who established those authorities (Rom. 13:1). That is why stubbornness and rebellion are called idolatry (1 Sam. 15:23). Someone who declares, "I am king and no one else can rule me" is worshiping self. This violates the first commandment (Exod. 20:3).

Teach the consequences of anger. Proverbs 26:23-28 teaches several truths about anger. Angry feelings lie to us. Verse 27 describes it as a trap. "He who digs a pit will fall into it, and he who rolls a stone, it will come back on him." We might call it a boomerang. It promises to obtain what the child wants, but it delivers more trouble (James 4:1-3). Angry words feel good in the moment, but "a fool's lips bring strife and his mouth calls for blows" (Prov. 18:6). Parents can point out ways in which these verses come true in the child's life. Because of vengeance or rebellion, Jeremiah 17:6 is true in his life. He misses "prosperity" and lives in lonely, salted wastelands. Anger destroys friendships like salt kills plants. The angry person is left alone and lonely and dissatisfied. Anger promises to make things right but delivers strife, broken relationships, pain, and guilt.

Teach from Psalm 37 what happens to the righteous and the wicked. Anger over being hurt by others leads only to evildoing (37:8), and God will punish evildoers (37:9). So it is better to be the oppressed than the oppressor. There are benefits to living God's way, benefits like hope, companionship, fun that is free of evil, lasting satisfaction, and inner peace (Ps. 37:6, 9, 11; Jer. 17:7-8).

Teach the cause and solution. According to James 4:1-3, angry people have grown their desires into demands so that they get angry when they do not get what they want. The angry person thinks that he needs what he wants. A need gives him a right to it. Therefore, he has a right to be angry when his so-called need is denied or when his so-called rights have been violated.

Overcoming anger will require putting off a claim to rights and putting on responsibility to obey God. It will require putting off selfish desires and putting on desires that please God.

Ownership is an issue in anger. The angry person thinks he owns himself and deserves that which he desires. The fact is that God made him. He needs to put off self-ownership and submit to God's ownership.

Teach him to put off brooding and put on thanksgiving (Ps. 37:8; Phil. 4:6). The angry person is proud, not grateful. He ignores the fact that he has nothing except what has been given to him (John 3:27). *Gratitude douses pride and anger.* It shows a person that he is not a victim but a recipient of many good things. In response to a pretty sunset or a pay raise for Dad, talk about God's goodness, beauty, and other wonderful attributes. List what God has done and use that list with him in praying thanks to God.

Teach him how God's goodness and sovereignty relate to his situation. Psalm 37:3-7 says, "Trust in the Lord *and do good*...Commit your way to the Lord...Rest in the Lord and wait patiently for Him." In the heart, trusting in God means believing that God is trustworthy, loves him, is in control of the difficulties, and will use them for his good if he loves God (37:5-6; Rom 8:28). The word "commit" is translated from the Hebrew for "roll." The child's fears and angers are too heavy; he needs to roll them off of his own back to Him who has the power and wisdom to handle them rightly. In thoughts, he must rest. The word "rest" means to "be silent, be still." Rest requires putting off those roiling thoughts and demands, giving up the right to have his way, and being content with whatever God provides. He can put on the truth, "Since God is in control, then He has put me under this authority (dad). So I will submit, trusting God to control my dad and protect me." Behaviorally, he can put off angry words and actions and put on doing good and self-control (Gal. 5:20, 23).

Teach him to put off rule by feelings and put on obedience to commands. Feelings are poor counselors. They are often mistaken and mislead us. We are to be Word-oriented. Psalm 37:1-3 says to put off anger and "Trust in the Lord, " Your child must not listen to his feelings but exert himself to do good in his situation no matter how he feels. You can tell him, "I know that your feelings feel strong right now, but you do not have to obey them. Feeling mad is uncomfortable, but it is no excuse. Your responsibility right now is to respect my authority and obey" (Eph. 6:2-3).

Teach him to put off self-love and put on service (love) to God and others (Matt. 22:37, 39; Phil. 2:3-4). An angry person is all about self. Service to others counters pride and selfishness, develops good habits and right thoughts, provides practice in showing kindness, invites development of compassion, and creates opportunities to experience reward feelings from well-doing.

Joseph provides a good example of how to handle anger-provoking mistreatment. He did not deserve to be abandoned, enslaved, and thrown into jail while the perpetrators went unpunished. Yet, instead of ranting about unfairness or demanding that people treat him fairly, he trusted God. He accepted that God was his Owner who deserved his obedience. He applied himself to his responsibilities, like serving his masters well. He even returned good for evil by forgiving his brothers and saving them from famine. Those hard times were what shaped Joseph into a man who could lead a country with integrity. He humbled himself and God gave him grace and exalted him (Gen. 37, 39:1-50:21; James 4:1-11).

Implement the Principles

* As a family with Dad leading, use Psalm 37 in daily readings. Teach the concepts in this section.

* Plan questions to ask that will challenge the logic of his/her false beliefs. "What did your anger really get you?" "Did your anger deliver on its promise?" "You got the pleasure that you wanted by retaliating, but what else did you get along with it?"

* As spouses together, pray with your child about those who mistreat him/her and situations that trigger his/her anger. Talk about what Romans 12:9-21 says to do when mistreated, and how he/she might apply it.

- Memorize Philippians 2:3-4, 1 Corinthians 13:4-8. Help your child do three kind acts for others this week.

- Read Luke 6:27-49 with your child each day for a week and let him/her choose one principle to apply that day. Plan how it might be implemented.

- Add humor when possible, though not to the minimizing of the seriousness of anger. It surprises and adds perspective. Observe that the spider trap of anger has caught him/her, or he's spilling salt again (an allusion to Jeremiah 17:6).

- With the child, list things for which he/she is, or can be, thankful (1 Thess. 5:18; Phil. 4:8). Read them together. Use them daily in prayers.

- Do family service projects and put the child in places where he/she must serve others.

- Use option cards. On cards, write options for what the child can do when he is feeling angry. For younger children, draw pictures representing the options. When needed, have the child go through the options and choose one to do. Options on the cards might include ideas from the points above and "Ask God for help," "Draw a picture of this verse" (on anger), "Ask for a hug," "Thank God for loving me," "Thank God for putting me in this family," "Read my thought chart," "Do my sister's chore for her," "Play a game," "Figure out with Mom why I feel so bad," "Ask for suggestions for kinds of things I can do," "Tell Mom I miss my birth family." [8]

Study what lies the child is telling himself. For example, frustration over learning a new task might be based in the expectation that life should not require struggle. In the thought chart below are some possible lies that an alienated child might believe countered by biblical truths.

Anger POPO Chart

Selfish or Angry Thought	Biblical Thought
This isn't fair.	I will let God take care of what is unfair. My responsibility is to love my neighbor and return good for evil. (Rom. 12:17-21)
This shouldn't happen to me!	Jesus did not deserve to die. It was unfair. But He trusted His Father. I will trust God and do what is right. (1 Pet. 4:19)
This shouldn't happen to me!	I will not fret; it leads only to evildoing. I will wait patiently for God. (Ps. 37:7)
I don't deserve this!	What I really deserve is hell, but God has had mercy on me. I know that God is good and loves me. If this is what God has for me, I will trust Him and obey what I know He wants me to do. (Ps. 37:1-11)
I am unhappy. I can't obey Mom when I feel like this.	What God wants is more important than what I feel. Because I love God I will do what is right and obey Mom. (Eph. 6:1-3)
I don't have to do what you say. I don't want to. I don't trust that what you want is a wise thing to do. (This may be anger rooted in fear.)	God wants me to trust Him and do good. That means obeying my dad even when I don't feel like it. God has promised that if I obey, I will reap blessings. (Ps. 37:3; Eph. 6:2-3)
I'll get you for this!	Since God gave me this parent, I need to trust Him and obey her. (Dan. 4:17; Rom. 12:19; 1 Cor. 13:5)

Teach How to Ask for Forgiveness.

When we sin we must confess to God and to others (Matt. 5:23-24; James 5:16). Confession is part of the put-off in the change process. Parents will need to teach how to do it.

First, in a respectful tone and facial expression the child admits what he did. "Mom, I turned my face away and spoke disrespectfully to you" (Prov. 30:17; Eph. 6:2; Prov. 26:4). This clearly identifies the sin.

Then he asks "Will you forgive me?" The words "I'm sorry" are not acceptable because they are vague and they hedge on full agreement that he is guilty. He may feel sorry because he did not get away with his manipulation. He does not show conviction seriously enough to pursue reconciliation or show that he wants the offense to be properly resolved. In contrast, the request for forgiveness seeks a clear and conscious transaction between both parties. It says, "Will you or will you not forgive me?" It provides an opportunity for the other to make a conscious commitment of forgiveness, which will help clear the forgiver's heart of the hurt.

In the request, there must be no "if," "but," or "maybe." Those words imply doubt that the offender sinned and are an effort to get the other person off his back. For example, "I'm sorry I snapped, but if you didn't make me dress before breakfast I would not have had to hurry so much." The word "but" cancels all that preceded it and shifts blame away from the person who sinned.

Anything but the right tone and facial expression with eye contact is unacceptable. Body language that contradicts words is a strong indicator that the heart is not in agreement with the words.

Only after the child properly requests forgiveness (right words and tone) should you respond as Luke 17:3-4 teaches by making a verbal commitment to forgive him. The commitment to forgive is also clearly stated, "I forgive you."

Forgiveness is a promise. When God forgives, He refuses to remember it against the offender (Isa. 43:25). The words "I forgive you" express a commitment by the offended to a) not bring up the offense against the offender again, b) not dwell on it in his thoughts, and c) not tell others about it.

Sometimes forgiveness is confused with trust. Manipulative children try to gain trust in order to hoodwink others. Because they are on the lookout for signs of trust, they might misperceive forgiveness as an expression of trust. The promise of forgiveness is not an expression of trust, only that the offense is no longer held against the offender. The child must still prove himself trustworthy.

Teach Relational Behaviors

The alienated child may be ignorant about behaviors that parents take for granted. He may not realize that they are not perceived by the other person as loving. For example, people are not put at ease when someone they do not know grabs them in a hug. When parents observe behaviors that are inappropriate, they need to ensure that the child knows what appropriate behavior is.

The child may need to practice skills as basic as how to greet people, how to be excused from the dinner table, and how to appeal for something. Many children rudely interrupt talking adults. Teach him how to communicate that he wants to talk but will wait quietly until you are done. Other skills to practice are looking someone in the eye when they speak to him and greeting new people without inordinate affection. Do not allow inordinate affection toward strangers, such as grabbing them in a hug or charming their attention; that is manipulation for selfish reasons (Prov. 7:13; 31:30).

Remember to teach the attitudes that fit the actions (Matt. 22:39; 1 Cor. 13:4-8). Outward behavior without a right heart is not the goal (Matt. 23:37). Constantly go for the heart.

Footnotes

1. Baker, "Reactive Attachment Disorder."
2. Ibid.
3. Ibid.
4. Ibid.
5. Ibid.
6. Ibid.
7. Ibid.
8. Ibid.

Chapter 11
Communication Methods to Aid Instruction

Proverbs 16:23 says that the wise will teach his mouth to use prudence and persuasion. Although it is the Holy Spirit who regenerates the heart and it is the child's responsibility to choose heart change, it is parents' responsibility to exercise wisdom so as to influence persuasively.

Choose appropriate timing.

At the end of His ministry, Jesus gave prolonged instruction to His disciples (John 14-17). Yet He knew when they reached a point where they could not handle more (John 16:12). Everyone swings between more and less teachable moments. Choose a time when the child is teachable and able to learn.

Get to the point.

Jesus consistently shot directly to the core problem. For example, when the Pharisees criticized Jesus for eating with the tax collectors, Jesus did not mess around defending his choice. He went directly to their problem, their lack of compassion (Matt. 9:9-13).

Children tune out long lectures. When correcting, keep it short. Get to the point.

Use a gentle tone.

Matthew 12:20 records Jesus saying that in His ministry He would not break a battered reed. What He meant is that He would be gentle to the weak and seek to restore them. The alienated child has been emotionally battered. He needs gentle answers that turn his wrath away and words that soothe his fear and make knowledge acceptable (Prov. 15:1-2; 16:24). A calm voice and tone create a sense of safety.

Be careful of facial expressions. They can provoke the child even when the words are calm. Frowns convey disapproval, which flips the alienated child's threat switch. Shock feeds his sense of control. An angry countenance conveys a multitude of silent harsh words

(Gen. 4:6; Prov. 15:1). When the child offends, stay engaged with non-accusing eye contact that conveys respect. Be aware of what your face and voice communicate.

There are likely to be so many negatives and corrections directed at the unruly child that negativity can saturate the atmosphere. Rather than constantly telling him the truth, it may sometimes help to pose questions that challenge the child to state the truth. This will not always work because he may use a question as an opportunity to compete with arguments. But a question can be stated such that the truth is obvious, and a parent can simply answer it if the child will not. Jesus frequently used questions with the Pharisees, directing them back to God's Word. For example, when the lawyer tried to trap Him on how to obtain eternal life, Jesus asked, "What is written in the Law?" (Luke 10:26). So, "Donnie, what does the Bible say about _____?"

Affirm correct answers. When Peter identified Jesus as the Christ, Jesus blessed him (Matt. 16:17). When the lawyer answered correctly that the Law said to love God and love your neighbor, Jesus responded with affirmation (and a challenge with a promise): "You have answered correctly; do this and you will live" (Luke 10:25-28).

Use positive phraseology. Jesus' answer to the lawyer held a positive tone. To the woman caught in adultery He said, "Go and sin no more." Putting the positive view on the statement conveys grace and a desire for the child's benefit. There will be times to firmly state, "No, you may not play right now. Do your homework," especially if a positive approach has already been stated. A first attempt like "I would be happy for you to play just as soon as your homework is done" communicates the loving intent of the parent, the responsibility of the child, and the reaping he will gain when he sows obedience.

Utilize visual and kinesthetic aids.

Jesus wove his verbal instruction with a visual and kinesthetic loom. "Kinesthetic" means movement and awareness of the body, as opposed to just hearing or seeing. For example, Jesus made Peter the first water skier (Luke 5:1-11). He assigned His disciples a short-term mission trip of their own. When the lawyer challenged God's command to love others, Jesus told the story of the good Samaritan. He drew attention to the birds of the air and flowers of the fields. Seed sowing, buried pearls, and sheep folds all created visual images. Narratives and verbal imagery engage the imagination and emotions, which hook their arms on either side of logic and carry it along to the truth.

Antisocial children like concrete ideas and pictures. So use role play, activities, videos, and pictures. Read the stories and parables in the Bible. Draw personalized pictures, such as of the child safe in Jesus' arms or safe in a fort labeled "God's Love." The implementation ideas in this book provide more suggestions.

Take a walk and draw attention to the flowers. Then teach from Matthew 6 about how God takes care of flowers. If He takes care of a flower, will He not much more take care of Donnie? So then, Donnie does not need to worry about situations and people. He just needs to be busy doing what is right and let God take care of the rest (Matt. 6:24-33).

Gardens can provide many illustrations of crucial principles, such as the fruit and root principle of Luke 6:43-45, the sowing and reaping principle of Galatians 6:7, and the lesson on condition of the soil (the heart) (Mark 4:3-20). God's loving protection noted in Psalm 139:5 might be illustrated by the little house dog that always wants to go outside. It dislikes the restraining will of its master. Yet the master knows that it would starve or freeze to death outside, that it needs the protection of limits even though it cannot understand why. So also, God uses parents to lovingly protect the child by the rules and limits they set.

Shape the verbal imagery to the child's situations and attitudes. For example, Control has bound him in his inner "house" (Matt. 12:29-30). The villains, Anger, Fear, and Hardheartedness prowl inside and rob him of companionship and joy. They let no one else inside to sit with him and share togetherness while sipping hot chocolate. He needs to ask the strongest Man of all creation to make him new inside so that his house will become a safe and welcoming place. Or, "Donnie, 'The good man out of his good treasure brings forth what is good; and the evil man out of his evil treasure brings forth what is evil.' Your words and actions are showing what is in your heart's piggy bank" (Matt. 12:35-36).

When you know that a situation new to your child is soon to come, use sequential pictures of how right behavior looks through different phases of situations he will be encountering. Introducing the child to Sunday school is an example. The fearful child cannot think past being left by you in the class and the sense of being abandoned again. He may not understand that you will be back. Draw pictures of each stage of what will happen on Sunday morning. Next, visit the class on a weekday and walk through what will happen.[1]

When teaching thoughts to put on, practice saying the thoughts aloud together. It gets the child speaking the thoughts and not just hearing them. Then role-play the situation while saying the put-on thoughts. Role play how to meet someone new or how to greet family first thing in the morning. Visuals and practice facilitate the child's comprehension of right behaviors.

Add fun with riddles. Jesus surprised his listeners with new ways of looking at things. When they demanded a sign, Jesus talked about Jonah, the Queen of the South, and an unclean spirit. Luke 11:37-41 records how, when accused about a hand washing law, He jumped from hand washing to heart washing. He did not explain every metaphor (Matt. 9:14-17; 12:43-45). Ask some posers (Luke 6:6-11). "Donnie, which shows more love to a child: disciplining or letting him have his way?" "For which do you think a parent is responsible to God: to train a child in wisdom or to give the child whatever he wants?" "Which shows more respect: to let a person experience the consequences of his choices or to interfere by saving him?" "What does this mean: 'Your compassion is like dew'" (Hosea 6:4)?

Memorize Scripture.

When He was in the wilderness being tempted by Satan, Jesus used Scripture to combat the temptations. How much more should we do the same?

Daily Scripture memory work with the family gets Scripture into the minds of the children (and you) so that their desires, thoughts, attitudes, and behaviors can be shaped by it (Ps. 119:11). Find the verses that relate directly to issues that arise and memorize one at a time. Talk about it and teach how to meditate on it. Scripture memory and meditation help in the application of putting off sinful desires and thoughts, putting on new godly desires and thoughts, and preventing future sins.[2] In the mind, it is readily accessible for discussions during the day and for application at the needed moments. When you refer to it in application to a situation, your child will already be familiar with it and able to more readily see how it applies.

Footnotes

1. Baker, "Reactive Attachment Disorder."
2. Priolo, *Teach Them Diligently*, 84.

Chapter 12
The Heart of Change

First thing in the morning, having had contact with no one so far, Donnie stomps down the stairs to the kitchen for breakfast. He ignores his mom. When she gives him a cheerful "Good morning," he averts his face and snaps a gruff, "What do you want?!"

How can Donnie change? How can his parents help him? They might take him to a behavioral therapist. They might also apply cognitive therapy to change his thinking. What if he then behaves? The DeSpares will be relieved, but will Donnie have truly changed, and is this the kind of change that pleases God?

How Heart Change is Made

God's change plan is outlined in Ephesians 4. Verse 17 commanded the Ephesians to no longer live like the unbelievers that they were before salvation. Change is not an option. Verses 22-24 teach that in salvation, they laid aside the old self, their minds were renewed, and they put on the righteous new self. God's way of change is a replacement process. Sinful desires, thoughts, and behaviors are put off and godly desires, thoughts, and behaviors are put on. Believers are to continue in that process. Putting off requires confession and cessation. Putting on requires planning, effort, and practice.

The replacement process is further elucidated by examples given in verses 25-32. What is the solution to someone who has a habit of lying? It is not just that he stop lying. He must put also on truth-speaking. It is not enough that the thief no longer steals. He has not truly changed until he stops stealing *and* works to support himself and give to others.

Even change of behaviors is not enough. When Ephesians 4:23 speaks of renewal "in the spirit of your mind" it means a change of the whole inner man, including heart desires. Someone who behaves well while maintaining sinful desires is still selfish at heart. Jesus used the term "whitewashed tombs" to reveal that under the good works (behaviors) were dead hearts repulsive to God (Matt. 23:27).

Without a change of heart, true change has not been made. The former thief might no longer steal (behavior) and might change his thoughts by not dwelling on what he can steal (cognition). Yet he retains desires of greed or of self-ownership rather than of submission to God's ownership of him. Therefore, though he does not steal, perhaps he builds bigger barns (hoards) (Luke 12:13-21). Or perhaps he develops a habitual reaction of anger if he does not get his "fair share" at work, parties, or pot lucks. Change must be made in heart as well as speech and behavior.

The Western mindset looks at that word "mind" and thinks of the intellect as distinct from the heart. We say, "I know it in my head, but not in my heart." We associate heart with emotions, but the Bible does not contrast the two so completely. Its use of the term "heart" never excludes the intellect. Psalm 14:1 says, "The fool has said in his heart, 'There is no God.'" Hebrews 4:12 says that the heart has thoughts and intentions. The heart is where plans, imaginations, and perceptions are generated (Ezek. 11:5; Mark 7:20-23). The heart reasons, doubts, and believes (Luke 5:22; Mark 11:23). These are all attributable to the mind. Therefore, what goes on in the head is the heart. Emotions like joy and fear may be associated with the heart, but the intellect is never excluded. Rather, our thoughts of the mind express the heart, produce emotions, and the emotions embellish our thoughts.

Proverbs 4:23 says to "guard your heart diligently, for from it flow the springs of life." The heart is the seat of your passions, intellect, character, attitudes, and desires. It is the well from which all thoughts, feelings, decisions, plans and, therefore, behaviors spring. As "heart" refers to the whole inner man, so does "mind." To renew the mind is to guard the heart.

What generates behavior

Let's start with Mrs. DeSpare. She bemoans to Pastor Helpin that she yelled at Donnie that morning. She agrees that her behavior must change, but doesn't connect her behavior to what is causing it. Pastor Helpin knows that yelling is a symptom, an expression of a motivation in her heart (Prov. 4:23).

Going for her heart, he asks, "What did you want to accomplish?"

She replies, "I wanted a decent conversation, and all he would do is argue. I wanted him to behave."

Pastor Helpin takes her to James 1:14, which says that "each one is tempted when he is carried away and enticed by his own lust." In other words, it is desires that drive behaviors. Jesus, too, attributed behaviors to desires when He said,

> The good man out of the good treasure of his heart brings forth what is good; and the evil man out of the evil treasure brings forth what is evil; for his mouth speaks from that which fills his heart (Luke 6:45).

A treasure is something we value. We want it. So treasures of the heart are the wants, or desires, that drive the behavior used to obtain that desire. We even speak this way when we say that a person has certain "drives." A drive says, "I want and must have."

Pastor Helpin teaches Mrs. DeSpare that she is a worshiper at heart. She treasures things in her heart and speaks and acts out of what she most treasures.

Jesus listed only two types of treasures (desires), good and evil. What constitutes whether a desire is good or evil? When Mrs. DeSpare tells Pastor Helpin that her desires are good desires, he suggests that she reconsider. So she asks, "How could peaceful conversation be considered a sinful desire? Peace is a good desire."

To answer, Pastor Helpin reads James 4:1-3, which says,

> What is the source of quarrels and conflicts among you? Is not the source your pleasures that wage war in your members? You lust and do not have; so you commit murder. You are envious and cannot obtain; so you fight and quarrel. You ask and do not receive, because you ask with wrong motives, so that you may spend it on your pleasures.

James told his readers that what generated their quarreling was unfulfilled desires. James was not saying that all desires are wrong, but that even the good ones are sinful when they cause fighting (sin). When people are willing to sin to get what they want, or react sinfully when they get something they do not want, the desire has become more important to them than pleasing (loving) God. It corrupts into a demand. So desire for peace became sinful when it became a demand such that when Donnie wouldn't give it to her she punished him with yelling. It became sinful when, in order to get it Mrs. DeSpare was willing to disobey God's command that speech be edifying.

This is a simple way for identifying when a person's good desire is sinful. Are you willing to sin to get it or sin if you get what you don't want? Has it become a demand over which you are willing to punish the other person?

Pastor Helpin might help Mrs. DeSpare further explore what underlies her stated desire. What was she thinking that peaceful conversation and no trouble would get her? It might be relief, which shows a love of comfort (2 Tim. 3:4). It might be a good relationship; is she seeking a sense of intimacy or companionship (Pss. 42:1; 73:25)? Perhaps she wants the family under control (3 John 9-10; 1 Cor. 13:5). Whatever it is, she wanted it more than she wanted to obey God with self-control and edifying speech (Gal. 5:23; Eph. 4:29).

It is right and good to want and must have God; then we won't sin. It is sinful to want and must have anything except God and His will (Exod. 20:3-5). Jesus said that man "cannot serve God and mammon." He meant that we cannot treasure God and something else (Matt. 6:24). We must choose. Since behaviors arise from what we desire, then behaviors are a worship issue. They show what we have chosen to treasure.

While behaviors are symptoms of desires, they do not comprise a simple one-to-one equation. Roots are not visible to people. A variety of desires may result in a particular behavior. Unless a person expresses his reasons, we cannot truly know his motives. Roots get all twisted so that sometimes even we don't know all of our own motives (Jer. 17:9). You are there to help your child in this process, not to be the expert on his heart. Be careful to not judge quickly; keep your conclusions tentative. If the child won't be honest about his heart, you can still speak to behaviors, teach on the heart-behavior connection, and ask the Lord to change the child's heart.

Although God does not allow one man to examine another's heart (1 Cor. 4:5), we can ask him to judge his own heart (Acts 5:1-4; 2 Cor. 13:5). Proverbs 20:5 says that "a plan in the heart of a man is like deep water, but a man of understanding draws it out." You can ask questions that draw out the child's desires and thoughts. Then compare them to Scripture because "the word of God is living and active and sharper than any two-edged sword, and piercing as far as the division of soul and spirit, of both joints and marrow, and *able to judge the thoughts and intentions of the heart*" (Heb. 4:12, emphasis added). No psychological therapy can do so. Even the methods taught in this book are useless apart from the Spirit's use of the Word. God's Word, by the power of the Holy Spirit, cuts apart the core and judges the motives. You are simply an assistant helping your child apply the Word to his heart in order to rightly discern it, be convicted, and apply the biblical solution.

A Step-by-Step Process

Following is an explanation for how to break a situation into its parts to evaluate and arrive at a biblical solution that will promote change.[1] Obviously, for change to occur, the child must willingly participate. An alienated child is not likely to do so. Persevere in formulating questions and statements that will, in a gentle manner, most effectively reveal your child's heart to himself and inspire him to reconsider.

It works well to use the following questions, but conversation will also work. They are adapted from Paul Tripp's book, *Instruments in the Redeeemer's Hands*.[2] Ask:

1. What was the situation?

2. How did I respond?

3. What was I thinking and feeling?

4. What was I seeking to accomplish? (What was I wanting?)

5. What does the Bible say about what I thought and wanted?[3] (Evaluation of thoughts and desires)

6. What does the Bible tell me to want? (What would please God?)

7. What will I choose? (What will I do?)

Let's talk through the purposes of these questions and how they can be used.

Identify the circumstances. What was the situation? What was happening? At this point, you are stepping into your child's world and inviting teamwork rather than conflict. Talking about his heart will likely be uncomfortable for the child. Being more observational and less personal, these initial questions make it easier for him to start talking rather than clamming up in self-protection. It simply observes the situation.

For example, Donnie might answer:

* It was time for breakfast.

* You (Mom) were in the kitchen when I got there.

* You said, "Good morning."

Identify the response. How did I respond? This is still simple observation. Donnie writes (or Mom writes for him):

* I asked what you want.

At this point, Mom does not make moral judgments, but she does insist that information be accurate. There was more to his response than what he recorded. So she will ask Donnie what his tone and behavior were. If he does not say, she will state them (in a calm, even voice):

* He stomped on the stairs.

* He refused to look at her.

* He used a harsh tone and disrespectful expression.

Identify his thoughts and feelings. What was I thinking and feeling as it was going on? This question turns the child's attention from his outward behavior to his inner machinations. It makes him aware of himself.

Thoughts and feelings are not the same. Thoughts are views or analyses. Feelings are physiological reactions to the thoughts. Examples of feelings might include angry, scared, or sad.

His thoughts should be recorded exactly. Encourage him to be honest. This is not the time for disapproval. The goal is for the child, not the parent, to evaluate his own heart. A few thoughts typical of alienated children are:

* Mom is mean!

* I hate you.

* That's not fair!

* Everybody hates me.

* I'll get you for this!

* I hate this family. I'm leaving as soon as I can.

Evaluate thoughts. What does the Bible say about what I thought? Find the biblical terms that describe the child's thoughts. Sinful thoughts or false beliefs are what the child must put off. Then find the biblical put-on thought. (This will be shown in a later chart.) Using these biblical labels for the speech clarifies the moral character of what is being said.

Thought	Biblical Evaluation
Mom is mean.	• False accusation (Matt. 19:18) • Disrespect (Eph. 6:2-3)
That's not fair.	• False accusation (Matt. 19:18) • False theology. God is not fair, He is just. (Prov. 21:3; Jer. 9:23) • He wants people to be just.
I can't wait to get away from this family.	• Impatience and ungratefulness (Eph. 4:2; 1 Thess. 5:18)
Everybody hates me.	• Vain imagination (2 Cor 10:5) • False accusation (Matt. 19:18) • Empty conceit (self-focus) (Phil. 2:3)

Identify desires. What was I seeking to accomplish? What was I wanting? This identifies motivations (James 1:14-15; 4:1-3).

Many times, children clearly know what they want, but sometimes they don't. Helpful questions include, "What would make me happy?" "What was I worried would happen?" "What did I think I might lose?" "If I could change my situation, how would it look?" Donnie might answer:

* I wanted to play in my room longer.

* I don't want to go to school.

* I want you to feel bad.

* I don't want to live with this family.

Evaluate desires. What does the Bible say about what I wanted? Evaluating desires identifies what to change. For example, suppose the child stole. The biblical evaluation of the behavior would be stealing and lack of self-control (Eph. 4:28; Gal. 5:23). What was his heart motivation? Was it out of greed (Rom. 1:29), envy (Rom. 1:29, Tit. 3:3), malice (Tit. 3:3), or revenge (Rom. 12:17-19)? Behavioral put-ons are clear-cut (Gal. 5:23; Eph. 4:28). Solutions for the heart vary according to his desire.

Find the biblical terms that describe the child's desires. As mechanics know, obscure diagnoses make solutions difficult to find. "There's a rattle in the engine" does not identify the exact problem. When the problem is not clearly identified, any sense of guilt is vague and dull. While a person may seek relief from the discomfort of guilt feelings after a conflict, how does he do it when his problem is called "conduct disorder"? Identify love of pleasure (of play) (2 Tim. 3:4) or love of control (over Mom) (3 John:9), and then it is clear what the person must put off in repentance. Use of biblical terms lays the particular violation on the table under a bright lamp for clear identification from God's perspective. A person is faced with how he offended God, so conviction is facilitated.

When evaluating desires, distinguish between desires that are sinful and desires that are not sinful. Desires like wanting revenge or wanting another's possession (envy) are sinful. It is not sinful to want a bike, to play longer, to attend a party, or to be loved. Good desires become sinful when the child is willing to disobey God to get them because then he is rejecting God's rule over him.

Here are some more questions to help determine whether a good desire was sinful and to insert God into the situation:

* Was I willing to sin to get what I wanted?
  If I got what I didn't want?

* Was I willing to punish whoever didn't cooperate
  with my plan?

* Did I love God and want His will done or
  did I want my way?

* Was I behaving as if I am my own boss or
  as if God is my boss?

The following chart demonstrates how various heart desires can produce the same sinful thought fruit. If you make a similar chart and keep a log of what you observe in your child, over time you may find that there are a few key guiding themes to his thoughts. The charts in this chapter contain samples to get you started in a deliberate process of learning to think biblically about behaviors, thoughts, and desires. I added a range of verses not in the charts in chapters 2 and 5. The Bible has more. Choose one or two for a topic that you can use repeatedly as that issue reoccurs so that in your child's mind it might become so associated with that desire, attitude, thought, or activity that it comes to his mind automatically in those situations.

Thought	Possible Heart Desires	Possible Biblical Evaluations
Mom is mean.	• I want you to feel bad. • I want you to get off my case.	• Revenge (Rom. 12:17-19) • Love of control, Power (Rom. 12:17-19; 3 John 9)
That's not fair.	• I wanted to play in my room longer. • I want life to be my way.	• Love of control (3 John 9) • Love of pleasure, Love of self (2 Tim. 3:1-4)
I can't wait to get away from this family.	• I want to be free of parental authority, to control my own life, to not risk having to relate.	• Love of control (3 John 9) • Love of self (Isa. 53:6; Matt. 6:24) • Love of safety (fear of man) (Prov. 29:25; Ps. 56:3-4)
Everybody hates me.	• I don't want to have to adapt to people. I want to feel safe.	• Love of self (John 12:25; Luke 9:23) • Love of security/Fear of harm (Ps. 37:1, 3; Ps. 56:3-4; Matt. 10:28)

Identify the replacement desire. What does the Bible tell me to want? What would please God? This step leads to the biblical *put-on*. The first question directs him to Scripture, the source of authority. The second question couches the same idea in the context of pleasing God, which leads to relationship. It steers him to the ultimate goal and offers hope of a solution to his guilt and enslavement (Col. 3:17; 2 Cor. 5:9). In this way, you are bringing the gospel to bear on your child's situation. The following chart follows possible tracks of four thoughts:

Thought	Heart Desire	Biblical Evaluation	Desire to Put On
Mom is mean.	• I want you to feel bad. • I want you to get off my case.	• Revenge • Love of control • Power (Rom. 12:17-19; 3 John 9)	• Desire to please and trust God (Rom. 12:17-19; 2 Cor. 5:15) • Desire to honor my parents (Eph. 6:2-3)
That's not fair.	• I wanted to play in my room longer (want life to be my way).	• Love of control • Love of pleasure • Love of self (2 Tim. 3:1-4)	• Desire to love God and live for His glory (Ps. 37:3; 2 Cor. 5:15) • Desire to love others as myself (Matt. 22:39) • Desire to tend to my responsibility
I can't wait to get away from this family.	• I want to be free of parental authority, to control my own life, to not risk having to relate.	• Love of control • Love of self (Isa. 53:6; Matt. 6:24; 3 John 9) • Love of safety (fear of man) (Prov. 29:25; Ps. 56:3-4)	• Desire to please God, trust Him with control (Ps. 56:3-4; Matt. 6:24; Prov. 29:25) • Desire to love others (1 John 4:18) • Desire to fear the Lord
Everybody hates me.	• I don't want to have to adapt to people. • I want to feel safe.	• Love of self (John 12:25; Luke 9:23) • Love of security/Fear of harm (Ps. 37:1, 3; Ps. 56:3-4; Matt. 10:28)	• Desire to trust God (Ps. 37:3; Matt. 10:28-31; Phil. 4:6-9) • Desire to love others (1 John 4:18; Ps. 37:1, 8; Phil. 2:3-4) • Desire to God's glory more than my safety (1 Cor. 10:31)

In the previous chart, some of the desires are not necessarily sinful. They are sinful only when the child turns them into demands. In particular, "I want to feel safe" is a legitimate desire. The problem with it is, in this case, the child has assigned it too great a valuation. He deems his comfort and safety as more important than God's glory. No one wants to be hurt, but the alienated child elevates emotional safety to a life-dominating demand. He needs to change what he treasures in his heart.

Plan a God-honoring thought. At this point, application requires engaging the gears of right heart desires with thoughts. You and your child can work together to plan specific thoughts to tell himself in order to live out a God-pleasing desire. Speaking these aloud reinforces the truth even more than merely thinking them.

Thought	Heart Desire	Biblical Evaluation	Desire to Put On*	God-Honoring Thoughts to Put On*
Mom is mean.	• I want you to feel bad. • I want you to get off my case.	• Revenge • Love of control • Power (Rom. 12:17-19; 3 John 9)	Desire to please and trust God (Rom. 12:17-19; 2 Cor. 5:15) Desire to honor my parents (Eph. 6:2-3)	Mom is trying to help me. I choose to respect my mom. I will "trust in the Lord and do good" by obeying her willingly. (Ps. 37:3; Eph. 6:2-3)
That's not fair.	• I wanted to play in my room longer (want life to be my way).	• Love of control • Love of pleasure • Love of self (2 Tim. 3:1-4)	Desire to love God and live for His glory (Ps. 37:3; 2 Cor. 5:15) Desire to love others as myself (Matt. 22:39) Desire to tend to my responsibility	Life is not fair, but God is good and just. I will do what He wants, not demand my own way. (Prov. 21:3)
I can't wait to get away from this family.	• I want to be free of parental authority, to control my own life, to not risk having to relate.	• Love of control • Love of self (Isa. 53:6; Matt. 6:24; 3 John 9) • Love of safety (fear of man) (Prov. 29:25; Ps. 56:3-4)	Desire to please God, trust Him with control (Ps. 56:3-4; Matt. 6:24; Prov. 29:25) Desire to love others (1 John 4:18) Desire to fear the Lord	God is good. I choose to accept the place God has chosen for me to be, and I will thank Him and my parents for what they give me. (Phil. 4:12; Col. 3:17)
Everybody hates me.	• I don't want to have to adapt to people. • I want to feel safe.	• Love of self (John 12:25; Luke 9:23) • Love of security/ Fear of harm (Ps. 37:3; Ps. 56:3-4; Matt. 10:28)	Desire to trust God (Ps. 37:3) Desire to love others (1 John 4:18; Ps. 37:1, 8; Phil. 2:3-4) Desire God's glory more than my safety (1 Cor. 10:31)	Being holy is more important that being safe. Whatever they think, I will trust in God (Ps. 56:3-4). I will stop thinking about me and focus on my responsibilities.
			*Or use the verses in the Evaluation column	

Challenge with choice. What will I choose? What will I do now? By calling for a commitment, these questions teach a child to be an active chooser. It also promotes hope by assuming that change is possible. There is, of course, risk of false promises. Also, remember that you are not to manipulate. You will have to make the judgment call on when to ask the child for a verbal commitment and when to simply pose the question and tell him that his actions will express his choice.

Offering Help and Prayer Support

As the process reaches the application stage, you can also ask, "How can I help?" Perhaps there is something you can do that will be a support, a reminder, or a guard. This question conveys your good intentions for his welfare.

Before the conversation is over, pray with your child. Be sure that you are talking to God and not to the child, but let him hear your concerns and desires for him lifted before God. Show him your reverence for and dependence on God as the One who has the power to help people in their weaknesses.

Working it Out

After this evaluation, what is the child to do with it? To put off his sinful behaviors, thoughts, and desires, he must put on godly desires, thoughts, and behaviors. You will probably have to help him determine the exact put-offs and put-ons. This is where the work at finding accurate biblical terms for behaviors, thoughts, and desires will pay off, making you able to shine the light on both the sins and the path out of them, and to speak to the heart.

Is an unruly child going to cooperate in this process? He is likely to balk repeatedly and need to be disciplined and/or sent to a quiet place to think about what God would have him do. You might not be able to coach him through the process, but you will be thinking through it yourself. Then you can develop the question or statement to say even when the child refuses to answer. You will develop insight into your child and skill at guiding him to godly responses. A question here and a statement there will help him a little at a time. Below are scenarios of how Donnie's parents might guide him.

Scenario A: Donnie's motive was to play in his room longer. He thought that his mom was mean for not letting him do so. He wanted revenge and to control her. Mom might say any of the following:

- **On desires:** "Donnie, instead of wanting revenge, you need to want to please God by honoring your mother." (Rom. 12:17-19; 2 Cor. 5:9; Eph. 6:2-3)

- **On thoughts:** "Thinking that I am mean is a false accusation. You can think what is true. You can think, 'Mom is making me breakfast. I choose to be thankful and respect my mom. I will "trust in the Lord and do good" by obeying her willingly.'" (Eph. 4:25; Ps. 37:3)

- **On behaviors:** "To honor your mother means to obey her cheerfully and speak respectfully. Will you please now answer my 'Good morning' as I have taught you to do?" (Eph. 6:1-3)

Scenario B: Donnie reacted in anger because he was worried about the morning bus ride to school because he thinks everyone is out to get him. Mom might tell him:

- **On desires:** "You are wanting to protect yourself. That is God's job. You can relax because He is trustworthy. Put on the desire to trust Him and think of the interests of others." (Ps. 37:3; 1 John 4:18; Phil. 2:3-4)

- **On thoughts:** "The thought that everyone is out to get you is not true. You are focusing on yourself. Instead, you can tell yourself what is true: 'Because God is trustworthy, I will trust in Him. Being holy is more important than being safe. I will stop thinking about me and focus on my responsibility to treat Mom with respect.'" (Phil. 4:8; Ps. 37:1, 3)

- **On behaviors:** "Your fretting led you to speak disrespectfully to me. You could put off fretting and instead ask me to pray for you. I would be happy to help you feel safe. You need to tell me what is bothering you and speak to me with a respectful tone." (Ps. 37:8; Eph. 6:2-3, 29, 31)

Now that we've seen the method, let's apply this to an actual case. At age ten, Delia insisted on a nightly bedtime ritual in which she said, "I love you, Dad" and "I love you, Mom," and each parent was required to answer, "I love you, Delia." She demanded that the ritual be repeated twenty to thirty times before they turned off the light, and if they did not do it she became hysterical. Her father said that Delia was obviously in "real pain."[4]

How can this dad help Delia? First, he needs to learn to think biblically, such as about the term "pain." If he thinks that Delia is in physical pain then he needs to have a doctor examine her. If there is no physical pain, then Delia is not sick. She is not really in pain but in want. Even if she has what we call emotional pain, it is still driven by an unsatisfied desire. In addition, even if she has physical or emotional pain, she is not handling it in a godly manner. Hysteria shows a lack of self-control (Gal. 5:23). The repeated pleadings and the demands for repetition demonstrate an attempt to manipulate, which shows desire for control (3 John 9-10). The refusal to obey and go to sleep is disobedience and her manner may indicate rebellion (Eph 6:1; 1 Sam. 15:22-23). Perhaps she has given herself over to fear (Prov. 3:24-26). Is she angry over something?

Before he jumps to fix Delia, Dad needs to evaluate himself. Is Delia's behavior a reaction to something that he and his wife are doing? Has Delia's dad provoked her by criticism, anger, indifference, or withdrawal that evening or in recent weeks? Has he spoken harshly to his wife or abdicated his leadership role? Is he irritable at Delia's bedtime because he wants to get back to a TV program? If he said bedtime is at 8:30 yet he stays and interacts with Delia until 9:00, then at the least he is showing unfaithfulness by not keeping his word; his "no" does not mean "no" (Matt. 5:37). He must confess his sin and begin to change himself.

Then, Delia's dad needs to draw out her heart by investigating what she is thinking and wanting. Is she prolonging awake time, postponing aloneness in her room, enjoying control over her parents, or is she afraid of something? He picks a time early in the day to question her about the bedtime situation. What was she feeling? What was she thinking? What does she gain by the "love you" ritual? He needs to become involved in her world and draw out her heart so that he can know how to help her. For the purpose of this discussion, we will determine that Delia was adopted eight months ago and is now postponing aloneness at night because she is afraid that her parents will leave her.

So, Dad begins to put right thoughts about fear of abandonment into her mind. Possible approaches include teaching that David saw God as a Rock, a huge rock cliff where he could climb and find a safe place out of reach of his enemies (Ps. 18:1-2). Or he might take her to Psalm 56:3-4 and teacher her that she can trust in God as her Rock and say what David said, "When I am afraid, I will put my trust in Thee... I shall not be afraid." God is everywhere and always with us. Rather than be controlled by fear of abandonment, she can believe God when He says that He encloses Delia "behind and before," so He is a protection around her all the time. She can go to sleep in peace in the shelter of her Rock knowing that when she wakes the next morning, He will be there to greet her (Ps. 139:18; Lam. 3:22-23). He is someone to love. She can desire to enjoy His presence.

In reminding her of his love, Delia's dad would emphasize God's involvement and authority. He might read Psalm 127:3, that children are blessings given by God to parents to raise, and explain that parents are responsible to God to take care of them. He might remind her of a memory verse, Ephesians 6:4, which commands him to teach her, and he cannot do that if he does not stay with the family. He also is accountable to God to teach her to put off being controlled by fear and put on being controlled by love for God.

Dad will tell her what she can do to overcome her fear. She can choose to love God (1 John 4:18). She can love God by praying to Him and obeying Him (John 14:21). The way she can obey Him is to put on self-control and cheerfully obey her parents. God promises blessing to her if she does (Gal. 5:23; Eph 6:1-3).

The dad would instruct Delia on a new bedtime plan or plan one with her input. The plan will include her actions and thoughts. Maybe he will tell a Bible story or read a short book. They will pray together and repeat a memory verse. Then he will turn out the light and Delia will stay in bed quietly and go to sleep. If she feels afraid, she can pray and think the memory verse to herself. If she has a hard time, she can thank God for items on her thank list, or repeat Bible verses, Bible stories, or hymn lyrics to herself. They might role play the plan in the afternoon.

I offered several ideas above. Delia's dad will teach her one truth pill at a time, not the whole bottle at once. In the first couple of days of working their new plan, he will remind her early in the evening about the new behavior he expects of her. As he leaves her room that night, he might remind her of God's loving presence, her responsibility, and an appropriate Bible verse. Each night, if she starts her old routine, he would briefly remind Delia to trust God and fulfill her responsibility, then turn out the light and leave. At that point, he himself might need to go do some Bible meditation and have prayer with his wife.

Necessity of Practice

An alienated child needs training because even if he wants to change, new right ways feel uncomfortable. It feels easier and safer to use the old habits. You should guide your child through practicing the words and behaviors you want him to learn. Parents do this with young children all the time, such as in the use of "please." Eventually, saying "please" becomes a habit and promotes an attitude. In the same way, you will find yourself repeating certain verses or questions over and over. That's a good thing.

This process breaks situations into bite-size pieces. All children benefit from this kind of training. A RAD-type child especially needs it. With some children, you may be able to shift more to guiding questions. "What does Ephesians 4:29 say? Was your speech unwholesome or edifying? What would be an edifying way of saying what you want to convey?" "What does Ephesians 6:1 say? What do you need to do right now?" "What does 1 Corinthians 10:31 say? How might you do that in this situation?" With an alienated child, you will likely be answering the questions most of the time, as outlined in this chapter and the next, countering his false thinking with truth.

Some parts of this chapter have been adapted from Lou Priolo's book, *The Heart of Anger*, Calvary Press Publishing, 1997. Read that book for a more detailed treatise on calmly, reasonably, biblically helping the angry child.

Is all of this processing overwhelming? It is if you try to do it all at once. Take it one step at a time, one conversation at a time, one thought at a time. Pray for wisdom and grace. Pray for your child. Persevere in godly responses in order to please God.

Footnotes

1. This process is adapted from several sources, but especially *Heart of Anger*, by Lou Priolo.

2. Paul David Tripp, *Instruments in the Redeemer's Hands: People in Need of Change Helping People in Need of Change*, (Phillipsburg, N.J.: P&R Publishing, 2002), 224-226.

3. From Priolo, *Heart of Anger*, 96.

4. Koplewicz, *Nobody's Fault*, 4.

Chapter 13
Respond to Manipulation Biblically

Mrs. DeSpare is mixing a cake when Jason, Donnie's older brother, walks out the door to play with Cole. Cole is a neighbor friend whom Donnie also knows. Jason had already asked Mrs. DeSpare if this time he and his pal might be allowed to play without the younger Donnie interfering, spying on them, and trying to take over as he often did.

A minute later, Donnie comes skipping out to the kitchen where Mrs. DeSpare has just opened the oven door to insert the cake. He grabs her in a tight hug over her arm which jostles her so that some of the batter spills on her hand, the oven door, and a red-hot burner on the stove. He proclaims, "I love you, Mom."

Thinking that this could be a time when maybe he is truly connecting with her, she takes a deep breath, sets the pan on the counter, and returns his hug, "I love you, too." Letting go of her, he heads for the door. Mrs. DeSpare stops him, saying that he can stay home and play with his own toys today.

Donnie drops his head and whimpers, "Please, Mom. I want to play outside."

She turns to wash her hand. "We already talked about this. I told you that Jason was going by himself to play with Cole and that you would stay inside. I also told you why you would not be playing with Jason and Cole, because you have been interfering and trying to control them. Remember what your dad taught about sowing and reaping? Today you are reaping and will say inside."

"But Cole is my friend."

Mrs. DeSpare stops herself from cleaning the pan, turns full attention to Donnie and says, "Actually, he is Jason's friend. You have other children in the neighborhood who are your friends."

"But Cole is my friend, too, just as much as Jason's."

Mrs. DeSpare firmly says, "Be that as it may, you will stay home this time."

"But I've been home all day. You told me yesterday that I need fresh air."

Mrs. DeSpare now wonders if she was inconsistent. Clenching her teeth, she says, "You stay inside."

Donnie suddenly explodes, "That's not fair! Jason gets to play with Cole, but I don't. You didn't let me have Kirk over on Saturday, either. Why can't I go? You never let me play with my friends when I want. You don't love me like you do Jason!"

Mrs. DeSpare was trying to get work done. Then Donnie's inconsiderately imposed hug caused a mess and she felt irritated. Now she suspects that the display of affection was a snow job and she got sucked in enough that she did not correct him for the selfish hug. She did well to have told him earlier about staying inside and by stopping her work and turning her full attention to Donnie. On the other hand, she is not addressing his manipulations and his accusations have her second-guessing whether she has actually been unfair. She was unjustly accused. She feels angry, guilty, and confused. She could get relief by giving in, "Oh, just go out then!" but knows that is not right. She is ready to explode at him with a long lecture recounting all of his infractions of the day.

Manipulation is an effective control tool. The antisocial child is a master at it. Therefore, response to manipulation is a skill that parents need to study and practice.

Manipulation is an effort to control another person by illegitimate means for selfish purposes (James 4:1-3). Usually, efforts are directed at emotions. The idea is to get the other person to react out of emotion rather than out of reasoned decision. For example, in Jesus' parable, the older son said to his compassionate father, "That's not fair! For your bad son, you throw a party and serve filet mignon. I've been good to you, yet you never let me have a party, even if I serve measly goat burgers!" (Luke 15:29, liberally paraphrased). He used exaggeration and false accusation to try to evoke guilt feelings in his dad. When the Pharisees told Jesus, "Go away ... Herod wants to kill You," they were using threat to evoke fear in Jesus and control His departure (Luke 13:31).

The approach explained in this chapter is not easy. You may fail many times in the face of the endless and repeated temptations that the child will throw your way. With practice, you will gain skill. Take heart from the truth of God's forgiveness and patience. If you sin, confess it and then press on again trusting God for the grace He promises (1 Cor. 10:13).

Parts of this chapter contain distillations from my own studies on both RAD-type children and manipulation. Parts have been adapted from *The Heart of Anger*, by Lou Priolo, applying his counsel in the context of RAD. His book is published by Calvary Press, Amityville, New York. It contains much additional counsel that I have not included. I cannot recommend that book highly enough. Looking to God's Word at every turn, Priolo simplifies and organizes complicated family interactions so that effactually pleasing God as you work through them is a possible and reasonable goal.

How to Answer Foolishness

Proverbs 26:4-5 says, "Do not answer a fool according to his folly, or you will also be like him. Answer a fool as his folly deserves, that he not be wise in his own eyes."

Manipulation tempts people to answer back in kind. They may defend themselves, argue, snap back, withdraw, pout, etc. Foolish responses in a parent are just as foolish as the child's provocations. When a child gains the satisfaction of having manipulated his authorities into foolish responses, he thinks himself a wise guy. A godly response answers in a way that maintains control, uncovers for the child where he needs to correct his ways, and does so in a way likely to be most persuasive.

Jesus' interactions with the Pharisees, who were manipulators, provide ideal examples for us. He never argued on the Pharisees' terms but persistently corrected their understanding in a way that revealed their hearts in order to draw them to God.

Remember your ambassadorship.

When attacked, Jesus kept turning the spotlight back on the attacker. This was not a control move. It was out of humility and love. He did not seek to defend Himself but to glorify the Father. He loved His attackers by trying to show them their sin against God that they might repent and receive peace with God.

Likewise, you must remember that the unruly child's control tactics are ultimately and tragically a rebellion against God. Your responsibility is not self-defense, but love for God and your child. Cast your hurt in the trash and get busy discerning the child's real problem and redirecting him to God.

To do so, you will need to plan wise, biblical answers to types of manipulations, keeping reconciliation always in mind. God "reconciled us to Himself through Christ, and gave us the ministry of reconciliation, namely, that God was in Christ reconciling the world to Himself, not counting their trespasses against them, and He has committed to us the word of reconciliation" (2 Cor. 5:18-19). You have the privilege of participating in reconciling your children to God.

Responding to manipulations is not about getting the upper hand. If you use these truths for that purpose, you will be guilty of the same sinful demand for control as your child. You will also contribute to hardening your child against God because he will perceive Scripture as just one more parental club for controlling him. It would not be an honorable use of the Word of God (2 Tim. 2:15). Instead, respond out of a heart of love in a way most conducive to reconciling your child to God.

For example, Mrs. DeSpare can remind herself that getting the cake baked is less important than her stewardship of the situation God has sovereignly handed her. She needs to get her own attitude right and think through a response that will speak truth to Donnie's heart. For example, to his words, "You never let me play with my friends when I want," she might reply, "That is a false accusation. The Lord wants you to speak truth and honor your mother."

Appeal to the mind.

Jesus responded to manipulations with a logical application of Scripture directed at the mind, not the will or emotions. Jesus did not whip up fervor or strong-arm with threats. He countered lies with the truth, darkness with light. For example, there was a man who said to Jesus, "Teacher, tell my brother to divide the family inheritance with me." In other words, "It isn't fair. Make him share."

Jesus responded, "Man, who appointed Me a judge or arbiter over you?" and went on to warn against greed (Luke 12:13-15). This exposed both the man's selfish motive of greed and his manipulation in appealing to the improper authority (Jesus). To do so, Jesus utilized a rational appeal to the mind rather than to emotions.

When the Pharisees tried to discredit Jesus over His eating with tax-gatherers, their premise was that God comes to good people (us), not bad people (them). Jesus reasoned that as doctors help sick people and not the well, so Messiah comes for sinners, not those who consider themselves too righteous to need a savior (Matt. 9:9-13).

We, too, are to appeal to the mind by speaking truth in an attitude of love (Eph. 4:15). Our methods are not the ways of the world, which appeal to the flesh in emotions or coerce the will by use of power (1 Cor. 1:18-25). We simply expose the darkness of sins and lies, and counter lies with truth (Eph 5:11; 2 Cor 10:5).

Mrs. DeSpare might apply this truth by observing to Donnie that he hugged her while she had the pan in her hand, a time most convenient for him and inconvenient for her. He would please the Lord if he considered others more important than himself (Phil. 2:3-4).

Apply God's standard, Scripture.

Jesus consistently referred manipulators to God's Word, even if only by allusion. When they accused His disciples of lawbreaking regarding the picking of grain on the Sabbath, He answered with two passages of Scripture, "Have you not read what David did?" and "I desire compassion and not sacrifice" (Matt. 12:3-7; 1 Sam. 21:6; Hosea 6:6). When they accused His disciples of breaking the hand washing tradition, He asked why they themselves broke the law and quoted, "Honor your father and your mother," and "He who speaks evil of father or mother, let him be put to death" (Matt. 15:4; Exod. 20:12; 21:17). The citing of Scripture redirected the manipulators from an attack on Jesus personally to how they compare to God's design.

If Jesus treated Scripture as authoritative and sufficient for use with manipulators, then parents need to be using it to help their children. Children need to see that God's Word is the authority to which everyone must defer.

Apply the Bible first to yourself (Matt. 7:5). Then, when you draw the child's attention to Scripture, do so in such a way that the child sees that you also are in subordination to it. Do not wield God's Word as a club to defend yourself or demand behavioral change. Hold it up like a mirror so that the child can see his reflection for himself. Minister Scripture to entice heart change. Show your child God's heart and will so that he can see himself in relation to God.

For example, to Donnie's begging, Mrs. DeSpare might reply, "Donnie, God says that you are to obey your parents. It may be hard, but it is not more than you are able to do with His grace. You can obey cheerfully by Christ's strength" (Eph. 6:1; 1 Cor. 10:13; Phil. 4:13).

Call to responsibility.[1]

Jesus consistently swiveled the camera around to the manipulator by observing that person's failure to fulfill his responsibility. This was not tit for tat; it was dealing with the real problem. For example, when Martha complained to Jesus that Mary was not helping, Jesus observed that Martha was being anxious, which He had taught His followers not to do, and that she was not focused on what was important (listening to Jesus).

The Pharisees tried to evoke guilt when they accused, "Why do Your disciples transgress the tradition of the elders? For they do not wash their hands when they eat bread." Jesus redirected from a focus on the disciples to the Pharisees' own responsibility, "And why do you yourselves transgress the commandment of God for the sake of your tradition? For God said, 'Honor your father and mother'" (Matt. 15:2-6). He calmly referred them to Scripture and reminded them of their own responsibility which they had not fulfilled.

Combine the skills.

Take another look at how Jesus calmly referred people to their responsibility and to Scripture. One day, the Pharisees asked Jesus' disciples, "Why is your Teacher eating with the tax-gatherers and sinners?" Many manipulation attempts by the Pharisees were indirect, taking the form of either grumbling to others or accusations of Jesus' disciples. By using the "why" word they tried to incite guilt. Instead of defending Himself, Jesus identified their problem. They were calloused toward people. They were failing to fulfill the law "love your neighbor." In this, they missed the heart of God. Jesus answered with an appeal to their responsibility, "Go and learn what this means," and to the Scripture, Hosea 6:6, "I desire compassion, and not sacrifice" (Matt. 9:10-13). He did so not to win the argument but to draw them to repent so that they could reconcile to God.

To develop a wise answer to a foolish manipulator:

- Observe the responsibility that is not being fulfilled by the manipulator.
- Identify the Scripture that teaches the responsibility.
- Combine these into a calm, reasoned answer (directed at reconciliation to God and others).

For example, Matthew 19:3-9 records the Pharisees' challenge of Jesus about certificates of divorce. The responsibility not being fulfilled was that of honoring the sanctity of marriage. The Scriptures teaching the high value of marriage were those that Jesus quoted from Genesis 1:27 and 2:24.

In the accusation over hand-washing (Matt. 15:1-9), the Pharisees were concerned about the breaking of their own hand-washing tradition. The responsibility not being fulfilled was obedience to God's law. They elevated their tradition over His law, their way over His way. Jesus pointed out one example, their lack of honoring their parents. The Scriptures used were Exodus 20:12 and 21:17.

What should Mrs. DeSpare have done? Right at the start, she needed to ask Donnie, "What does the Bible say that love does?" It is not rude. It considers others (1 Cor. 13:5; Phil 2:3-4). "When you insisted on a hug in your timing, you took no thought for what I was doing and so you caused the batter to spill. Take this cloth and clean it up while I wash my hand. When I get the cake in the oven, I'll be happy to receive your hug." She conveys loving gentleness while refusing to accept manipulation, and directs Donnie back to God's Word and his responsibility.

This is the ideal. But I found myself often slow to realize the principles involved in the conversation evolving before me. I was sometimes more like Mrs. DeSpare, reaching the boiling point and exploding into harsh words. What is the solution then? Mrs. DeSpare remembers Ephesians 4:15 which says that truth is to be spoken with love. Crying to God for help, she stops. She tells Donnie to go to his room while she and he both consider what God would have them do. She prays and ponders how to answer. If Mr. DeSpare is home, she seeks his counsel. She goes to Donnie's room, confesses her harsh words as sin, and requests Donnie's forgiveness. Mr. DeSpare goes with her to oversee the process and reinforce her teaching if necessary. Then she goes through the process of identifying his deceitful show of affection and his arguing, what the Bible says about them, and what he needs to do.

Appeal to the Conscience.

A good conscience displays two primary characteristics: it holds to the right standard (God's) and sensitively responds to it (1 Tim. 1:5; Heb. 4:15). It sees the self in light of God's standard. It agrees with God's evaluation, whether good or sinful. If good, the person is affirmed and proceeds with confidence. If sinful, there is a conviction of guilt which produces the emotion of guilt feelings (2 Sam. 24:10; Rom. 2:14, 15; 1 Tim. 1:5, 9). The person responds with remorse and repentance.

Children labeled RAD are known for a hardened conscience. A hardened conscience was explained in chapter 5. The child's conscience became calloused by repeated hardening against its warnings (1 Tim. 4:2; Rom. 1:21, 25). Now it functions by lies instead of truth, so it follows a wrong standard. This conscience lacks sensitivity; it does not feel guilty when it should (Tit. 1:15). Instead, it glories in shame (Phil. 3:19; Rom. 1:32).

Hardening does not just happen to a person. People deliberately harden themselves one decision at a time through rebellion against what they know to be true (Ps 95:8; Heb. 3:8, 15). They choose a lie and function accordingly (theology produces function). Determined that Jesus not be the Messiah, the Pharisees hardened themselves against Jesus' evidence (Mark 8:11-12). Rather than admit that Jesus healed a blind man, they put the blind man out of the synagogue (John 9)! Even the disciples hardened themselves a few times against the truth that Jesus taught or demonstrated (Mark 6:45-52; 8:1-10, 14-21). Hardening oneself inhibits learning.

Since Hebrews 5:14 indicates that a discerning conscience is developed through training, there is hope for a child with a calloused heart. You can teach the right standard (Deut. 6:4-9; Eph. 6:4). Instruct his mind in truth. Jesus retaught the hardened Pharisees. Regarding their lack of compassion He reminded them, "I desire compassion." When they would excuse themselves from the "love others" standard, He corrected their definition of "neighbor" (Luke 10:25-37). They believed in easy divorce; Jesus retaught them on the sanctity of marriage. They disputed His teaching by citing Moses' "command" to "give [the wife] a certificate of divorce and send her away." Jesus corrected that Moses did not "command" divorce. He "permitted" it, due to their hard-heartedness and sought to limit serial remarriage (Matt. 19:3-9). You can reteach your child regarding the lies he is believing.

Truth in hand, appeal to the conscience. By that I mean, ask for decisions based upon the truths of God's Word. Examine how Nathan induced conviction in David (2 Sam. 12). He led David to examine himself before God. He did so by uncovering David's sin so that David could see himself in light of God's standard (Eph. 5:11). Nathan appealed, "What say you, Conscience?" Although Nathan didn't pull his punch when David needed it, he kept himself to the role of a guide or witness by using a story and having David make the judgment. Nathan left David's response in David's hands. He allowed the Holy Spirit to do the convicting.

This method of answering manipulators emphasizes bringing the child to the standard so that he can examine himself. The conscience then has two witnesses to consider—his actions and God's standard. Like in the Nathan and David situation, the sinner is left facing God (by Scripture) with his own unfulfilled responsibilities. This method respects the child and honors God.

Do not usurp the role of the Holy Spirit to convict or the responsibility of your child to respond. A conscience is self-examining. Therefore, your child's response is his responsibility. Your role is like Nathan's. You bring your child to the standard in a way that the contrast is apparent. You trust the Holy Spirit to do as He will with your child's heart while you stay out of the conviction business.

There are communicative devices that do not awaken a conscience or induce a godly response. Criticism provokes shame; the shamed person will react by justifying himself. Accusation provokes guilt; the guilty will defend himself. The "why" question provokes hurt and guilt; the hurt person will explain himself. None of these responses leads to remorse before God in a way that prompts repentance. They cut God out of the picture as the parent tries to force a conviction and, thereby, becomes a manipulator.

People sometimes ask "why" in order to gain information about a person's reasons or motives. But because the "why" question can provoke hurt and guilt, it must be used with care, especially with children who are already defensive. Rightly applied, it can lead to conviction. When misused, it aims to hurt. Listen to these misused "why" questions. "Why do Your disciples transgress the tradition of the elders?" (Matt. 15:2). "Why is your Teacher eating with the tax-gatherers and sinners?" (Matt. 9:9). "Son, why have you treated us this way?" (Luke 2:48). To prevent unwittingly provoking guilt, consider using a "what" question like, "What were you trying to achieve?" or "What were you thinking before you _____?"

In his book *Teach Them Diligently*, Lou Priolo points out that Jesus used "why" questions not for gaining information but primarily for convicting His hearers. He asked, "Why did you doubt?" (Matt. 14:31) and "Why do you call me 'Lord, Lord,' and do not do what I say?" (Luke 6:46). Of Mary He asked, "Why is it that you were looking for Me? Did you not know that I had to be in My Father's house?" (Luke 2:49). Priolo suggests other conviction-moving questions like "Do you know what God calls what you just did/said?" and "How did those words build up or minister grace to that person?" [2] They convict because they remind the child of the Bible's evaluation of his sinful behavior. Such questions are not to be used for attack or humiliation or in sarcasm; that is manipulation. They must be spoken in gentleness for conviction and teaching. [3]

When Jesus dealt with hypocrisy, He did not point out just any inconsistency. He compared the complaint with the higher standard of Scripture, especially of loving God and others. Did they complain about the breaking of their traditions? Jesus shifted the focus to the higher standard, observing how they violated Scripture.

Jesus did not compare one person with another. He compared the inconsistent actions of the manipulative person. For example, when they censured healing on the Sabbath as work, He asked which of them does not work on the Sabbath by walking his donkey to water (Luke 13:10-17). You may show the child his own inconsistencies, but you must not compare one child with another.

Jesus especially held the Pharisees to account in the area of compassion. Compassion is reflective of the very heart of God and the core of the law (Matt. 22:37-39). So lack of compassion demonstrates a lack of love for people and God (Matt. 9:9-13; 15:1-9). The Pharisees demonstrated greater concern for their donkeys than for people, which was really a greater concern for themselves and their religious system than for God and His ways.

Like the Pharisees, alienated children lack compassion while being sensitive on the issue of rule-keeping, their own rules, of course. Their sensitivity makes it a gateway to their conscience, a place of appeal to utilize like Jesus did. Loyalty, or faithfulness, may be another portal. The RAD child demands loyalty from others but does not loyally love God. You might also be on the lookout for other doors. Remember, the goal is to draw the child to God, not to hammer his faults or gain control.

Use Jesus' responses to the Pharisees as models. For example, "Donnie, you want your teachers to think you are great, but at home you hit your brother. God desires compassion, not good appearance" (Matt. 9:13). Or, "Donnie, you accused me of being mean. Your accusation is not loving. You need to honor your mother" (Matt. 15:1-9). Or, applying Luke 13:10-16, "Donnie, do you not treasure and take care of your bicycle? Yet you did nothing to help your little brother when he fell and skinned his legs. Of how much more value is a person than a bike?"

No person can force conviction upon another. Verbal clubs will only provoke defensiveness and anger. Take the time to find the appropriate Scriptures, to approach with gentleness, and to plan questions worded to persuade the conscience to consider the truth. Teach him his need to confess, to seek God's forgiveness, and to turn from his sin.

It is not easy to "answer a fool as his folly deserves," especially in the heat of battle. The Lord will give you grace to be able to do so and forgiveness when you fail (1 Cor. 10:13; 1 John 1:9). Your child's salvation is not in your power. Rest in Christ.

Challenge lying.

An antisocial child lies as a lifestyle. He lies so habitually that he can be characterized by lying (Prov. 17:4; 19:22). Lying is a difficult manipulation to handle.

First Corinthians 13:7 says that love "believes all things." Christians are called to give others the benefit of the doubt. How can you give benefit of the doubt when your child lies as a matter of course?

This will be a wisdom issue requiring prayer and Bible study. As much as possible, deal with what you know. Don't play detective. Pray and trust that God will reveal what is needed. Trust God to work in your child's heart regarding what you don't know.

Your child's lying will require attention. Proverbs 22:3 says that "the prudent sees the evil and hides himself, but the naive go on and are punished for it." Proverbs 26:23-28 specifically warns against believing those prone to anger and charm. Verses 23-25a say,

> Like an earthen vessel overlaid with silver dross
>   Are burning lips and a wicked heart.
> He who hates disguises it with his lips,
>   But he lays up deceit in his heart.
> When he speaks graciously, *do not believe him...* (emphasis added).

If you naively trust a liar you will suffer. Love demands prudence to safeguard yourself and others and to effectively expose lies to the light of truth. Maintain your desire to think the best of your child. Keep the goal that one day he will gain a reputation for honesty. Speak in ways that set him up for integrity and do not provoke lies. But since he has a history of lying, since he is characterized by lying, prudence and love require that you be slow to believe him.[4]

First, evaluate how you might be provoking lies. Parents who avoid conflict (evasion) or react angrily (attack) will discourage honesty. Patient listening and a gentle tone prevent provoking self-defensiveness in the child, invite obedience, and produce an atmosphere making it as easy as possible to tell the truth.

Pray that God will expose the child's lies to authorities in his life and provide consequences to motivate change. Teach from Proverbs 6:16-19 that God loves truth and hates lying, both those spoken and those in the child's heart (Ps. 51:6).

Teach about reputations. Proverbs 20:11 says, "It is by his deeds that a lad distinguishes himself," which means that people gain reputations by what they do. You might illustrate it with sowing and reaping crops. Or you could illustrate it by depicting words as boards in the building of your reputation. People who see a building made of boards with "Lie" written on each one will label it "Liar" and "Not Trustworthy." Cities label unreliable buildings "Condemned." If you build with truths, people will label it "Honest" and "Trustworthy." If your lying child wants a different reputation, if he wants to be more quickly believed, then he needs to be truthful. He is the one who needs to prove his word trustworthy.

What is likely to be the child's response? "You never believe me. You never trust me." A constructive answer is, "You know what Proverbs 20:11 says about building a reputation. I would like to trust you, but you have built a reputation for not telling the truth. Change the boards you're building with. When you show yourself to be consistently honest, then you will build a reputation for honesty. We look forward to that day."

If in some situation the child has been truthful and yet receives punishment, this injustice is not a catastrophe. It happens to everyone. Besides, he has also had the injustice of not paying for many of his misdeeds. Unjust punishment provides an opportunity for him to see the truth of Galatians 6:7, that we reap what we sow, and he has sown a reputation of deceit. You can help him consider how he might have prevented his connection to the situation or how he might handle it better next time. At this time, he can thank God for the opportunity to learn how behaviors can have long-term consequences. Your child's responses to these points will show how serious he is about loving God with honesty and trustworthiness.

Giving the child opportunities to be truthful in situations where his truthfulness can be verified could help to build a habit of honesty. Offer hope that if he practices truthfulness he will build a reputation of being truthful.

Look to Yourself

Galatians 6:1 says, "Brethren, even if a man is caught in any trespass, you who are spiritual, restore such a one in a spirit of gentleness; each one looking to yourself, lest you too be tempted." You must not run from the responsibility to confront your child's sins. But a manipulative situation is a field of land mines. By its deceptive nature, manipulation is stealthy and hurtful. Emotions quickly run amok. You can easily step into the trap of trying to control your child just as much as he is trying to control you. Be examining your own heart and words as you correct your child.

What is your goal? Are you demanding self-defense, relief, cooperation, to win the word battle, or respect from the child? Seek to glorify God by fulfilling your responsibility in the process of helping your child toward a right relationship with God. Seek to reconcile him to God.

What is your life like? Matthew 7:1-5 says that someone who would correct another must first take the log out of his own eye.

What is your manner of communication? Galatians says to restore "in a spirit of gentleness." Be sure that your tone is gentle, that your word choices are respectful, true, and gracious (Eph. 4:15; Col. 4:6; Prov. 16:24). Be sure that your facial expressions and body language are non-threatening.

While Jesus applied prudence regarding people, He constantly led toward relationship. Even though the Pharisees hated Him for it and clung to their impersonal works-righteous religion, Jesus kept leading them back to relationship. When they kept manipulating with accusations and tests, Jesus did not cry, rage, flinch, or run. Their attacks seemed to have no effect. Jesus never retreated unless there was physical danger. Even then, it was for God's glory and timing, not for His own sake.

Remain faithful and move toward your child by the doing of good (Ps. 37:3; Rom. 12:21). Stay engaged and convey to the child by eye contact, body language, and voice tone that you are there to minister grace to him. Calmly, gently, firmly speak truth in love. Keep placing before the child the hope of God's love for him and his responsibility to love others and God. You will fail at times. But ask God to give you the wisdom for answers and the love that will motivate perseverance (James 1:5).

Ponder How to Answer

Answering manipulations is a skill. Improvement will require practice. Proverbs 15:28 says that "the heart of the righteous ponders how to answer." Consider these questions:

- What was the situation? What did the child say?

- What responsibility is he not fulfilling?

- What Scripture teaches on this responsibility?

- What can I say that gently refers him to Scripture and his responsibility?

In the response to the child, you do not always have to quote the verse, but you should be sure that you are responding on biblical authority. Knowing of the verse allows you to refer to its truth with confidence. Choose words that will edify him (Eph. 4:29). Practice a biblical answer with the help of your spouse to ensure that your tone and nonverbals are gracious.

In the heat of a conflict, if you find that you cannot think of godly responses, it is wise to stop the situation and go plan. Better that than to pour out evil things (Prov. 15:28b). "He who restrains his lips is wise" (Prov. 10:19). Come back to the child with a planned, godly response. If you fail to respond wisely or even to detect the manipulation at first, do not be discouraged. When you do detect it, start responding wisely.

There may not be one right answer. For example, how might a mother answer "My real mom cares; you don't," or "I want my real mom"?

- If this comment sounds like a plea of fear, an answer might be, "It sounds like you are worried about something," which might lead to a discussion of Matthew 6:24-33.

- If this is a vengeful attempt to hurt but is one of those battles not to fight, a disarming and compassionate answer is, "I've been praying for your birth mother. Do you want to pray together for her right now?" (Prov. 15:1; Matt. 9:13)

- An answer that points out the sin and corrects it might be, "You are trying to manipulate me and that is sin. The Lord says to speak the truth in love. If you have a problem with me, I will listen when you speak with respect." (Eph. 4:15; Col. 4:6; Eph. 6:2)

It is important to identify the specific kind of ungodly communication because only then can repentance be specifically carried out. The corresponding solution will also be clearer. Then your child will know accurately what to put off and put on. Search the Scriptures to learn what it says about specific types of communication.

Below is a small sample to get you started:

Arguing (Phil. 2:14)
Blame-shifting (Gen. 3:1-13)
Complaining (Phil. 2:14)
Deception, Charm, Flattery
   (Prov. 23:7; 26:28)
Gentle answer (Prov. 15:1)

Harsh words (Prov. 15:1)
Interruption (Prov. 18:13)
Nonstop talking (Prov. 10:19)
Raising the voice (Prov. 15:1)
Rolling the eyes
   (Prov. 30:11-13)

For example, Donnie accuses, "You never let me _____!" What kind of communication is he using? He is lying (Col 3:9) and making a false accusation (Matt 19:18).

What responsibility is he not fulfilling? At the least, he is not speaking truth or honoring his parent and is thinking of his own pleasure more than pleasing the Lord.

What Scriptures teach on this responsibility? Some options include Colossians 3:9, Matthew 19:18, Ephesians 6:1-2, and 2 Corinthians 5:9.

What can Mr. or Mrs. DeSpare say that calmly refers him to Scripture and his responsibility? There are many options. Below are samples of responses to manipulations. Notice that Mr. and Mrs. DeSpare study to find the biblical evaluation of each of Donnie's manipulations. Then they find what responsibility Donnie is not fulfilling and the Scripture to support that conclusion. See chapter 12 for more details on this process.

Samples of Answering Wisely

Manipulations and Responses	
Donnie sneers to his sister, "Serves you right!" – Spiteful (Rom. 1:30)	**Parent response:** "How did your words minister grace to your sister?" (Eph. 4:29) Or: "How was God's grace evident in what you said?" (Col. 4:6)
Donnie: "You believed Lucy and not me!" – False accusation of injustice (Matt. 19:18)	**Parent response:** "What boards have you used to build your reputation? Build with truths and you will be believed." Or: "If you consistently tell the truth, you will build a reputation for honesty and I will be more likely to believe you."
Donnie laughs incessantly. – Evasion or Reviling (Prov. 29:9) – Scoffing (Ps. 1:1) – Strife (Gal. 5:20	**Parent response:** "Do you know how God describes your incessant laughter? He says that the person who laughs without rest is a foolish person. Your attempt to control me is disrespectful. You must control yourself." (Prov. 29:9; Eph. 6:2; Gal. 5:23)
Donnie keeps laughing and says, "But I can't stop!" – Lie (Rom. 1:25; 1 Cor. 10:13)	**Parent response:** "God says that no temptation has overtaken you that you cannot resist with God's help. Turn your thoughts to how you might love your family by participating respectfully in their conversation. Ask for His help and then determine to please Him by self-control and love for others." (1 Cor. 10:13; Gal. 5:16; Phil. 2:3-4)
Donnie keeps laughing, "But I can't." – Lie (Rom. 1:25) – Arguing (Phil. 2:14)	**Parent response:** "God says that you can. You have not controlled yourself as I told you to do. That is disobedience to parents. You should be more concerned about pleasing the Lord than trying to control others. Go to your room now. Examine your thoughts and behavior in light of what the Bible says about them. When you return, put on right desires and self-control." (2 Cor. 5:9; Gal. 5:23)

Samples in a Series

"Let Me Go to Cole's House!"	
Donnie: "You never let me go to Cole's house!" – False accusation (Matt. 19:18) – Lie (Col. 3:9)	**Parent response:** Mom skips the manipulation to go for the demand (inordinate desire/lust) that started the situation (James 4:1-3) and says, "How does your demand to go to Cole's house reflect a desire to please the Lord?" (2 Cor. 5:9)
Donnie: "Who are you to talk! At least his house is more fun than this place." – Stubbornness (1 Sam. 15:23) – Love of pleasure (2 Tim. 3:4)	**Parent response:** Mom nearly explodes in anger, so she stops and tells Donnie to go to his room to think on what the Bible says about his words. Meanwhile, she prays, makes her heart right with God, and plans a wise answer. Rejoining Donnie, she says, "Love of pleasure is not the most important value; loving God is. I must discipline you for stubbornness. Then you must consider what you need to do that is right." (1 Sam. 15:23; Matt. 22:37)
Donnie: "That's not fair!" – False accusation (Matt. 19:18 – Arguing (Phil. 2:14) – Ingratitude (Col. 1:17)	**Parent response:** "God wants me to parent you rightly, not fairly. Your responsibility is to obey your parents with thankfulness." (Eph. 6:1; Col. 1:17)
Donnie: "But I never have fun with my friends." – Lie (Col. 3:9) – Selfishness (Phil. 2:3)	**Parent response:** "Learning to obey is more important than time with friends. You need to grow in godliness. It would be better to enjoy some time with God." (Ps. 73:25)
Donnie: "I'll write on the wall if you don't let me go!" – Threat (Ps. 37:12)	**Parent response:** "Then you will be sinning. If you do it, you will be disciplined for that also. God will give me grace to handle it His way." (1 Cor. 10:13)
Donnie: "I'll get you for this!" – Threat, Plotting revenge (Ps. 37:12)	**Parent response:** "How does that threat reflect trust in God? Plotting is sin. Trust in the Lord and do good, and you will be blessed." (Ps. 37:12, 27, 39)

────────── **Implement the Principles** ──────────

* Journal in order to ponder how to answer (Prov. 15:28; 26:5). Record the conversation. Go back through it and prayerfully attach biblical labels, determine Bible verses that apply, and plan what you can say that will "answer a fool as his folly deserves." Ask your spouse to help.

* Refer to other chapters for responses that fit your situation.

* In the Gospels, study Jesus' responses to threats, "why" questions, no-win questions, and others. Formulate answers like His adapted to your child's statements.

* To equip yourself with a useful tool, extend the list in this chapter on types of speech.

* As a couple, read *Shepherding a Child's Heart*, by Tedd Tripp, and *The Heart of Anger*, by Lou Priolo. You'll find especially helpful insights on lying and other manipulations.

Ideas in these chapters may seem clear on paper, but in real life it is going to be messy. Pray for wisdom and grace (James 1:5; Col. 4:6). Examine yourself for any logs in your eye (Matt. 7:5). Persist in speaking truth out of love and in a loving manner (Eph. 4:15). When necessary, step away from the situation to pray and plan a wise answer (Prov. 15:28; 26:5). You can tell your child to be considering wisdom at the same time. Discipline as necessary. When you fail, confess and trust in His grace, get back up and try again (Prov. 24:16). Persist in thanking God for this training of yourself (James 1:2-3).

Wouldn't it be easier to just make Ephesians 6:1 (obedience) and 1 Corinthians 10:31 (glorify God) your default appeals? Use those as needed, but remember that an alienated child is full of false beliefs, lies, and hardening. He needs to have his mind renewed specifically.

Do you have the time for all of this work? Is it difficult and exhausting? God says that you can do all things through Him (Phil. 4:13; 1 Cor. 10:13). Your time and effort spent in godly parenting is time and effort spent glorifying God. It is also time and effort spent in holding before your child God's character (standard) to shine light on his responsibility so that his conscience might be retrained. You will be loving your child in the way that will be most effective to draw him to repentance and trust in Christ.

Footnotes

1. Priolo, *Heart of Anger*, 129.
2. Priolo, *Teach Them Diligently*, 144.
3. Ibid., 42-45.
4. Welch, *Addictions*, 89.

Chapter 14
Guidelines for Discipline

Mrs. DeSpare removed what was left of Donnie's burnt curtains. Then Mr. DeSpare removed the brackets. They decided to leave Donnie's room bare of curtains. That evening, when Mrs. DeSpare opened a drawer to obtain her pajamas, she found human feces on top of her clothes.

The degree of the child's antisocial behavior can stymie parents. How do you discipline a child impervious to punishment and pain, who turns parental discipline into his own tool against the parents? Proverbs says that a foolish son is a grief to his mother and gives his father no joy (Prov. 10:1; 17:21). In the face of grief and sorrow, parents must persevere for the glory of God and love for the child. This chapter offers more guidelines for persevering in godly discipline.

Parent in obedience.

The Lord commands parents to be parents (Eph. 6:4). You may play with your child, but you are not his playmate. You may be a friend to your child, but you are not his brother or sister. You may discuss ideas, but you are not his classmate. He may appeal a decision, but you are not a business partner, so don't negotiate. You are his parent.

If you negotiate, your child will learn that rules are suggestions and that if he can wear you down you'll give in. What does that teach him about God's commands and God Himself? How does it demonstrate your own obedience to the Lord? Rules are not up for debate. There are situations in which exceptions or changes can or even should be made. You may teach your child how to appeal to an authority and listen to his appeal with grace, but the final decision is yours and should be accepted without argument.

When requests or reasoning don't work with parents, some children try whining. Whining is a method of complaint and manipulation. It manipulates by irritation applied at a degree just under the threshold at which it would precipitate disciplinary action. It demands that a parent come back to the negotiation table or suffer the punishment of eternal nagging. Whining expresses rebellion. After teaching a biblical view of whining, from then on, correct or discipline it at the first whimper. Don't negotiate, bargain, or compromise. Obey the Lord; be the parent.

Overcome evil with good.

It is said that children think concretely. How much more concrete can it be than in giving you the defecation that many people shout about when angry or when actually urinating rather than just verbalizing it as an expletive.[1] It is hard to not take offenses like these personally. Disciplining in anger is retaliation, not training. It is returning evil for evil and demonstrates that the parent is more concerned about his or her own hurt than about God's glory or the child's welfare.[2] God gives us the hope that a pure heart will be impervious to temptation, like to anger, because it is fixed on loving God and His wisdom (Prov. 23:26-27). Develop a pure heart.

To relieve emotional pain, some suggest depersonalizing. Reckon that your child would retaliate against any authority, not just you in particular. While this rationale is true, is depersonalizing a biblical response? How does it image Christ?

Depersonalizing is usually self-defensive rather than other-loving. It can lead to indifference or cynicism rather than a pure heart pursuing love.

A better alternative is to remember the gospel. Even while persecuted, rather than think self-defensively Jesus entrusted Himself to His Father and moved toward man with means of reconciliation (1 Pet. 2:23). Remember that your child's real problem is his offense toward God and that you are responsible to love in order to lead him to see his need for Christ. Rather than take offense and rather than prevent your own hurt feelings by depersonalizing, put on the pure heart of Christ by thinking of God's heart and the child's spiritual welfare (Phil. 2:3-4). Grieve for the price Christ paid for your child's sin and the punishment coming to him if he does not repent. This will motivate you to apply God's solution.

God did not advise depersonalizing; His solution is to overcome the evil, overcome it with good. Even a cursory reading of Luke 6:27-36 and Romans 12:9-21 reveals the aggressiveness of this command. It is not a matter of passively enduring. We are to go on the offense with good done in love.

Choose battles carefully.

There will be a multitude of infractions on a daily basis. Constant conflict is not productive. Choose the battles that are important. Place the priority on issues of the heart, safety, or the most serious of the life-dominating habits.

If you are just starting to make parenting changes, don't try to do them all at once. Neither you nor your children can change everything right away. Choose one or two points of change and build from there.

Study the child.

There will be surprises, but awareness can reduce the number. While an antisocial child can seemingly erupt out of the blue, extreme events may be preceded by warning signs as the child stews and plots. Study him. When he suddenly becomes cooperative or seems unusually edgy or hyperactive, what happens in the days following? You may not become aware beforehand of the exact nature of the coming storm, but you might, and might be able to take some preventive action (Prov. 22:3).

Plan ahead.

Antisocial children are more likely than other children to cause serious events. In the midst of a crisis or difficult situation, your perspective may not be accurate. Having a predetermined plan can steady and guide you (Prov. 20:18a). Don't magnify your child's case, but don't ignore symptoms, either. As you see the need arise, plan at least a big picture of what you might do, contingent upon further godly counsel. Slip the plan in your mental hip pocket until needed. Meanwhile, trust in God. Planning is not a license for worry or extremism.

Encourage pause and think.[3]

In the midst of conflicts, emotions rocket our words and actions into trouble (Prov. 16:32). That is why Proverbs warns, "When there are many words transgression is unavoidable," and "He who makes haste with his feet errs" (Prov. 10:19; 19:2). The child needs to pause and think about his circumstances and responses.

A practical aid to pausing and thinking is to stop all words and actions and go to another room to think. There, he begins with prayer. Then he plans right attitudes, words, and actions that will glorify God. You will find this a productive practice for yourself as well.

Determine to discipline.

As an ambassador of the Lord to teach this child about Him, you must command obedience and discipline disobedience (Prov. 6:20; 13:24; 19:18; 23:13-14). Discipline is training for the benefit and restoration of the child (1 Tim. 4:7). "The rod and reproof give wisdom" and "reproofs for discipline are the way of life" (Prov. 29:15a; 6:23), preventing misery and reaping blessings. So what are some reasons that some parents do not discipline diligently?

Some parents view corrective discipline as the opposite of love or a last resort. On the contrary, "He who withholds his rod hates his son, but he who loves him disciplines him diligently" (Prov. 13:24). The reason that Proverbs 23:13 says, "Do not hold back discipline from the child" is that holding back discipline from an unruly child is like refusing to call the fire fighters until the house is engulfed. Love disciplines the sparks to stay in the fireplace (Prov. 3:11-12).

Relentless unruliness can wear a parent down. It seems easier to do the child's homework for him, to not enforce rules "this time," to pay for what the child stole, or to pay bail. This is parental laziness and selfishness. "A child who gets his own way brings shame to his mother" (Prov. 29:15b).

In pity for his past or for his "disorder," some parents may excuse the child or try to make life easier for him. This is a serious failure to believe God's Word when it teaches that it is by *discipline* that we learn. God never excuses sin. This child needs more discipline, not less, to give him greater opportunity to learn wisdom. Discipline, not pity, is the way of life (Prov. 6:23).

Behaviors like strange eye motions and hyperactivity may have become so automatic that they seem physiological rather than volitional, but inability is not the problem. Self-control is possible. Changing habits is hard, but discipline makes it easier. So discipline diligently.

Is it contradictory to teach a child that he is helpless in his sins (Rom. 5:6) and can do nothing apart from Christ (John 15:5) while also teaching that he can obey his parents (Eph. 6:1)? No, unbelievers (who do not have the Holy Spirit's empowering) obey rules, laws, and authorities every day. It is just that they, outside of Christ, cannot transform their own hearts and their good works are not acceptable to God (Isa. 64:6). Apart from Christ they can do nothing to please God. The child is capable of temporal obedience and needs to learn habits of obedience so that if/when he trusts Christ, his good habits will aid him in sanctification. You can and must call him to his responsibility.

Allow consequences.

Behavior and consequences are a package deal (Gal. 6:7). It is like the game "The Price is Right." When a participant chooses a door, he also chooses what is behind the door. In this way, consequences are educational.

Some parents interfere with their child's education by saving the child from experiencing natural consequences of his hurtful behavior. Proverbs 19:19 warns that "a man of great anger shall bear the penalty, for if you rescue him, you will only have to do it again." Parents who rescue the child from his penalty will have to do it again and again and again. They will prevent him from learning to do right. They are facilitating him to become enslaved to his sinful behaviors.

The loving father of Luke 15 did not save his prodigal from harsh street life. For the good of your child, and within the limits of safety according to his age, allow him to experience the consequences of his actions while he is young, both the rewards for good and the penalties for bad. If he is not allowed to eat the fruits of the seeds he has sown, he will not be motivated to take responsibility when he is older.

For example, a few years ago the manager of an RV park in Missouri related this incident to me. One of the rules at the park is that pets must be on a leash when outside the motor home. A twenty-seven year old man had repeatedly ignored that rule. One day he returned to his motor home to find that his cat had been shot with an arrow. Furious, he went door to door accusing people of shooting his cat. He even called a radio station, the staff of which took pity on him and started a fund to pay for the vet bills. He grew so obnoxious that the park manager ordered him to leave and finally called the police to evict him.

So the man called his mother, who came to the park and blamed the manager. The manager answered that she was the one to blame because she had not disciplined her son when he was young and so he was out of control now and not man enough to be responsible for his actions. She then tried to interfere with the policeman. He ordered her to sit in her car and be quiet.

The manager was right. Mommy was still rescuing her boy from consequences he had earned. The most loving thing that mother could have done would be to confess her sinful parenting to her son, counsel him to submit to his authorities, and then drive away.

Do not save the child from consequences. If he gets into trouble at school, check the facts. Be open to accepting that your child may be guilty in the matter.

Homework is a common trouble spot. A seven-year-old may need coaching, but a fifteen-year-old needs to know that although his parents are available for truly needed help, they will not help with homework that he is capable of doing. Flunking the test or the class would provide a greater motivation to learn responsibility than if the parents do the work for him.

Or perhaps one day, similar to the cat owner, the older teen or grown child calls on the phone, "Mom, some stupid cop says I lifted software at a store. He threw me in jail. Will you bail me out?"

Mom lovingly answers, "Did you steal it?"

"Mom, you know cops. They have it in for me."

"You did not answer my question. Your reputation inclines me to believe the policeman. If you stole, then you were not loving others or obeying God. That saddens me. I will let your dad know and will follow his lead. Perhaps we can visit you."

"Will you bail me out?"

"You know I wouldn't do that without talking to your dad. Besides, it is not our responsibility to take your consequences from you. They are for your benefit. Hopefully we can visit you. I'd like to pray with you before we hang up."

"But I didn't want to go to jail!"

"Son, you know God's Word says that you will reap what you sow. The way of the transgressor is hard. This is a chance for you to learn to do right. I love you and will come to visit you. May I pray for you now?"

True compassion realizes that hope for change is not in keeping the child comfortable or making him feel good about himself. It is in confronting his wrong thoughts and behaviors as well as in helping with his positive efforts.[4]

Deliver consequences.

Allowing consequences is passive. Parents must also discipline actively.

Deliver consequences at the first infraction. Do not keep warning or giving more chances. This models laziness, manipulation, and empty words. Counting to three gives tacit permission to test you. It teaches that you do not really mean what you say. It trains in diso-bedience to both the command and counts one and two. It does not teach that delayed obedience is disobedience. It sets the stage for your own anger as the child keeps pushing your limits until you erupt. No wonder a child is provoked to anger by a parent who does not enforce a command. God did not give Adam a pass, a second warning, a louder threat, or a three-count. Adam received consequences at the first sin. Put off temptations to lazy passivity and deliver the promised consequence. Consequences need not be harsh, just delivered.

Persevere in the discipline you apply. Numbers 14 relates a beneficial example. Through two years of wilderness travel, Israel had complained, rebelled, argued, and tested God. God disciplined repeatedly. Eventually, Israel reached the border of the promised land. When the people heard of giants in the land, they refused to go forward, refused so stubbornly that their resistance turned violent. Like the antisocial child, self-preservation was uppermost in their minds. God punished them with a sentence of death in the wilderness. Hearing this, they suddenly complied, but not really. Numbers 14:40 says that the next day "they rose up early ... saying, 'Here we are; we have indeed sinned, but we will go up to the place which the LORD has promised.'" God told them it was too late. They went up anyway and were beaten into a rout by the Canaanites (Num 14:39-45). Their belated "obedience" was not obedience. It was avoidance of consequences. It was also another act of rebellion in that they again refused to go where God said to go (because they didn't want the discipline). The alienated child will try the same ploy of seeming compliance. Do not relent just because the child changes his mind when he learns of his penalty. The penalty stays in force. If he really does obey anyway, he can also receive a reward after the discipline has been delivered. But receiving consequences for the initial offense is crucial for the child to learn self-control.

If there is physical assault or serious intentional property damage, it may be best to call the police and press charges. Your child needs the consequences and your other children need to see that you will take measures to protect them. In a situation this serious, remember also to call your church leader to seek his prayer and counsel, and to make yourself accountable to him.

Providing consequences for disobedience is not retaliation and should never be done in anger. Discipline is for training in godliness and reconciliation of relationships, and you won't accomplish that with anger (Prov. 6:23; Matt. 18:15-18). Rather than sin in anger, it is better to leave the room, pray, and put off all anger (Prov. 16:32).

Also, discipline is not complete until there has been reconciliation of the offended parties. Coach your child through this process. However, you cannot force a true reconciliation. Stay focused on pleasing the Lord.

Wrap discipline in compassion. Although God did not relent on the death sentence for Israel's rebellion, He did graciously pardon them (Num 14:20). He also stayed with them throughout the remaining thirty-eight years in the wilderness. He supplied all of their needs during those years; their clothes and sandals did not wear out (Deut. 29:5). Compassion tenderizes correction without subverting it.

Choose suitable discipline.

The alienated child subverts all types of discipline. For example, while parental approval is a motivator for most children, it is not for antisocial children because they are not people pleasers.[6] For them, affectionate behaviors are often tools. They may obtain for the child a sense of control, winning an ally against parents, or schmoozing others to prevent suspicions of himself. Taking praise as an indicator that authorities think he is doing well, he complies for a while to lower their guard. One mom began to trust her newly cooperative son only to learn later that at school he had been stealing and extorting money from other children.[6] Parents who use the tools of disapproval and praise will find them usurped if the child perceives those tools as a means to control his parents' emotions. The child performs to make them feel sad or happy as he wills, while they view themselves as trying to motivate with praise and finding it futile.

Proverbs 10:1 speaks to the fact that a child's conduct affects the emotions of his parents. It says that "a wise son makes a father glad, but a foolish son is a grief to his mother." Solomon, a very wise parent and author of this proverb, was referring to wise parents. Biblically wise parents would want godly children. So, when a child lives wisely he pleases his parents. And when he pleases a godly parent, it indicates that the child is also pleasing God. When appropriate, parents ought to communicate their joy over a child's wise choices and their grief over his sin. "When appropriate" will be a wisdom call. Parents must not allow their emotions to be controlled by the child or use their emotional responses in an effort to manipulate him.

Whether or not it motivates, recognition of and appreciation for desired behavior is important. It instructs, demonstrates respect, and encourages. Guarding your own motives, affirm and then leave his response between him and God.

You can also phrase recognition of work well done in ways that steer your child toward God and emphasize his own change and rewards. This is a positive adaptation of Jesus' method of handling manipulations. It compares your child to truth from Scripture and his own responsibilities so that he sees how he is doing right. "You tried hard on your homework today. You are behaving wisely" (like the ants, Prov. 6:6-11). "Look at what you accomplished. Do you feel that sense of satisfaction?" (Gal. 6:7). "Your tone and words honored your mother. Good job" (Eph 6:2).

What about spanking? Many prospective adoptive parents, at least in the United States, will repeatedly hear through required reading or instruction that they should never spank children who have been physically abused. While space prevents a lengthy discussion on this teaching, here are a few observations to consider. What constitutes physical abuse? The U.S. culture has inclined toward such extremes that a mere comment may be deemed verbal or even sexual abuse. Similarly, some do not distinguish between beating and spanking; they view spanking as physical abuse.

Never is a long time and does not take into account growth in a child's understanding and in relationship. The teaching of total abstention from spanking of children who have truly received physical abuse underestimates children. It presumes that they are not intelligent enough to distinguish between the beating of an angry, selfish parent and the corrective discipline of a parent who has the child's interest in mind.

Wise parents are not going to resort to spanking first thing after adoption. Proper spanking will not be done before there has been love consistently demonstrated in the relationship and clear instruction given about spanking, why it is done, and the loving intent of the parents. There will be clear instruction given about the behavior in question and its consequences. Especially in adoption, there will have been time allowed for the child to adjust to expectations new to him, all the more in cases of physical abuse. Parents will make full use of other means of correction as well, understanding that there is a broad principle behind the term "rod" in Scripture, that of structure in discipline.

Usually, spanking *done correctly* motivates to repentance and reconciliation with the parent. Because an alienated child conquers pain and fights anything he views as a threat, he may sabotage this effect and choose defiance instead. Then, since the parent has spent the biggest ammunition in his arsenal, there is nothing left. Considering the amount of conflict an alienated child will instigate and how extensively he will push, if a parent resorts to spanking too quickly, he will be spanking too often, dulling the effect. Still, Scripture teaches that there is a use for spanking. When spanking is carried out in a wise, loving way, the alienated child can understand that in this case, what he might reinterpret as a "threat" is truly for his good and shows the love of his parents. Used judiciously, it has beneficial effect, down the road if not in the immediate situation. Seek counsel and apply wisdom regarding your particular child.For more information on the topic of spanking, study Scripture, consult your church leaders, and read the books in the resource list at the end of this book.

Alienated children, being familiar with deprivation, try to subvert the impact of loss of possessions. If they can't have something, they just determine to stop wanting it. Parents see shrugged shoulders, a total disinterest, disdain for the object, or perhaps increased trouble-making. So at times, the child's success in changing his desires is only partial. After all, if he really did not want the object, there would be no anger, revenge, or overdone indifference. Indifference can be a facade. By nature, antisocial children tend to be greedy and possessive, which means that they have strong desires to possess things. The sin nature is too strong for him (James 1:13-15); his desires are not so easily self-manipulated as he would like. In the moment, the child talks himself out of wanting the lost item. But if the object was truly treasured, loss of it will have an impact in the long run because the child, though he denies it to himself, does feel some unhappiness (if only due to the loss of his control over the object). Also, the loss demonstrates that the parent delivered a consequence. That means that the parent might do it again.

God has made man to love and worship Him. That requires desire. Therefore, though our desires have been corrupted by sin, the human heart constantly generates desires (Prov. 4:23; James 1:13-15; 4:1-3). The child cannot get away from the fact that no matter how many things he determines to not want if deprived of them, he will continue to want those or other things. He cannot escape the impact of loss.

You might allow the child to earn back a confiscated treasured possession. This adds a behavioral aspect to loss of the item, providing the child cares enough to earn it back. It will be his choice. In this case, the option to earn it back allows him an opportunity to enjoy some legitimate control under your authority.

Decide discipline limits.

Choose discipline that has an end point. Some of God's discipline incorporated time limits. He assigned Israel to the wilderness for forty years and to Babylon for seventy years. I wouldn't suggest couching your discipline in terms of years, but you get the idea.

Rather than submit, an antisocial child is likely to escalate disciplinary situations. Then, "Go to your room until you are ready to apologize" might result in either a five-day stay in the room or the parent rescinding his order, which is unfaithfulness to his word. The child can sabotage any form of discipline, so discretion will be necessary to prevent escalation. Because you must persevere in delivering consequences, you need to think ahead and incorporate limits.

Be careful about establishing consequences that cause you or the other children more penalty than the offending child. For example, grounding the child also grounds you and maybe the other children if they rely on your transportation. Inconvenience is a reality of parenting, but you need to be judicious about it.

Finally, even when discipline seems futile and the child persists in a stubborn attitude of rebellion for days on end, do not stop disciplining in a godly manner. Disciplining children is the parents' responsibility to God (Eph. 6:4), not just a pragmatic tool to use if it happens to work. "Do not lose heart in doing good, for in due time you will reap" (Gal. 6:10). Many times, though the discipline bears no fruit in the immediate, your child will feel the cost enough that later he will restrain himself to avoid a similar expenditure. Even if your child does not respond, you will reap godly character.

Consider restitution.

Consider restitution as a training tool, especially for property damage and theft from siblings and others. Making restitution reminds the child that sins require a payment and that evildoers will pay (Rom. 6:23; Ps. 37:8-9). It teaches compassion as he experiences loss connected to the loss that he caused to another. It counters the child's pride and offers a sense of justice to the siblings.

Restitution works well when the offense involves property, whether the loss occurred through negligence or a deliberate act (Num. 5:6-7).[7] It is best if it fits the loss in kind (Lev. 24:18-21).[8] An act of service for the offended party is an option.

Restitution should be just, not vengeful (Lev. 24:19-21; Matt. 5:38-42). The goals are restoration of relationship and training through consequences.

Be a watchman.

Antisocial children commonly exploit parents' desire to trust them. They must be held accountable to limits. This will require close supervision and a willingness to be uncomfortable in a conflict situation. In response to supervision, the child may resort to an accusation like, "You don't trust me!" You might answer something like, "Are you fulfilling your responsibility? I am responsible to God not for trusting you but for training you. You have shown me that you do not behave responsibly. I love you so much that until you show me that you are trustworthy, I will continue to check on you" (Prov. 20:11; Gal. 6:7). See chapter 13 for guidance on responding to manipulations.

One way a rebellious child gains cunning in deceit is by getting parents to explain how they knew what he was doing. He asks, "How do you know?" This is manipulation. First, it diverts attention from his responsibility and puts parents on the defense explaining themselves. Second, it tempts the parent to doubt his own judgment and might get him to back off. Third, if it works, the child learns what to do next time so as to not get caught. Do not allow the topic to switch from the child's guilt to your defense, nor coach him in evildoing. Evidence is for the judge, not the defendant. A sample answer may be, "A guilty person does not need evidence to know that he is guilty. You need to ask for forgiveness and do what is right."

What about the right to privacy? It is the Constitution, not Scripture, that promotes a right to privacy.[9] Which is more loving toward a child known for deceit and sinful behaviors, to blindly trust with freedoms or to practice prudence and protection? A room search that uncovers the butcher knife stolen from the kitchen may prevent a crime. It is not that you refuse the respect of a knock on the door, but the last thing this child needs is total privacy (Ps. 10:5-11; Prov. 9:17; 18:8; Rom. 1:18, 25). For his own good, he needs to have his deeds exposed (Eph. 5:11-13). Watchfulness is wise, not disrespectful. You may find that for his good or the family's you have to forego the warning knock or remove the door altogether. If he gets angry over your entrance into his room without permission, perhaps that says more about his heart than the issue of privacy.

Insist on pattern change.

Just because a child starts behaving well does not mean that you should quickly lift restrictions. Since lying and charm are the antisocial child's lifestyle, it is automatic for them to fake a change. So be slow to believe that real change has occurred. Habits and character are like gardens; they take time to develop. The roots of old habits don't die easily. Look for evidence of true change in established patterns over time.

You may have to coach church friends on this. They are, thankfully, enthusiastic about child evangelism. The manipulative child may take advantage of that enthusiasm for his own gain. For example, he may fake a salvation when under their care. While God can at any time grant him forgiveness and a new heart, before any parent or church authority affirms his salvation there must be insistence that the child with a reputation for manipulation live a changed pattern over many months. If his heart has been transformed by the Holy Spirit, this insistence won't be a problem. The Spirit promises to preserve His own (1 Pet. 1:5). Since people are known by their fruits, fruit grown over the long term will be the evidence of true heart change (Mark 7:20).

Deliver up for restoration.

As the child grows, so may the magnitude and intensity of his behaviors. Some alienated children persistently declare that they want nothing to do with the family. They eventually demonstrate their commitment by running away, vandalism, or violence. Some people view these actions as cries for help. Need for help (dependency) is far from what an alienated child is about. He prizes self-sufficiency. He is more likely trying to carry out his intention to separate from his family.

Some people never change. There are Cains, Absaloms, and Korahs (Gen. 4:3-8; 2 Sam. 14-18; Num. 16). They adamantly refuse to reconcile or to submit to legitimate authorities. Correcting them only invites escalating trouble (Prov. 27:22; 9:8).

Is removal from the home ever an option? There is precedent for removing the child. God put His children out of the Promised Land after centuries of rebellion (Deut. 28:64; Neh. 1:8; Jer. 9:13-16; 2 Kings 17:6, 22-24; 18:11; 25:9-11; Ps. 106:40-43). He did so again when they rejected His Son.

Removal involves the loss of parental influence and possibly removal of other restraints on evil. Depending on how it is done, the child is given over to other authorities or to his sins and their consequences.

The child may view moving from the home with relief, as a release from bondage. People like having less restraint. What they do not realize is that in God's economy, withdrawal of restraint is a punishment. When He gives someone "over to their own devices," the person's own sins reap back on him a harvest of strife, desolation, and barrenness (James 1:15; 4:1-3; Jer. 17:5-6; Pss. 1:4-5; 81:11-16; Prov. 1:24-32; 13:15b).

The biblical term "deliver up" conveys the intent. When Paul instructed the Corinthians to put an unrepentant person out of the church, he used the term "deliver" (1 Cor. 5:5). It is the English translation of *paradidomai*. It is a judicial term for handing a sentenced criminal over to those who will carry out his sentence upon him. John the Baptizer was *paradidomai* to prison (Mark 1:14). Jesus was *paradidomai* to death (Rom. 8:32). "Deliver up" is used in Romans 1:21-32 to describe what God does with unrepentant people. He gives them over to their sins as a judgement.

Matthew 18:15-20 records Jesus' explanation of a disciplinary process in which after repeated efforts to reconcile a person back to right living, if he is still unrepentant, he is put out of the church. He told of the prodigal son who sinfully separated from his family and the troubles that followed motivated repentance (Luke 15). Paul's purpose for his instruction about the unrepentant Corinthian was "that his spirit may be saved in the day of the Lord Jesus" (1 Cor. 5:5). The man did repent (2 Cor. 2:6-7). Putting the child out of the house prior to what would occur with a normally maturing young adult should be done as a form of discipline on the same principle as church discipline. The process requires allowing the child to have at least some of the independence he so strongly demands and the negative consequences that go with it.[10] The goal is restoration (Prov. 23:14).

Sadly, there are times when it may be in everyone's best interest to remove the child from the home before he turns eighteen. Such a severe action should be reserved for serious violations such as habitual, unrepentant use or storing of drugs in the house, behavior that has damaging or pernicious effects on the siblings, physical violence or threats thereof, and theft. "In these situations, the child is clearly saying that he is unwilling to be part of the family, and he should not receive the protection that a family normally affords."[11] He wants out so badly that he will do anything, even harm himself or others, in order to force his goal.

Parents are legally responsible for minor children unless there is a court-approved emancipation. Government agencies will not take responsibility for unruly children unless they have been in trouble with the law. The police will not interfere until property has been damaged or blood drawn. Aside from these resources, options include boarding school, residential treatment, and granting guardianship to someone else. Boarding schools cost a cart of gold, residential treatment a truckload, so some families who cannot afford these options have to endure until the child is of legal age for independence.

Before you consider the step of removing a child from your home, ascertain that you have taken the log out of your own eye (Matt. 7:1-5). Have you lived what you preach? Have you made the rules clear and enforced them consistently and with grace? Have you persevered in godly parenting, and then persevered some more? Consult your pastor, elder, and/or a biblical counselor who can help you evaluate to be absolutely sure that you have not provoked continued anger in your child. Seek their counsel on whether this serious transition should be made and, if so, how to go about it.

Your attitude regarding the removal is vital. This is not about relief, retaliation, or conceding defeat. Those are self-focused responses. Israel's rebellion earned chastisement as horrific as war, famine, and exile, yet as Hosea recorded in 11:8, He grieved:

> How can I give you up, O Ephraim?
> How can I surrender you, O Israel? ...
> My heart is turned over within Me,
> All My compassions are kindled.

And "Oh that My people would listen to Me...I would quickly solve their problems and bless them abundantly" (Ps. 81:11-16, paraphrased). Centuries later, Jesus mourned, "O Jerusalem, Jerusalem...! How often I wanted to gather your children together, just as a hen gathers her brood under her wings, and you would not have it!" (Luke 13:34). Punishing Israel was extremely painful to Him. He longed for their reconciliation.

Like God, you must be so full of love and compassion that you are moved to grief over the child's loss of the blessings that he could have had in the family and the connection with God that you provide. Cultivate in yourself a fervent desire for reconciliation and a heart prepared to forgive (Gal. 6:1-2; Matt. 18:15-17; Luke 17:3-4). Remember, you don't know the future. As long as there is life, your Absalom could repent.

The process of moving the child elsewhere needs to be in the context of relation to God, which will need to be explained.

A. According to the circumstances, tell the child in biblical terms the reasons for his removal.

B. Tell him the purpose of discipline.
1. You are handing him over to God's discipline that he might experience the pain that his sins will cause and turn back to God's gracious love (Jer. 17:5-6; Matt. 18:17; 2 Cor. 2:6-7).

C. Warn him of coming consequences.
1. You have decided to give him over to his ways. He may be very happy about that right now, but he will suffer for it (Ps. 81:12; Rom. 1:21-32).
2. Proverbs 13:15 says that the way of the transgressor is hard. He is sowing stubborn, hardhearted, rebellion. He will reap trouble.
3. In leaving the house, he is losing the protection and comfort of those who love him most. He will reap aloneness, strife (conflicts), broken relationships. He will not have peace of mind or heart, but anger, fear, and anxiety (James 1:15; 4:1-3; Jer. 17:5-6; Ps. 1:4-5).

D. Remind him of hope in God's love.
1. You love him and want good to come to him.
2. You stand ready to grant forgiveness and reconciliation if he repents.
3. You will be praying that he will be caught for every sin. You pray this way so that he might learn to do right, which will reap blessings for him. You will pray that he will never be able to forget that God sees him, that God scrutinizes and judges even his private sins, even the sins in his heart (Prov. 5:21; 15:3).
4. God will favor him with peace and grace if he repents (Ezek. 18:32; John 5:24, 40).

When moving a child out of the home, you may be tempted to worry, doubt, and vacillate. You know that this child almost certainly will choose more extreme sins away from home. Drugs, sexual sins, hunger, and physical threats from strangers are possibilities. He will likely suffer a harder life and you do not want him hurt. You may fear onset of regrets should your child be harmed. There may be a baby born to the homeless daughter. You may grieve or feel guilt over the times that you failed to parent in a godly manner. Therefore, you need to have solid reasons established for your decision. Again, consult wise counselors like your church leaders to help ensure that you have done all that you can and to plan for what you will do should grief, doubts, or regrets arise.

The child may leave and never look back or he might come looking for handouts. If he comes back, remember his skill at manipulation and do not be quick to don the elated robes of the prodigal's father. Once you remove the child, you must keep your word and hold firm.

You may feel pity for the poor sufferer or worry that a refusal to help equals lack of love. On the contrary, Proverbs 13:24 says that the one who *withholds* discipline is the one who lacks love. Ecclesiastes 8:11 teaches that when punishment is delayed, people think that they can get by with sin, so they do more of it. If you relieve him of consequences, you encourage him to think that he can get away with sin. You interfere with God's work in his life by relieving him of the pressure that God may be exerting to motivate repentance.

A return to the home is possible if there is demonstrated repentance. Rules must be established. Those might include daily Bible reading, cessation of manipulative language, regular church attendance, continued education with passing grades and/or holding a job, paying rent, cheerful work around the house without you reminding him, etc. It should be clearly established ahead of time that he will be evicted if it turns out that he has not repented.

God calls parents to their task. Keep sowing godly parenting and wait for God to produce the harvest He chooses (Gal. 6:7, 9; James 1:2-4; Rom. 8:28-29).

Footnotes

1. Baker, "Reactive Attachment Disorder."
2. Priolo, *Teach Them Diligently*, 38.
3. Michael R. Emlet, *Angry Children: Understanding and Helping Your Child Regain Control* (Greensboro, N. Car.: New Growth Press, 2008), 20.
4. Adams, *Christian Counselor's Manual*, 149.
5. Baker, "Reactive Attachment Disorder."
6. Samenow, *Before It's Too Late*, 160.
7. John F. MacArthur, *The Freedom and Power of Forgiveness* (Wheaton, Ill.: Crossway Books, 1998), 91.
8. Ibid., 188-189.
9. Welch, *Addictions*, 99.
10. Ibid., 101.
11. Ibid., 100-101.

Chapter 15

Handling Parental Heart Responses

Parents, you can and must trust that God will provide the wisdom and strength that you need in order to rightly respond to the situation in which God has sovereignly and lovingly placed you (1 Cor. 10:13; James 1:5). To turn temptations into growth situations, apply to yourselves the same truths and practices that you teach your children. This chapter contains implementation ideas. It is not intended that you complete all of them. Choose those which will most effectively help you to put off sinful responses and put on loving obedience to the Lord.

Identify your Problem Biblically

As we saw in chapter 12, Pastor Helpin taught Mrs. DeSpare that she is a worshiper at heart who speaks and acts based on what she most treasures. Some desires are inherently sinful. Some desires are good but become sinful when we demand to have them (James 4:1-3). When Mrs. DeSpare wanted peace and decent conversation more than she wanted to respect Donnie and control herself, she was desiring peace and intimacy more than she was desiring to please God.

To change, Mrs. DeSpare can use her anger as an alarm for herself rather than a club against another. When she feels anger coming on, she needs to immediately put on self-control by the power of the Spirit (Gal. 5:16, 23), then ask herself questions like, "Did I sin to get what I wanted?" or "Did I judge and punish the other person?" If the answer is "yes," then she knows that her desire was more important to her than pleasing God and must be repented.

Use the heart evaluation questions explained in chapter 12. "How did I respond and what was I feeling and thinking?" "What was I trying to achieve?"

Applying the Solution Biblically

Once sinful heart desires are identified, then you can change them and the sinful behaviors by applying the put off/put on process (Eph. 4:22-24). What desires and behaviors does Scripture say I must put off? What desires, thoughts, and behaviors does it say I must put on? Putting off requires confession and cessation. Putting on requires planning and effort. Renewing the mind through Scripture study is essential in that process because thinking truths from God's Word will realign your desires with God's desires.

To illustrate the change process, recall Delia. Her dad's analysis of her "love you" routine and hysteria is that she is in "real pain."

What is the father thinking? He says that he thinks that Delia is in pain.

How is he responding? He is obeying Delia. At her demand, he stays and says "I love you."

What does he seek to accomplish? He has not exactly said. Certainly, he wants Delia to get the sleep she needs, but his actions show that her sleep is less important to him than something else. Perhaps it is easier to give in because then he can get back to his TV quicker than if he takes the time to train her. This is love of pleasure (2 Tim. 3:4). Maybe he is afraid of losing Delia's affection. This is love of approval (Prov. 29:25; John 12:43). Maybe he, like Eli, sees cooperating as the easiest way to keep the peace. This is love of peace (Gen. 16:1-6; 1 Sam. 2:22-25). For the sake of this discussion, I will assume that his statement about "pain" demonstrates that his most motivating desire is to keep Delia comfortable. He wants her to be happy. This family is in for much trouble because discipline is not comfortable, so Dad is likely to refrain from disciplining Delia (Heb. 12:11).

What does the Bible say about his desire? While this father probably has a sincere desire for what is best for Delia, his actions demonstrate that he so wants Delia to be happy that if she becomes unhappy he will withhold what is best for her, which is training in self-control. He takes more pleasure in her happiness than he does in her godliness, which means that pleasing her has become more important than pleasing God (Luke 14:26-27).

If Delia's father is a Christian, his professed theology would be something on the order of belief that godliness is the most important value for a child and a parent's priority is to glorify God. He is functioning, though, as if he believes that at bedtime happiness is the most important value for a child and a parent must ensure it.

The father needs to put on godly desires and thoughts. He should rethink his valuation of happiness. God wants us holy more than happy. Holiness requires sorrow in repentance, discipline, and strenuous work all of which do not initially engender feelings of happiness (Matt. 5:4; 2 Cor. 7:9-11; 2 Tim. 4:7-8; Heb. 12:11).

What does the Bible say he should want? His strongest desire for himself should be to glorify God by his parenting. It is not wrong to want Delia to be happy, but he should seek her holiness more than her happiness. When she is unhappy, he can remind himself that he is not responsible for making her happy but for teaching her to please God by honoring her parents and being obedient and self-controlled.

His self-talk might sound like, "I am responsible to parent in a way that pleases God even if my daughter is not happy with my decisions" (Deut. 6:7; Eph. 6:4). "If she is afraid, I know that I instructed her to trust in God; I will allow her to choose what she will do." "My daughter is demanding her own way; I must help her learn to submit with a quiet spirit" (Phil. 2:3-4; 1 Tim 2:2). Diligent practice at putting on right desires, attitudes, thoughts, and behaviors will develop godliness in the parent.

This is a general paradigm for rightly handling your negative reactions. The sinful desire of the heart is identified and confessed as sin, and then a desire to please God is adopted in its place. False or sinful thoughts and behaviors are stopped; true thoughts and godly behaviors are practiced. God's Word is used to learn truth, and thoughts are aligned with it. This process is practiced so that it becomes a part of the person's life.

Implement the Principles

- If you have provoked your child or reacted sinfully against him, make a thorough confession and ask his forgiveness. Do this any time there is clear sin against him.

- Memorize Proverbs 4:23, 1 Corinthians 10:13, Galatians 5:16, 1 Corinthians 13:4-8, and Philippians 4:6-9, 13; 3:12-14. For each passage, write at least two applications to your situation. Apply one. After you do, encourage a friend by telling how God's Word affected your life.

- Use the questions in this chapter to do self-evaluation.

- Read Ephesians 1:18-23 twice daily for five days and answer these questions:

- What resources does God give me to live for His glory?

- How can I use them today?

- Use this passage in prayer for yourself and three other people today.

Change Weak Areas

The balance of this chapter will relate how the general principles above can be applied to emotional problems common to parents of antisocial children. These problems include anger, fear, depression, grief, guilt, and regrets.

Anger

Much as you do not want to be angry at your own child, you might be. Many parents of alienated children find themselves frequently irritated, frustrated, and even furious. Their parenting is not "working." They can't enjoy the reciprocal relationship of which they'd dreamed, or they want relief from the child's relentless goading and manipulations.

Often an angry parent has an underlying expectation of his ideal family or how the adopted child would turn out. Mothers are not "supposed to" be prison wardens. Children are not "supposed to" be unresponsive to love, destructive of property, or violent toward others. Unmet expectations are matches to the fuel of anger.

Expectations, demands, and anger are worship issues. This attitude, "I must have _____, and if you don't give it to me I have the right to be angry," expresses what we love and who rules our hearts. "I have a plan for my family and you must follow my plan" indicates that I most want a certain kind of family. If I become angry over being disrespected then I love/worship being respected. Anger is a worship issue because at the heart is an assumption, "In my kingdom, I rule and you cooperate." This position loves self and usurps God's rule.

To deal with sinful anger, don't settle for anger management. Put it off completely. Start by submitting to God's plan that includes trials and disappointments for you. Romans 8:28-29 teaches that if you love God, everything that comes into your life is part of God's sovereign, loving plan to shape you into the image of His Son, to make you like Christ. To what end is that Christlikeness? It is that He might have the preeminence. In Ephesians 1, Paul three times expresses the ultimate goal this way. We are in Christ "to the praise of the glory of His grace" and "to the praise of His glory" (Eph. 1:6, 12, 14). When we are like Christ is when we can best glorify God..

How do we become like Christ? Put off love for self and put on love for those at whom you are angry. "Let all bitterness and wrath and anger...be put away from you, ... and be kind to one another" (Eph. 4:31, 32). To do this, will require putting off the angry reactions and putting on self-control by the power of the Spirit (Gal. 5:19-23). A plan for change might look like this:

I WILL Put Off Anger

PUT OFF:
Stop angry words and behaviors (by putting on self-control – Gal. 5:20, 23).

Pray.

Identify: What am I trying to accomplish? What am I getting that I do not want, or wanting that I am not getting?
What is the biblical evaluation of my desires?

Confess the sinful desire.

PUT ON:
Pray for God's help. Pray Galatians 5:16.

Thoughts. What desires and thoughts does the Bible say to put on?

Actions: What kindness can I do to love the other?
Thank God.

Plan godly desires and thoughts to put on in place of selfish desires and thoughts. Create a POPO chart for desires and one for thoughts, or one in which they are combined. See the chart on the next page for an example.

Anger POPO Chart (Parents)

My Agenda	God's Agenda
I want my child fixed.	God has given me the privilege of sharing His love with this child. Only God can change my child's heart, so I will pray and trust Him. My goal is to love and please God in my parenting. (Matt. 22:37; 2 Cor. 5:9)
I want to enjoy a warm relationship with my child. (This is a good desire, the loss over which I am angry or despairing.)	I may feel grief over loss of relationship, but I will thank God for His grace to me and plan biblical responses that demonstrate His grace and love. (1 Cor. 13:4-8)
This is too much to bear. I want relief.	God owns me and has chosen to give me this stewardship. I choose to be content with His plan. God has promised to give me strength to obey Him. (Phil. 4:11-12; 1 Cor. 10:13; Phil. 4:13)
My family does not fit my ideal.	A happy family is not a bad desire, but that is not what God has given me. He owns us. I will be content with God's will and pursue loving my family. (Phil. 4:11-12; 1 Cor. 13:4-8; 2 Cor. 5:15)
My child should not speak to me this way!	How often have I rejected and dishonored Jesus who died for me? My child needs Him. I will correct graciously to please my Lord and help my child. (Rom. 3:23; Col. 4:6; Prov. 26:5)

As parents respond in love, then even if the child never changes, they can still have the joy of knowing that they walked with God and pleased Him.

——————— Implement the Principles ———————

❖ Stop Sign. If you have a problem with outbursts of anger (Gal. 5:20), use a Stop Sign method to get it under control. It is based on Galatians 5:19-23, which contrasts the fruit of the flesh with that of the Spirit. On several 8½ x 11 pages, write in big letters "Put off: Deeds of the flesh … outbursts of anger," and "Put on: Fruit of the Spirit … self-control," and "Galatians 5:19-23." Post these papers in rooms and the car, where they serve as quick stop signs for oncoming anger.

- Use parent teamwork. Whenever one parent notices another becoming angry with the child, the calm one speaks a previously agreed-upon word or statement. Upon hearing the signal, the angry parent immediately steps away from the situation to pray, get control of himself, and plan a wise answer. If he sinned against the child, he needs to confess it to the child. He will not speak to the child about the conflict until he knows that he can speak in a way that conveys God's grace.

- Every time you sin against someone in anger, confess it and request forgiveness. This is a vital part of repentance.

- Anger Change Plan. Make a plan for submitting to God's ownership and agenda. Write your plan on a card to carry with you for reference.

- Thank List (Phil. 4:7). An angry person is not a grateful person. Every day, list twenty blessings from God. Thank God aloud for each one.

- Renew your mind. With your spouse's help, list the expectations that trigger your anger. Personalize the POPO chart and use it in daily prayer to change desires and expectations.

- Use one of these passages for daily time with God: Romans 8; Galatians 5; Colossians 3:1-17; 2 Peter 1:3-9. Answer the questions.
  - What is God's goal for me? Do my goals agree with God's?
  - Find in the passage attributes of God. Spend time praising Him aloud for those.

- Grow in adoration of God. A person who clings to unbiblical expectations holds a high view of himself and a low view of God. He needs to exalt God's greatness and grace and choose to worship and enjoy Him. Meditate on Psalm 73:25-26, Psalm 139 and 145, Isaiah 40-48, Job 38-42, Daniel, and Matthew 5-7 to put on a high view of God. Record principles that you learn, and plan how to apply one that day or week.

- Memorize Galatians 5:13; Philippians 2:3-4; 1 Corinthians 13:4-8; Colossians 3:12-17. An angry person is not loving others. Plan loving acts toward your child and do them.

Fear and Anxiety

As with anger, you may be baited by a smorgasbord of fears. Depending upon the age of the child and degree of the problem, fears might include what he will do to himself, what in the house will he damage, whether some night he will pick the lock of a bedroom door and harm someone, or what the long-term effects on the siblings will be. Fear is also one of the control tools in the arsenal of the alienated child. He may threaten to run away, to destroy something, to tell authorities an incriminating lie, or to hurt someone.

Some fears are good. There is a protective fear, like what parents teach children to keep them out of the street. A good fear becomes an ungodly fear when it, rather than God, rules the person. For example, a person so terrified of cars that he will not walk on a sidewalk has an ungodly fear. So we must learn to balance self-controlled trust in God with prudent awareness and caution. Fear is ungodly when it immobilizes a person so that he does not carry out responsibilities. Fear of losing an idolized desire is sinful, such as the fear of losing control. When we fear that which God commands us to not fear, such as people, it is sinful. Ungodly fear demonstrates a functional unbelief in God's goodness or ability to keep His promises.

The solution to fear is love. First John 4:18 says, "There is no fear in love, but perfect love casts out fear." A person engrossed in loving God and others will not have room for fear.

Philippians 4:6-9 teaches what to do with fear. It starts with "be anxious for nothing." Put off worry.

Then, put on right prayer. "By prayer and supplication with thanksgiving let your requests be made known to God." Requests combined with gratitude exercise trust. In prayer, you bring your desires in line with God's. Verse eight adds the putting on of right thoughts. This works to conform heart desires and thoughts to God's will. Verse nine adds the practice of right actions. So to put off fear and anxiety, put on love for God and others. Practice right prayer, right thoughts and desires, and right words and actions. A plan for change might look like this:

I Refuse to Fear!

Pray for help.

PUT OFF:

Identify: What am I wanting or fearing more than God? Confess.

PUT ON:

Thoughts: What godly desire can replace my selfish desire?

What godly thought can replace my fearful thought? (Perhaps use Psalms 27; 34:4 and 138:8.)

Actions: What can I do now that would be loving toward God and others?

What constructive action will I now take? (1 John 4:18)

Commit yourself and your children to God's hands in trust of His sovereignty, wisdom, and love. Loving Him, you will make His glory your reward (Ps. 37:3-5; 1 Pet. 4:19; Rom. 8:28-29).

Implement the Principles

* Meditate on one of these passages: Philippians 4:6-9; 1 John 4:18; Isaiah 26:3 and 41:10; Psalm 73:25-26. Plan one practical application that counters fear and implement it for the next two weeks. Then do the same for another passage, and so on. Tell a friend what God did for you by this exercise.

* Think list (Phil. 4:8). The fearful person is likely to brood on imagined catastrophes. He needs to direct his thoughts to what is true and good. On an index card, write a list of five or ten thought topics. When you notice yourself brooding, direct your thoughts to one of your topics. Or meditate on a particular verse. Ask a friend to pray for one week that you would be diligent in putting off brooding. Report back on how you did.

* Put off fear-inducing desires. Identify the desires that cause fear at the thought of losing them or that motivate you to worry or anger. Do you want peace in the house and avoid conflict? Do you want your child to be happy so much that you worry over his future and try to control situations? These are idolatrous desires. Confess them to God and practice replacing them with thoughts and acts of love for God.

- Grow in the knowledge and adoration of God. A fearful person maintains misperceptions about God's sovereignty, wisdom, love, and goodness. Choose a passage from the following to read three times a week: Psalms 27, 34, 37, 139; Isaiah 40-48; Job 38-42; Matthew 6; John 6, 9, and 11; 1 Peter. Record what you learn about God and how that applies to your fear. Plan how you will implement one application that day or week.

Despair and Depression

Proverbs says that "hope deferred makes the heart sick" (13:12). Despair hinges on a hope, on expectations. If there is no hope (expectation) for something, then the heart has no cause to be made sick if that something is not achieved.

No wonder depression is common to parents of alienated children. Their hopes for relationship, or a happy family, or a sense of success in parenting are totally thwarted.

Add other factors. Parents feel overwhelmed from the endless watchfulness and fending off of manipulative ploys. Mothers, especially, are often singled out by the child for the most aggression, provoking fear and a desire for safety. The mom feels like a prison warden, trapped with a child who needs constant supervision and enjoys plaguing his warden. It seems that only trouble lies ahead with no relief in sight. All of these factors and more can tempt parents to despair and depression.

Non-physiologically induced depression starts with a sinful thought or reaction. That produces guilt feelings. If the person confesses and repents, he is forgiven and continues in the obedience to God that produces joy. But if in trying to relieve the feelings or other pressures the person sins again in attitude or action, more guilt is produced. Discouraged, he doesn't feel like doing what he should. He stops fulfilling responsibilities. Guilt feelings and sinful reactions heap one upon another in a downward spiral until the person is habituated into a pattern and becomes increasingly immobilized. Exaggerated false beliefs complicate the problem.

Cain provides a good example. Genesis 4:1-14 relates that when God did not accept his offering, Cain became angry. Rather than confess, "his countenance fell" (4:5). Next, rather that do what was right, he compounded his problem with bitterness and murder. Then, rather than confess, he made excuses. When he heard his punishment, he declared his "punishment ... too great to bear" and said that everyone would be out to get him. Paraphrased, it was "Woe is me! I just can't take it!"

In the case of loss of relationship, grief might eventuate in depression. God empathizes. Through Hosea He says, "What shall I do with you, O Ephraim? What shall I do with you, O Judah? For your loyalty is like a morning cloud and like the dew which goes away early" (Hosea 6:4). In Luke 13:34 we read that centuries after Hosea, Jesus cried, "O Jerusalem, Jerusalem...!" God's grief roils out of intense but rejected desire for relationship and for the good of His child.

Feelings of depression can, in themselves, feel debilitating. To walk the hill back out of depression, the depressed parent must stop paying attention to feelings. Believe 1 Corinthians 10:13 and can the "cannot" in the trash. Yes, you can. Get active doing your work and renewing the mind with truth. Most of all, make your central desire that of pleasing the Lord. *Pleasing the Lord is an attainable hope and gives joy no matter what other hopes are thwarted.*

Gratitude and trust in God's sovereignty are essentials. Both Paul and the Philippians receiving Paul's letter were suffering in trials. Yet Paul opened his letter to them with words of thanks to God (Phil. 1:3) and trust that God would continue to work (1:6; 2:13). He expressed his perspective of what God was going to do despite mistreatment that he received (1:12-17).

How could he be so positive? His heart desire was for God's glory (1:18; 1:28). As long as he was in fellowship with God and God was being glorified, Paul was content with whatever happened to him (4:11-12). He could be content in suffering because he completely trusted in God's provision of the Holy Spirit's power to be obedient (4:13), and claimed that the same was true for the Philippians (4:19). It is true for you also. *Gratitude and obedience are chisel and hammer to chip away depression.*

Use the chart on the next page frequently to renew your mind. Watch for any other desires and thoughts that depress you. Find biblical responses to use. Add them to the following chart.

Depression POPO Chart

My Agenda	God's Agenda
This isn't the family I dreamed of!	Lord, I choose to desire to be satisfied with pleasing You in the family that You have given to me. (2 Cor. 5:9; 1 Cor. 10:31)
When will it end! I just want relief!	Lord, I choose to be joyfully content with serving You to Your glory under whatever conditions You have ordained for me. (2 Cor. 4:7-11; Phil. 4:11-12)
I feel like I have failed again!	Lord, I confess_____. Thank you for Your forgiveness. (1 John 1:9) Thank You for not condemning me. I will do my next responsibility, trusting in Your grace. (Rom. 8:1; Rom. 5:1-2)
I feel trapped and helpless.	Lord, I know that You are here with me. Thank You for this situation which You are using to develop perseverance and Christlike character in me. (James 1:2-3; Rom. 8:28-29)
I am losing my child!	Lord, I am very sad, but my grief is nothing compared to Yours. Please soften my child's heart toward You. Please convict him of sin and woo him with grace.
I feel sucked dry.	How I feel does not matter. You want me to keep loving my child and You give me the power to do so. I choose to obey You with joy. (1 Cor. 13:4-8; Gal. 5:16)
It will never end!	Trials are temporary. I trust that You will use this one to produce godliness in me. (Rom. 5:3-5; 2 Cor. 4:16-18)
I can't do it anymore!	Lord, You say that I can obey You. I choose to ignore my feelings and believe You. I will now_____(right action). Please help me. (1 Cor. 10:13)

 Depression makes life seem overwhelming, so a person stops trying. Therefore, to start your change, choose just one option from the implementation ideas list and work diligently at it for a week. As you improve, make other applications in grateful service to the Lord.

─────────── **Implement the Principles** ───────────

* Seek help from someone who will not commiserate but will give counsel that leads you to change.

* Practice gratitude (Phil. 4:7). Every day, list twenty blessings from God. Thank God aloud for each one.

* List three of today's responsibilities. Do them to please the Lord. Do them first thing. Do the hardest one first. Check them off as you complete them. Thank God for your abilities.

* Read Psalm 139 twice daily and answer these questions:

  – What does this passage show me about God's relation to or involvement in my daily activities and troubles with my difficult child?

  – What does God want? Are my desires the same as His?

  – For what can I praise God? (Do so.)

  – What would keep me from praying verses 23-24 with a whole heart?

* Study Psalm 77 and answer these questions:

  – What was the psalmist feeling?

  – What was causing his feelings? What was his view of himself and of God?

  – What did he do about it? What solution did he apply?

  – What about God did he choose to remember?

  – Mimic the psalmist's solution in your own life. List God's deeds, and then thank God for them.

* Read John 18-20. If Jesus did so much for you, what might you do to show your love for Him?

* Apply Philippians 2:3-4. Perform three acts of loving service to someone each week. A depressed person is self-focused. Loving others will move your focus from self to others.

* Choose to rejoice (Phil. 4:4). List ten reasons over which a Christian can rejoice. (See 1 Peter 1 and Ephesians 1 for a few ideas.) Thank God for them. Meditate on them. Choose your favorite song of praise and sing it at least once every morning no matter how you feel.

•   When you are with people, choose to smile and give positive responses no matter how you feel. Speak of God's goodnesses to you. After all, if you are not in hell, then you have better than you deserve. Put off thoughts of self; put on interest in others.

Guilt and Regrets

We often peg more than one meaning on the term "guilt" so let's define terms. The state of guilt is different from guilt feelings. A state of guilt is a judicial position based upon the evaluation that a moral standard has been violated; the person is guilty. The state of guilt causes physiological reactions, and bad feelings which we call guilt feelings. They act as an alarm which tells us that something is wrong and corrective action is needed.

Sin causes a state of guilt before God. The corresponding guilt feelings are intended to drive us back to Him for reconciliation. Guilt feelings might also result from violating one's own, unbiblical standard. For example, a parent may expect himself to respond perfectly to his children, whatever "perfectly" means to him. Perceiving himself to fail frequently, he makes a self-evaluation and judges that he is guilty, so he experiences guilt feelings. His feelings are responding to a standard as they should; it is his standard that is inaccurate. Regrets follow close on the heels of guilt.

Guilt and regrets complicate parenting. They provoke parents to uncertainty or indecisiveness. Regrets can seduce a parent to try to make up for failures by being too permissive.

List the reasons that you feel guilty. Then identify which ones are clearly sinful attitudes or actions. Confess and ask forgiveness of the people against whom you sinned (Matt. 5:23-24). Do the same with God. Then, those sins need no longer be a cause for guilt (1 John 1:9). Take action to change.

With what is left on your list, distinguish which of your standards are God's and which are of your own making. It is not wrong to have an extra-biblical goal. It is wrong when that goal becomes a standard so important that it produces guilt if not achieved. Confess any setting of your standard above God's. Otherwise, determine to live by the grace in which you stand as a believer (Rom. 5:1-2).

There is absolutely no biblical warrant for a selfish idea promoted in recent years, that of forgiving oneself. If after confession and repentance you still have bad feelings then either you did not really repent or you are refusing to believe God's promise of forgiveness in 1 John 1:9 and need to repent of unbelief. Deal with your bad feelings God's way. Put on biblical thinking.

 Clarify responsibilities. As long as you obey God in your relation to the child, it is not your responsibility if the child does not improve. According to the commands of Deuteronomy 6:4-9 and Ephesians 6:4, parents are responsible for their influence, not the child's response.

God is sovereign. Proverbs 16:33 relates that people make choices, but God's will rules in the end. He even uses people's sinful actions to accomplish His purposes (Gen. 50:20; Eph. 1:11). Therefore, there is no question that God put your family together as the best way for all of you to participate in His plan, share His good news of grace, and glorify Him. Be looking for the good that God will bring out of the situation (Rom. 8:28-29).

Since Christians on earth are not yet perfected, they still fail at perfect obedience. The apostle Paul failed, too. In Philippians he wrote, "Forgetting what lies behind and reaching forward to what lies ahead, I press on toward the goal ..." of Christlikeness (3:12-14). The preceding context indicates that he is saying that he puts no faith in his past good works. We know, however, that he also murdered Christians in his past. Apparently, Paul refused to be distracted by his whole past, whether achievements or failures. If all sin is confessed, we must put off thoughts of the past and put on present efforts to please and glorify Christ.

Take advantage of failures and learn. Proverbs 24:16 says that "a righteous man falls seven times, and rises again, but the wicked stumble in time of calamity." Failures are endemic to men. What is important is to rise again and keep pursuing Christlikeness for the glory of God. If you want to conquer a habit of regretting, you must keep current on confession of sins, vise-grip your mind to the truth, put off the past, and press toward glorifying God..

Implement the Principles

* Ask your spouse to help you evaluate by a biblical standard the desires, thoughts, words, or actions that produce your guilt feelings or regrets. Enlist his or her help in creating a plan of action to deal with them biblically.

* Memorize Proverbs 24:16. Each time you are tempted to bemoan a failure, quote this verse aloud to yourself, thank

God for His grace at work in you, and then apply your mind and body to the next task of the day.

- Each night at bedtime, examine your heart to be sure to have confessed all known sins. Then read Romans 5:1-2 and meditate on the grace in which God has placed you.

- Before you get out of bed each morning for a week, read Romans 8:1. At salvation, all of your sins were forgiven. What is your response?

Battling regrets, guilt, fears, anger, grief, and loneliness requires an honest evaluation of the desires of the heart and a constant guard upon the heart (Prov. 4:23). It requires confession, repentance, putting off the sins and putting on God's ways by renewing the mind in the power of the Holy Spirit. Anyone with problems in these areas will facilitate overcoming them if he/she seeks godly counsel.

God has given this child to you for a purpose. It was not a mistake. He will give grace in time of need. There is joy in pleasing the Lord no matter your circumstances and feelings. Godly responses can become your lifestyle.

Persevere Toward Relationship

There is no way that you will perfectly practice all of the ideas recommended in this book. Take it one idea at a time. Build your skills. When you fail, rise again (Prov. 24:16). God promises grace to those in difficulties who humble themselves to draw near to Him (James 4:1-10). The moment you return to doing what is right you are succeeding even when you aren't perfect.

Progress will also be very slow with your child because habit is hard to change. You will water the soil of his heart. You will fertilize, aerate it, and pull weeds, and still the tree may seem lifeless. You do not have the omniscience of God to decide that your little tree is a hopeless case. Patiently work fertilizer into the soil of his heart and leave the outcome to God, who owns us all. Persevere in putting on compassion. It will hedge you from digressing into anger, indifference, or hardheartedness.

 Persevere in right parenting to please the Lord. You are responsible for loving, not for having the love accepted. As long as the Lord is pleased, you gain the joy of obedience no matter the child's response.

Always keep in mind that the goal for the child is not modified behavior. The end toward which your discipline and instruction should lead is adoration of God out of a recognition of how much God has loved him. The child starts with fear and anger entrenched in the battlefield of his mind. By the time he leaves home, even if he has not turned to God or significantly changed his ways, he needs to also have these mental redoubts from Matthew 22:37-39 and Jeremiah 17:5-8 firmly built:

"Love the Lord your God with all your heart ...
and your neighbor as yourself."

and

"Cursed is the man who trusts in mankind ...
Blessed is the man who trusts in the Lord."

Chapter 16

Teach and Guide the Siblings

It is said that the squeaky wheel gets the grease. In families with alienated children, siblings and their problems tend to be overlooked because they do not squeak louder than the angry child's wheels. This chapter is intended to put some oil on their squeaky parts. We will identify likely difficulties that siblings might face, encourage further investigation of what your children might be experiencing, and introduce a few major topics that bear on the situation. Since some topics have been discussed in greater detail in previous chapters, this one does not make thorough studies of each topic. Refer to other chapters in this book. Do further Bible study. Read other books on these topics and consult with your deacon, elder, or pastor.

Consider the Siblings' Situation

Siblings live in the same house with a person who enjoys deliberately and relentlessly provoking them. Siblings are spied upon, stalked, bullied, manipulated, ridiculed, and baited into arguments they never intended to have. Their belongings are stolen, broken, or mysteriously disappear. They see their parents receive verbal and maybe physical maltreatment and see both the godly and sinful reactions of parents. In a Christian home, siblings have to live all week with provocations, but then at church on Sunday have to respectfully listen to charmed adults tell them what a sweet person their antisocial brother or sister is. Some are physically and/or sexually abused by the antisocial child while parents remain unaware.

How Siblings Might Naturally Respond

In response to the frequent conflicts ignited by the angry, alienated child, siblings are prone to a range of responses like irritation, humiliation, sadness, hurt feelings, fear, and anger. They may be jealous of the boldness and fun that the angry child appears to be having on easy terms while they work hard to be responsible and obedient.

When an accusation arises and friends or authorities believe the alienated child's lies rather than the innocent sibling, there is disillusionment or loneliness. The injustice of being shunned while the charmer gets attention provokes resentment. In a child's view, adults should be knowledgeable, so it is confusing when the sibling sees them being deceived. Pride can rattle its tail in the heart, poisoning with the attitude of the Pharisee who thanked God that he was not like sinners (Luke 18:11-12). Siblings experience some tough temptations and need counsel for how to deal with them in a godly way.

What Parents Can Do

You are the front line of aid to your children. Teach and train them to pursue the goal of pleasing the Father who loves them. Chapter 12 holds vital truths for them about the heart. The following added points pertain especially to helping the siblings:

Offer physical protection.

Tell the children that you want to know about any serious physical aggression. Establish preventive measures as the need arises. Perhaps bedroom doors need to be locked at night, or all knives kept in a locked drawer. If physical danger seems likely and all other measures have been exhausted, there may come a time when it is wise to remove the persistent offender from the home.

Keep the marriage sound.

Marital division is frightening for children. If you maintain marital harmony, you will provide security, solidity, and a sense of peace in the home despite other conflicts.

Listen, teach, and be attentive.

The antisocial child becomes a master at manipulating family members against each other. If the siblings know that they can express their thoughts and feelings to you in an environment of understanding, they will be more open to expressing their problems and to receiving and applying your counsel.

Siblings are stewardships from God just as much as the antisocial child is. Therefore, be deliberate about spending time, money, and attention on them as well. There should be times when the antisocial child is required to take a back seat to other children in the family, just as they have to him.

Honor reputations.

Proverbs 20:11 says, "It is by his deeds that a lad distinguishes himself if his conduct is pure and right." When approaching conflict situations among the children in which the alienated child is involved, parents need to take reputation into account.

Persevere.

Paul's perseverance in trials for the gospel was a testimony that the Philippians could follow (Phil. 3:17; 4:9). Never give up on the belief that the alienated child can change by the power of God. The siblings are watching. Parental withdrawal from one child can stir the siblings to wonder about their own security. Also, they may one day have difficult children of their own; they need to see perseverance modeled. Moreover, perseverance is a testimony of God's faithfulness and ability to meet the needs of those in difficulties.

Have fun.

Proverbs 15:15 says that although there are daily trials, a heart filled with goodness will experience joy in the midst of trials. Philippians 4:4 commands us to rejoice. Christians have much over which to rejoice and can therefore take delight in the pleasure of laughter. The antisocial child will spoil many fun moments and drag everyone down. Stop the trend and lighten the atmosphere.

What Parents Can Teach

Like every person, the first thing that siblings need is the gospel. They also need to know God's character, to be taught about God's sovereignty, wisdom, and love as it relates to a family environment that sometimes seems, and sometimes might be, out of parental control. They need to know about trusting God, how to guard the heart, how to change, and what to do with specific temptations. Difficulties in the family will stimulate growth through learning to glorify God in the midst of injustice and suffering.

Daily disciplines

 Children need to be taught how to enjoy relationship with God. Teach how to pray and spend daily time in God's Word. Encourage obedience in thought and behavior, repentance when they sin, and rejoicing in the Lord. There are excellent books on these topics. See the list of resources in the appendix.

Some children, especially the people-pleasers, will try to become super good. It may start as a reaction to the antisocial child's exaggerated rebellion. It may be an attempt to make life easier for the parents or an attempt to reduce the discomfort of conflict in the home (love of peace). It might be a way of controlling what they can in a way that is acceptable. Perfectionism can result and cultivate pride, a constant drive to earn approval, exaggerated guilt over failures, and fear of disapproval. Teach children that the goal of spiritual disciplines is never to complete a checklist to be a "good Christian." It is to cultivate delight in God by walking in His grace in an intimate relationship with Him (Rom. 5:1-2; 2 Pet. 3:18).

Growth process

Learning general principles of spiritual growth will help children to stay right with God in the daily vicissitudes of life. These principles include the role of desires in their behaviors, guarding the heart diligently, confession and repentance, and the putting off and putting on process of change, all in the context of grace and relationship, not of merit-earning. These principles are discussed in previous chapters.

Trials

A sibling needs to know how to use trials and testings for spiritual growth. Truths on God's sovereignty, wisdom, and love, and the need for dependence upon the Holy Spirit, provide a foundation for the sibling to hope and to trust and obey God. God is in the harness with him. Rather than chafe in the harness of a trial, the child can thankfully rejoice that God will use the trial for his benefit (Rom. 8:28-29).

Many people in the Bible were set into families with difficult people. You can use the stories of siblings in the Bible to build empathy, show Scripture's relevance, and teach lessons on godliness. For ideas, see the implementation ideas listed at the end of this chapter.

Psalm 37 is a good passage for showing that God understands and that the Bible is relevant to his situation and gives direction. To build reasons to trust God in the trial, teach that God is good (Ps. 31:19) and just (Exod. 34:6-7) and is in control (Job 9:23-24). Teach that trials in this particular family are a part of His loving and wise plan for helping him to become like Jesus (Rom. 8:28-29). God will be faithful to help him, and he can please God in his situation (1 Cor. 10:13). The Holy Spirit will give him strength to do what is right as he steps out in obedience (Gal. 5:16; Phil. 4:13).

Second Corinthians 4:17 can help a struggling child gain the long-term perspective that affliction is temporary and tempered by God's compassion. Developing gratitude for what God is doing in his life through the difficulties prevents sinful attitudes (Phil. 1:12; Eph. 5:20). The book of 1 Peter is full of help for pleasing the Lord amidst trials.

Responsibility

Siblings of angry, manipulative children may perceive, accurately or inaccurately, many situations to be out of control. Insecurity can tempt him to manipulate or otherwise try to get a situation back into his concept of order. His efforts can become habituated. You want him to habituate to God's way of handling those things that are out of his control.

Talk logically through control and responsibilities with your child. What does the Bible say about our responsibilities in situations where we have control and where we don't have control? In situations outside of our control, do we still have responsibilities? What can (and should) we do? In other words, for what are we responsible regarding that for which we are not responsible?

Controlling the situation, making up for another's sadness caused by the antisocial child, or manipulating to ensure that justice is done, are not the child's responsibilities. His responsibility is simply (not easily) to love God (Matt. 22:37). Love is shown by obedience. He obeys God by being kind, submitting to parents, doing what is right, speaking truth with love and humility, and loving his enemy. He trusts God to take care of what he is not responsible to do.

Loneliness

Siblings may think, accurately or not, that they are misunderstood by friends and adults, so they feel lonely. Teach the lonely child what to value, the difference between perceptions and feelings, and what to do with both. The child feels lonely because he perceives himself to be alone in his views or having no one who supports him, and evaluates his situation as undesirable. Feelings are untrustworthy counselors.

Correct perceptions. A perception of being misunderstood might be inaccurate. Perhaps the other person understands but disagrees with him. He may need to apply Proverbs 18:1-2 and not stubbornly cling to his opinion but consider the other's view. Perhaps he is not as alone as he thinks he is. He needs observe facts, then put off inaccurate perceptions and put on right thinking.

If his perceptions are correct, truths about trials and relationships apply. He needs to examine his heart for what he most values. The child who is a believer can take comfort in God's presence; Hebrews 13:5 promises that God will never leave His children. There is also the example of Jesus. He was misunderstood and abandoned, yet He did not dwell on His loneliness but concentrated on pleasing

His Father. He often went off to pray alone with His Father—not alone, but alone with His Father. While he takes comfort in God, a child also needs to be busy loving others (Matt. 22:39). Loneliness is put off as service is put on.

Fear

Discord in the home can tempt a child to anxiety. He may fear for his physical safety. Siblings vulnerable to being manipulated can be baited or bullied into doing things they would not otherwise do. If the action was wrong, they feel guilty. Added to guilt feelings is the shame of being used or violated. Guilt and shame both create fear of admitting the truth to you. Guilt, fear, secrecy, and lack of reconciliation cause more problems. Teach about fear. Useful passages include Psalm 37, Proverbs 29:25, Jeremiah 17:5-8, Philippians 4:6-9, and 1 John 4:18. See exercises in the implementation ideas below.

Anger

Besides the anger responses already mentioned, siblings may also feel resentment toward parents for not controlling the situation better, for not preventing harm, or for putting so much time into the one child that they get shorted (in their perception). There may be anger because of expectations. Life should not be this difficult. Families are "supposed to" be warm, safe, and fun. Symptoms might include frequent stomach upset, insomnia, depression, abnormal eating, cutting, or overindulgence in books, electronic games, or TV. These are all ways of escaping unpleasant realities, expressing anger, or grabbing for control.

If your child thinks that he is being neglected, evaluate whether he is right. Putting yourself in his shoes, how would it look? Perhaps you need to change something.

On the other hand, refuse to be manipulated by a false accusation. Perhaps the child needs help correcting his perceptions. Consider the topic of fairness. Fairness often means getting a piece of cake of equal size (or more) even if the little body eating it is half the size of the other person. Parents are not called by God to be fair but to do what is right and kind (Prov. 21:3; Col. 3:12-13). They are to instruct and discipline each child (Deut. 6:7; Eph. 6:4). They help whoever needs help, teach what the particular child needs to be taught, withhold whatever that child needs withheld, and give whatever that child needs given. It means that each child is given what is best for him, not what is fair among all.

The sibling may benefit from the story of the older son in Luke 15. He was resentful, unforgiving, and manipulative. When his repentant brother was given a party he told his father something like, "You killed the calf for him, but you've never given me a single party with even so much as an old goat! And I've been so good to you!" Mean old dad did not fall for this guilt trip. Instead, he rebuked the son. Each child needs to be responsible for his own heart and behaviors. Gratitude for blessings will cut the legs from under anger.

Conflicts

Some people advocate leaving children to themselves to learn how to settle their differences. It is true that children need to learn through experience. It is also true that lack of adult guidance leaves two foolish, selfish persons unaided, each trying to convince the other foolish, selfish person by foolish, selfish means to allow him to have his foolish, selfish way. How does this carry out Ephesians 6:4?

If adults leave training in conflict resolution to foolish instructors, bad habits will be learned (Prov. 22:24-25). Ephesians 6:4 tells parents to teach God's ways. So teach how to handle conflict. If you don't know biblical principles of conflict resolution, read *The Peacemaker*, by Ken Sande, or get other biblical training. Instruction in childhood will bear fruit for the rest of their lives.

Peace time, not war time, is the best time to begin instruction. Teach the child to first take the log out of his own eye (Matt. 7:1-5). Then, if there was clear sin, he needs to talk to his brother about it (Luke 17:3-4). The goal is a restoration through confession by the offender and forgiveness by the offended. Help your children plan wording that honors God. If you instruct your children in the biblical method of dealing with conflicts, they will learn how to handle them in a way that pleases God even without supervision.

It is likely that many conflicts between an alienated child and his siblings will not be resolved to the satisfaction of the siblings, so there will be times when they will appeal to you. This is in keeping with the confrontation process of Matthew 18:15-17 as they first try to reconcile with the offender and then appeal to a higher authority. They need to feel comfortable doing so, which means that you need to communicate that the door is open. Especially tell them that if there is risk of harm to anyone involved then informing you is not gossiping or tattling, but is right and loving. It is for the good of others.

Whatever brings the child to you, an appeal over conflict is a teaching opportunity. Discern what he is wanting by telling you (guidance? gossip? revenge?) and address that as necessary. A question like, "What is your situation?" slows the child's thinking so that he can make clearer observations. "What are you wanting to achieve?" helps him examine his heart. "What does the Bible say to do about it?" steers him to a biblical solution. "What are you going to do?" asks for commitment to an action. As the children grow, you involve yourself less and less. Eventually, if the child comes for help, a question or two from you will remind him of what is right and provide inducement to do it.

He needs guidance on understanding sibling to sibling responsibilities. When offended, it is the responsibility of the offended to do what he can to make peace, but it is not his responsibility to pursue peace so much that he compromises what is right to gain it. If the offender absolutely will not be at peace even though the offended child has done all he can within the boundaries of truth and love, then the offended must leave it in God's hands. Punishing evil is God's responsibility, not the child's (Rom. 12:17-20). Leaving justice in God's hands and doing good in return will require love for and trust in God. In the end, the offended child must decide to be content with God's will in his life and love his enemy.

Forgiveness

Inherent in confrontation over a wrong is a need for forgiveness. There are many aphorisms about forgiveness which children hear and from which they may draw erroneous conclusions. "Turn the other cheek." "Forgive and forget." "If you don't forgive, then you won't be forgiven." "We should not judge others." Hearing these maxims, children may conclude that they have to "just take it" from their abusive sibling. Passively letting someone do to you whatever they want is not what the Bible teaches. Principles of God's justice, trust in Him, confrontation and appeal, and love for enemies will put the topic of forgiveness in the right context.

Forgiveness is a promise. In Isaiah 43:25 and other passages, we see that God remembers their sins no more. He doesn't forget; He is omniscient. Instead, He refuses to hold it against them ever again. When we forgive, we promise to not bring up the offense against the offender, to others in gossip, or to ourselves in brooding about it.

To prevent resentment and desire for revenge over the frequent injustices, a sibling needs to develop a heart willing to forgive. Teach Matthew 18:21-30, about an unforgiving servant, to help an offended sibling identify with being a debtor by thinking about his position before God outside of forgiveness in Christ. He offended God, yet God offers mercy to him. His anger and desire for revenge in the present situation deserve God's punishment. In that way, he is like his provocateur and just as much in need of forgiveness from God. If he is to be like Christ, he must have compassion on the one offending him and be willing to forgive.

However, that does not mean that he offers forgiveness before it is requested. According to Luke 17:3-4, the offended forgives *if* the offender asks for it. This is different from being willing to forgive; it is the actual transaction between the parties. If the offender requests forgiveness, it should be immediately granted. But if the offender does not ask for forgiveness, do not make your child say the words, "I forgive you." First, his promise prevents him from bringing the offense up again in the Matthew 18:15-17 pattern for the good of the offender. Second, it backhandedly accuses the offender of a wrong. Third, the antisocial child may view unsolicited forgiveness as evidence of the other's weakness, that he can do what he will and the offended party will let him off the hook. It is a blank check inviting more. Fourth, it robs the offender of guilt feelings that might motivate him to reconcile.

Lack of reconciliation puts a person at risk of becoming bitter. Forgiveness and bitterness are related but separate issues. Forgiveness or not, Luke 6:27-36 and Romans 12:9-21 forbid bitterness. Please see the next section "Loving enemies" for an introduction on how to respond to one with whom reconciliation is not achieved.

What if the alienated child asks for forgiveness as a ploy? This is not likely to happen, but Luke 17:3-4 would indicate that if it appears genuine then forgiveness must be granted. If subsequent words and actions indicate that this is indeed a ploy and becomes a pattern, then the dishonesty and manipulation must be confronted. After so many years of offense, it is not wrong to expect evidence before believing that the repentance is genuine. John the Baptizer refused baptism when the Pharisees had not lived in accord with their profession of repentance (Matt. 3:8; Luke 3:8).[1] Jesus pointed to lack of behavioral evidence when He asked, "Why do you call me Lord, Lord, and do not do what I say?" (Luke 6:46). Someone known for misrepresenting himself (lying) should be expected to back his words with actions, but it will require wisdom to manage this.

This section has only skimmed the surface of the topic of forgiveness. Study it to prepare yourself.

Loving enemies

Rightly responding to those who behave as enemies toward you is some of the hardest work in the battlefield of life. This section is only an introduction to the topic. You need to study the issue to give effective counsel to your child.

In spite of efforts at forgiveness, reconciliation, and kindness, the angry child is likely to persist in offending his siblings. Explain Luke 6:27-36 and Romans 12:9-21 to them. These are rich passages. Mine them deeply. Emphasize the aggressive nature of doing good out of love. Especially note the two commands given in Romans 12:21: "Do not be overcome by evil" and "overcome evil with good." There is no allowance for sinning in response to the evil done to us. And we are to actively, aggressively, and persistently do good to the offender.

The siblings will not feel affectionate toward the offender. Remind them that according to 1 Corinthians 13, love is an action, not a feeling. Therefore, they need not wait for feelings of love before they act. They need not worry if they never feel loving. They simply need to take action according to 1 Corinthians 13.

Teach that loving others, which includes enemies, is first and foremost a response to God's love and done out of a desire to please Him. First John 4:19 says that "we love, because He first loved us." Teach that even if they cannot love the offender as a brother, they are commanded to love even their enemies (Luke 6:27).

Explain from 1 Corinthians 13 that love is self-sacrificing. It "does not seek its own." Therefore, love is not done to change the other person. It is not bait but is self-sacrifice for the welfare of the other person.

Love for others is commanded by God (Matt. 22:39). The child is responsible to love, but he is not responsible for having his love accepted. Therefore, if it is not, he can still be satisfied that he obeyed God.

Implement the Principles

For Parents regarding their Children

- Evaluate the children and family relationships. For example, do they harbor anxieties? Might they be resentful that you did not control a situation better? Are you being permissive out of a sense of guilt? Have you equipped them to handle bullying and manipulation or do you leave them to learn by trial and error? Do you lean on them for comfort that is not

their responsibility to give? Are you modeling self-pity, worry
or anger? Ask your spouse to evaluate you also, knowing that
we all tend to be blind to our own errors (Prov. 16:2). Be slow
to disagree; apply yourself to seeing through his or her eyes.
Plan how you can help each other to improve.

* As a couple, study how to handle conflicts. Teach your
children. Resource: *The Peacemaker*, by Ken Sande

* Study to understand forgiveness.
Resource: *From Forgiven to Forgiving*, by Jay Adams

For Parents with their Children

Choose assignments from the options below or make up your own.
Depending on the age of the child, read or tell the Bible passages to
the children. Guide them through the questions, or create worksheets
to guide independent study.

* Do a daily devotion with your children. Ideally, do a weekly
Bible study with them, also. Keep it simple, but choose something that requires study time in the Bible according to the
level of each child's ability. These habits can bear good fruit
early in adolescence and last a lifetime for your children.

* Teach and encourage your children to have daily devotions
of their own.

* With your child, memorize 1 Corinthians 10:31 and
2 Corinthians 5:9. Discuss questions like, what is God's
purpose for you? How can you fulfill it? What is a reason
for wanting to please God?

* Clarify responsibilities for a particular situation in which your
child is tempted to try to control it or is responding sinfully
because he can't control it. Organize your thoughts into a
chart. Find Bible verses instructing on the following questions:

1. In the particular situation, what do I want to happen (or
not happen)?

2. What can I control?

3. For what am I responsible and what does the Bible say to
do about it?

4. What can't I control? (For what am I not responsible?)

5. What does the Bible say to do about that which I can't
control?

- Use Psalms 27 and 37 for devotions with the children. Read one of these psalms three times in a week. Together, answer these questions:
  - What was David feeling?
  - What was he, or might he have been, tempted to think?
  - What was he, or might he have been, tempted to do?
  - What did he believe about God? How was God involved in his situation?
    - How is God involved in my situation?
    - What resources does He give me?
    - Stop. Thank and praise Him.
  - What did David choose to *want*?
    - What do I now choose to want? What desire do I need to put off, and what shall I put on?
  - What did David choose to *do*?
    - What do I now choose to do? What behavior do I need to put off, and what shall I put on?

- Teach and memorize verses in this chapter. Refer to them at appropriate times in conversation to make their application practical.

- Read about Joseph in Genesis 37. Help your children consider:
  - What might you have thought?
  - How might you have felt?
  - What would you be wanting? Or not wanting?

- Story of Joseph, continued (Gen. 39-50):
  (His situation grew worse, then up and down, with final reconciliation.)
  - Did Joseph get angry at God and sin to get even with God or others? (Gen. 39:11-18; 40:8; 41:16; 45:1-15; 50:15-21) How did Joseph respond?
  - What did he believe about God?

    — What were the results of his belief and response ...

        ᐧ– ... for himself?

        ᐧ– ... for others?

        ᐧ– ... for God?

    — How can you be like Joseph when you face difficulties in your family?
      What can you put off and what can you put on?

* David and Goliath (1 Sam. 17). Ask questions similar to those about Joseph.

* Read Psalm 37 or 139 with your children and ask:

    ᐧ– What does this passage teach about God?

    ᐧ– What can God do for you in your difficulty?

    ᐧ– What desire could you have that would please God?

    ᐧ– What do you think God is doing in your situation?

    ᐧ– Redraw the picture in the assignment above.

* Plan service. Serving others pleases the Lord and gets us busy loving others rather than pitying or worrying about ourselves.

* With your children, use the following passages to list the benefits of trials: Heb. 12:11; James 1:2-3; 1 Pet. 2:23, 4:19; John 15:5; Gal. 5:16; 2 Cor. 12:9; Rom. 5:3-5.

* Read or tell Bible stories about mistreatment by siblings, like Cain and Abel, Jacob and Esau, Rachel and Leah, Joseph and his brothers, Amnon, Tamar, and Absalom, and the two sons of the compassionate father (Luke 15). Other helpful duos include wives (concubines) stuck in the same household by marriage, like Hagar with Sarah, and Hannah with Peninnah. How did these people respond? Where was God in these relationships? What did the offended sibling do right and what Bible verse teaches it? What should the offended sibling have done and what Bible verse gives that direction? What do you learn that you can apply to your life?

* With an offended child, use 1 Corinthians 13, Luke 6:27-28, and Romans 12:17-21 to plan a practical way to overcome evil with good in his particular situation. Lead the child to pray for his sibling and think out blessings that he can return for insults.

- Clarify responsibilities. In a given situation, what is the parents' responsibility? What is the child's? What is not the child's? What can be done with those things that he cannot control? What can be done with those things that he could influence but are not his responsibility? List these on paper or create a chart or drawing to help illustrate. Help him plan ways to implement what he learns when the same situation arises again.

- With your children, read and discuss *When People Are Big and God Is Small*, by Ed Welch.

- Choose appropriate exercises from preceding chapters in this book.

Footnote

1. MacArthur, *Freedom*, 187-188.

God has sovereignly, wisely, and lovingly placed your children in a home with a difficult person. As they trust in Christ for salvation and obey God by the power of the Holy Spirit, they will see His sufficiency and will grow in joy and love for God.

Your children may take great hope in the fact that they will be glorifying God and growing more like Christ who died for them.

Part 3: Viewing RAD Through the Lens of a Psychologist

To this point in the book, we have been using a biblical lens to understand a child who presents the symptoms that today's psychologies group under the label Reactive Attachment Disorder. Part 3 examines the prevailing view of RAD in our culture. I know that many who read this book will have already read other popular books and websites on attachment. If you haven't, you will likely read of these theories in the newspaper or hear comments by parents or counselors shaped by the presumptions in attachment theories. The theories can sound persuasive. I was once convinced of them myself. I did not realize what the foundations of attachment theories were nor that the word "attachment" meant one thing to therapists and another to me in my layman's understanding.

Some of you may consider therapy or residential treatment for your children. Therapies are developed and applied from the theoretical stance of the developer and/or therapist. So attachment theories affect the methods to be used on your child and the philosophies he will be taught.

With all of this in mind, I would like to offer Part 3 as a straightforward examination. Here, we will put on the lenses used by psychologists. We will consider their definition of attachment, their etiological theories, and how theories affect therapies. Since it is important to take a serious look at the possibility of physiological factors, there is a section on research efforts. Then we will examine their theories under the lens of Scripture, adding some observations on research, to expose false beliefs while honoring accurate ideas.

I hope that you will gain greater awareness of psychologies as philosophies, learn more truths about God and man, and gain greater appreciation for the unsurpassing superiority of counsel from the Word of God over any inventions from the mind of man.

Chapter 17
Understanding "Attachment"

The dominant theme in today's popular theories is that Reactive Attachment Disorder is an infant psychopathology and it is caused by lack of attachment in infancy.[1] Therefore, attachment is a key element.

How do Psychologists Define Attachment?

Attachment, in a simplified sense, is defined as an intense, selective, enduring attraction to a specific individual.[2] Attachment describes the drive to be physically and emotionally close to a specific figure, especially in situations when the attached person feels afraid, tired, or ill.[3]

Many psychologists teach that attachment developed in humans through evolutionary adaptations and that it is an outworking of an innate mechanism in the brain of an infant, causing the child to attach to a primary caregiver. So psychologists' more precise definition refines it to an intense, selective, enduring disposition in an infant, produced by a biological process, to seek proximity to a specific individual for the gaining of security. It is different from an affectional bond in that it is not a reciprocal social bond which requires mutual commitment, like peer friendship. Rather, it is a biologically driven complementary bond. In strict attachment theory literature, the word "attachment" is used in reference to only the child. The mother bonds; the child attaches. The parent is committed; the child is attached.[4] Seeking for security from an attachment figure is the defining feature of an attachment.[5]

How Important is Attachment Considered To Be?

Psychologists consider attachment to be essential. As both illustration and evidence, they frequently cite Harry Harlow's famous discoveries about rhesus monkeys publicized in 1959. Harlow compared rhesus monkey babies raised by surrogate cloth moms with those raised by

surrogate wire moms. Even though the wire moms held the bottle, all
of the babies spent their time cuddling the cloth moms. They went
to the wire moms only for food. Seeing that the babies valued soft
contact over hunger satisfaction, Harlow concluded that, "Food is
sustenance but a good hug is life itself." [6]

But even the monkeys raised with cloth surrogates, when they
matured, demonstrated aberrant behaviors, clinging to the cage bars,
screaming at passing people, rocking themselves for hours, and muti-
lating themselves by biting their own arms and pulling out their own
hair. Many of them became unresponsive to the environment. They
sat in strange positions or huddled in corners and did not appear to
see or hear anything.[7] To Harlow, the importance of relational give
and take responses from mothers was demonstrated. Harlow used
his studies to promote mother-love in America, stressing that if the
monkey or the human does not learn to love in infancy, he or she
"may never learn to love at all." [8]

John Bowlby was the founding father of today's theories on
attachment. He was a British psychologist and researcher trained
as a psychoanalyst. In his day, behaviorists had established the
consensus that fundamental to emotional health was the meeting of
physiological needs. Bowlby formed a different opinion. Correlating
juvenile criminals with a deprivation of their parents' emotional
closeness, he concluded that mother-love matters more than the
physiological needs.[9]

Psychologist Robert Zaslow, who developed rage reduction therapy, built on Bowlby's conclusions. He hypothesized that unless there
is clearly an organic cause, all mental disorders originate in some
abnormality in early attachment.[10]

Although attachment theorists agree that not all later problems
can be attributed to lack of attachment, attachment is considered so
vital that it forms a predictor of what social relationships will be like
for the rest of life. For example, adult depression can be traced to
despair due to detachment in infancy.[11]

In *High Risk: Children Without a Conscience*, Magid and McKelvey
say that if a child becomes unattached in infancy, his ability to
make and maintain stable, intimate relationships as an adult will be
impaired.[12] They write that studies from the 1960s and 1970s show
that the degree of antisocial behavior in adult psychopaths is correla-
tive to pathological parenting and loss of attachment in childhood.[13]
As examples of the extreme result of lack of attachment in childhood,

they cite Helter-Skelter murderer Charles Manson, David Berkowitz (the Son of Sam), and Ted Bundy, one of America's most famous mass murderers.[14] As inability to form intimate bonds with another is a distinguishing characteristic of a psychopath, so it is of the antisocial child.

How are Psychologists Organizing Attachment?

Psychologists have organized what they view as attachment strategies into categories.[15] Attachment categories were developed by Mary Ainsworth, who worked with Bowlby during the early 1950s. She designed the "Strange Situation" test. This test begins with a child, his mother, and a supervisor in a room. Both supervisor and room are unfamiliar to the child. The mother leaves the room for a designated period of time, and then returns. The researcher observes the responses of the child to his mother when the mother leaves the room and again upon her return. From her testing, Ainsworth categorized the responses and then labeled the attachment categories: secure, avoidant, and ambivalent or resistant. Later, a fourth category, disorganized attachment, was added.

In a Strange Situation test, when the mom returns, the securely attached child seeks to be near to his mother but then quickly leaves to explore and play. A child with avoidant attachment ignores the returned parent and does not seek proximity. The ambivalent child seeks to be near, yet remains anxious, not easily soothed, and does not quickly or readily leave the parent to play and explore despite the mother's continued presence. The disorganized child is disorganized in seeking proximity; he approaches and retreats, approaches and freezes.[16] Some researchers carry attachment theory so far as to hypothesize that specific attachment classifications can be correlated to certain behavioral disorders that manifest later.[17]

Footnotes

1. Samantha Wilson, "Attachment Disorders: Review and Current Status," review of current developmental research on attachment. *Journal of Psychology* 135, no. 1 (Jan. 2001): 42.

2. Thomas R. Insel, "Is Social Attachment an Addictive Disorder?" Review of research relating attachment to reward neural circuitry. *Physiology & Behavior* 79, no. 3 (2003): 353.

3. Bowlby, *Attachment and Loss*, 371.

4. Ibid., 377.

5. Jude Cassidy, "The Nature of the Child's Ties," *Handbook of Attachment, Theory, Research, and Clinical Applications*, eds. Jude Cassidy and Phillip R. Shaver (New York: The Guildford Press, 1999), 12.

6. Blum, *Goon Park*, 159.

7. Ibid., 178.

8. Ibid., 5.

9. Ibid., 58.

10. Magid and McKelvey, *High Risk*, 209.

11. Roger Kobak, "The Emotional Dynamics of Disruptions in Attachment Relationships," *Handbook of Attachment, Theory, Research, and Clinical Applications*, eds. Jude Cassidy and Phillip R. Shaver (New York: The Guildford Press, 1999) 35.

12. Magid and McKelvey, *High Risk*, 67.

13. Ibid., 63, 67-69.

14. Ibid., 2.

15. Charles H. Zeanah, Angela Keyes, and Lisa Settles, "Attachment Relationship Experiences and Childhood Psychopathology," *Annals of the New York Academy of Sciences* 1008 (2003): 23.

16. Siegel, *Developing Mind*, 75-76.

17. Wilson, "Review and Current Status," 41-42.

Chapter 18

How do Psychologists Explain Attachment?

Many therapists incorporate today's three main attachment theories into one big picture. To help clarify, I have separated them. After each, I summarize how the theory affects what therapy a psychologist will apply to the child.

Malfunctioning Mechanism

Behavioral System Theory. Why do infants generally pursue close relations with the mother? Freud assumed that infants, out of hunger, seek sustenance from a breast and then learn that their food source has a person connected to it. John Bowlby disagreed. He postulated that babies are born equipped with an inherent mechanism of attachment by which they emotionally connect with the one person, usually the mother, who most sensitively responds and nurtures. Just as a gosling imprints the first moving object as its "mother," so a baby attaches to his primary caregiver and looks to her for safety, provision, and comfort.

Bowlby theorized that the attachment mechanism is a behavioral control system. A behavioral system is a set of behaviors working together to achieve some goal. Behaviors in a behavioral system are not learned, but are genetic. We know they are genetic because they appear without practice within the right circumstances. Examples of behavioral systems are preening in birds and prey-catching in mammals.[1] Examples of human behavioral systems include the exploratory, caregiving, and fear behavioral systems. So, the attachment behavioral system is an organization of unlearned, genetically preprogrammed behaviors oriented for establishing attachment.[2]

The system's behaviors are called attachment behaviors. Crying, calling, and following are examples. The goal is to gain nearness to the attachment figure[3] by inducing the caregiver to approach.[4]

There are three important aspects of attachment behavior. Attachment behavior is prewired, is employed to achieve attachment, and requires a response. Being genetic, or prewired, the set of behaviors is, like breathing, automatic and inevitable. So, a behavior like crying is a preprogrammed behavior.

Not all theories consider relationship-building behaviors to be prewired. Learning theory, for example, proposes that there is no inherent mechanism, but that the infant learns by trial and error which behaviors gain reward and then associates the mother, who answers his calls, with those rewards. But attachment theory notes that even abused children, who receive minimal reward and strong punishment, attach to their parents. Attachment theory considers reward as irrelevant to the behavioral system. In neither theory is relationship primary; it is only secondary to the cause.[5]

In common usage, the word "attachment" infers a relationship and intimacy. By contrast, in systems theory, the infant is not seeking an actual person; it is seeking a state of proximity to a particular object. So the word "attachment" refers to an infant's attraction to a specific individual in which the infant zealously pursues proximity to that attachment figure. Emotional proximity is deduced from the attachment figure's responsiveness,[6] such as attentiveness and eye contact. Being near produces feelings of security and comfort.

Response is part of the system. The attachment behavioral control system is a control system in that, like a thermostat with a furnace, it uses feedback to determine which behavior to implement and to refine behaviors. The system is activated by stimuli such as the mother's departure or feelings of fear. When activated, the baby or child will display attachment behavior in order to regain proximity. When proximity is regained, the system is deactivated.[7]

Bowlby proposed that mothers have a caregiving behavioral system complementary to the child's attachment system. When the child expresses attachment behavior, the mother's caregiving behavioral system causes her to reciprocate. She responds with eye contact, a certain voice tone, smiling, and touch that all signal physical and/or emotional proximity to the infant. These behaviors deactivate the infant's attachment behavioral system. So then, according to Bowlby, "the child's tie to his mother is a product of the activity of a number of behavioural systems that have proximity to the mother as a predictable outcome."[8]

Detachment and lack of attachment also occur. In a house, if the furnace malfunctions and does not produce heat, the thermostat keeps signaling while the house gets colder and colder. In an infant, if the mother fails to provide caregiving behavior, the child's attachment behavioral system stays activated. If the lack of response is prolonged, the child digresses through three stages. First is protest. The attachment behavior, like crying, cannot be shut off because the attachment figure remains missing. The second stage is despair. When the attachment behavior does not achieve proximity the child mourns the loss. In the final stage, he will detach. Lack of attachment is a defense position against ever being hurt again by loss.[9]

Relational experiences in the first months and years build representations into a child's mind. This set of representations is called the internal working model (IWM). The IWM is his set of perceptions, attitudes, and expectations about his environment, relationships, and self. That mental model filters subsequent experiences and forms the basis for directing behaviors in response. The child anticipates how his caregiver will behave and organizes his attachment behaviors according to those expectations.[10]

The IWM of an attached child is composed of a set of expectations of positive responses from his environment. The IWM of a detached child contains expectations of negative responses.

Children respond to others according to their mental model. For example, an anxious child may view himself as an abandoned and threatened victim. In response, he may develop simple anxiety or maladaptive behavior. The avoidant child's IWM tells him that no one else will satisfy his needs and so he must. He becomes angry and aggressive. To avoid the guilt of his aggression, he may practice mental convolutions to believe himself the victim of persecution and, therefore, the innocent seeker of justice.[11] This expectation grid becomes his internal working model.

How does systems theory affect treatment?

In Bowlby's systems theory, because the diagnosed source of present misconduct is lack of attachment, attachment is considered to be the solution and, therefore, imperative for healing. So, attachment is the targeted therapy goal. Because lack of attachment originally resulted from how pathological care in his past environment affected his biological system, therapy methods include changing the child's environment by providing an "attuned" caregiver. The attuned caregiver helps him to rethink and change his internal working model, in order to induce him to attach to a caregiver.

In a Nutshell

Bowlby's theory proposes a genetically preprogrammed behavioral control system motivating an infant's behavior. It is biological, not learned. It uses feedback to activate and deactivate, determining particular behavior and developing behavioral refinement. System goals are external (proximity) and internal (felt security). The caregiver's responses develop in the infant an internal working model of perceptions, attitudes, and expectations to interpret future experiences and determine future behavior. A positive IWM produces attachment; a negative IWM produces lack of attachment. Many therapists follow Bowlby's theory.

Disrupted Process

Developmental Theory. The developmental theory of attachment makes a fitting overlay to Bowlby's theory. It stems from developmentalism, a philosophy formulated by psychologist Erik Erikson. The developmental view moves the discussion of attachment into the realm of brain development. It attempts to explain the behavioral control system, development of attachment, and the IWM neurologically. It is also cited as an explanation for development of the conscience and trust. Concisely summarized by Dan Siegel, "Human connections shape the neural connections from which the mind emerges."[12]

Erikson espoused that personality develops in stages, predetermined genetically. Each stage is dependent upon having successfully completed the previous stage. For example, teen-age rebellion is considered an inevitable and necessary stage of growth.[13] It is on the basis of Erikson's theory that an educational consultant working with a grade-schooler who has learning difficulties may test the child's ability to crawl, a necessary developmental stage, and prescribe lessons in crawling. The idea is that people can get stuck in a stage and not mature out of it. Brain cells do not develop or do not organize properly. In this way, learning may be inhibited if the child never learned to crawl. Going back to learn how to crawl causes brain cells to develop properly, and then other learning will progress more normally.[14] Similarly, since since trust, according to developmentalists, is the first developmental stage after birth, if the infant does not learn to trust he will always mistrust and that leads to psychopathology.

Developmentalism recognizes that babies are not born with completely constructed brains. Because nerve cells are still reproducing and organizing by migrating to different locations in the brain, many nerve connections have yet to form.

Memory function in the brain is a key element resulting from brain structure. Memory can be categorized into implicit and explicit memory. Implicit memory is that of which a person is not conscious. It is long-term memory used unconsciously for activities such as tying a shoe or driving. Explicit memory is what people can consciously recall for thought, discussion, or guidance in an activity. It may be short-term, as in memory of recent events or statements used to think and respond in the moment. It may be long-term, recalled to consciousness from the implicit memory.[15]

Implicit memory is built into brain structure. Brain structure includes nerve cells, or neurons, and the spaces between them, called synapses. Synapses are filled with chemicals. An activated neuron sends an electrical impulse from one end to the other. At its end, the signal is sent to adjacent neurons by chemical transfer across the synapses. The signal activates the adjacent neurons in circuits, or pathways, also called neuropathways.[16] Repeated firing increases probability of future firing and stimulates the repeatedly-activated nerves to build more cells and more synapses. Brain structure is built by repeated activation of the nerve cells. Because stimulation affects growth of neurons and their connections, experience alters brain structure.[17]

According to developmental theory, the IWM is developed as repeated similar experiences in a relationship cause implicit memory to become embedded in those neural pathways which are repeatedly fired. The internal representation becomes more indelible as experiences are repeated. Therefore, the IWM as a state of mind is a product of brain chemistry. For example, say a toddler has a frightening experience with a dog. His body reacts with increased heart rate, facial expressions, and possibly with crying or running. Why? Because in response to perceived danger, his hypothalamic-pituitary adrenal (HPA) axis, part of the fear behavioral system, was activated and produced hormones and cell responses that produced his feelings and behaviors. The child will connect the unpleasant feelings and thoughts of fear with the dog that stimulates them. Repeated fearful experiences with that dog strengthen the neuronal wiring [18] for feeling fear when exposed to the dog. These reactions embed in implicit memory and form the child's perceptions and expectations about what the adults around him label "dog." Neural responses can become sensitized to decreasingly intense exposures to the dog until merely thinking or dreaming about dogs may activate the fear behavioral system. Fear responses can also become generalized in relation to all dogs so that fear feelings and behaviors become automatic reactions to the child's IWM labeled "Dog."

Because neurons work in association with each other, stimulation of one neuron can activate others even when not needed or intended. This is why the smell of baking turkey in July can stir thoughts and feelings usually associated with Thanksgiving. So, while a young child may not consciously think, "That dog face frightened me," the next time he sees the face of a dog his neural network may automatically trigger fear feelings and behaviors. This will happen even if he is safe in his father's arms and the dog face is a happy one. His fear response to dogs has become a trait.

According to developmentalists, the IWM is established by age three. Because children under age three have undeveloped explicit memory systems, they cannot recall and discuss what they experience to gain more accurate perceptions. The implicit IWM unconsciously affects the individual's understanding and behavior for the rest of his life unless he consciously identifies and changes those perceptions and revises his model.

What does developmentalism mean for the child's character?

The application to attachment theory logically follows. Because the securely-attached child forms a generalized representation—"My caregiver is dependable and kind"—appearance of his caregiver activates neural networks developed to respond with feelings of calmness and pleasure. In contrast, the insecurely attached child's IWM of indifference, rejection, or pain directs his neurons to react with anxiety and a disorganized, unpleasant state of mind.[19] These neurons become more sensitized and numerous than neurons used for peacefulness, so sensitized that everyday stressors may activate them. Patterns of negative "affect" (defined below)* and misattuned** and

---

* In psychology, the term "affect" (á fect) refers to how an internal state of emotion is revealed externally. It can include actions, words, tone, sounds, body position, facial expressions, anything that expresses emotion or signals to others. It is a handy term for generalities or all-inclusiveness. "Affect" helps to keep the discussion neutral and amoral, which is really no help at all.

** Simplified, "attunement" refers to being tuned into, sensitive to, another's emotional state of mind. Like "negative affect," "misattuned," and "self-defensive responses," the word "attunement" is a term common among therapists and theorists. If parents talk with attachment specialists, knowledge of these terms may increase understanding.

self-defensive responses ingrain into the implicit memory, becoming traits. Experience develops the brain.[20]

Attachment theorists teach that the development of a healthy attachment causes proper brain development, which then causes proper behavioral and social development. If early attachment does not occur, neither does optimal brain development.[21] Neglect and traumatic experiences can disrupt neuronal cell division, misdirect neuron migration, cause cell deaths, and prevent formation of new synapses, all of which result in disorganization of the brain. That is why psychologists call the brains of children labeled RAD "disordered." They are missing the brain cells required for a conscience, for trust, for feeling empathy, and for controlling their emotions and behaviors.[22] Due to a lack of, and/or disorganization of, neurons used for congenial behaviors, the child will continue to have no capacity for intimate interpersonal relationships once he matures.[23] The reason an antisocial child cannot behave in a socially acceptable way is because he has "soft neurological damage."[24]

Apply this theory to something practically affecting a family, like a child's conscience. Developmentalists teach that conscience develops at age two or three. For example, a baby who sticks a finger in another's eye does not feel guilt but is simply fascinated by the reaction of the other person. At age two or three, he develops a sense of guilt for similar behavior and may express remorse. But the unattached child, because of developmental delay, does not develop neuropathways (brain structure) for emotions and behaviors such as guilt and remorse.[25]

To developmentalists, RAD is a brain structure problem. Dysregulated behaviors are explained by neural disorganization and implicit memory. As reactivity to fearful stimuli increases in his unconscious implicit memory, he develops intense, automatic, physiological responses to ever smaller stimuli. This is called hypervigilant reactivity.[26] As a skill like skating is mediated by memory in the motor control area of the brain, so a state of fear in the RAD-type child is a built-in memory in the midbrain and brain stem regions. Since the child experienced the mistreatment at an age prior to his ability to reason and talk about it to organize his thoughts into accurate perceptions, his implicit memory resides in dysregulated neural networks.[27] His thoughts are disorganized. He is incapable of organizing information or regulating emotions. He is unable to organize himself in relation to others.[28] Because these children have such ingrained fear reactions, they become just a bunch of defenses and do not know why they act as they do. They live in a state of fight or flight. "They live in the brain stem." [29]

How does developmentalism affect treatment?

As with Bowlby's theory, attachment is the solution to the lack of attachment. Additionally, because brain structure is key and lack of attachment caused neurological damage, the solution is to build new neurons and new, organized neural circuits.

Therapy requires an attuned caregiver. Methods include play therapy, a highly structured environment, and narrative discussion. Narrative therapy involves the child telling his feelings within a historical framework, meaning within a context of events during which he felt his feelings. This brings the internal working model to the surface in order to rethink beliefs and then create a new and accurate implicit memory. Role play gets the child practicing positive behaviors, such as those that show remorse, so that neural pathways for positive affect are built. Through these experiences, the brain will gain neural pathways for trust, for a conscience, and for showing remorse.

In a Nutshell

Developmentalism teaches that although genetics have a role (as in Bowlby's theory), it is experiences and relationships that significantly impact whether neurons develop or die, and to which circuits they connect.[30] Messages conveyed by the quality of caregiving from the primary adult directly shape the child's brain into states of mind [31] that continue into adulthood, coloring the person's perceptions and motivating behaviors. Negative caregiving causes a disorganized brain from which RAD can result. To developmental psychologists, a behavioral problem is a brain structure problem.

Broken Connections

Needs Cycle Theory. Another foundational theory is the needs cycle theory. This is a needs-based behavioral theory proposing that babies will bond with whoever satisfies their needs. Needs, rather than an innate behavioral system, drive the child. It can also be called a rage cycle or a bonding cycle.

The four basic stages of the cycle are need, rage reaction, gratification, and trust (thus the interchangeable labels "bonding," "rage," and "needs"). The baby feels a physiological need, such as hunger. In response, he may start sucking on his fist. If his hunger pains are not quelled, he cries—a rage reaction. The gratification stage of the cycle occurs when the parent feeds the baby. As hunger is relieved, rage dissipates. The baby has just had a lesson in the idea (not yet fact to him) that he can trust his parent to relieve his hunger and meet his needs. As the completed bonding cycle is repeated for any number of circumstances, the child develops trust that the parent will satisfy his needs. Over time, he learns to distinguish which person is the one who most effectively responds to him. This will be his attachment figure.

Similarly, emotional needs are met as the baby gurgles, waves his arms and calls for a parent, and the parent responds with eye contact, speech, and smiling back at him. The interplay of eye contact, smiling and verbal cues has been called the mother-infant dance.[32]

The cycle is broken when one member, usually the caregiver, refuses to dance. The causes of broken cycles include neglect, abuse, adoption, foster care, hospitalization preventing contact with a parent, or pain from a chronic illness that the parent cannot prevent.[33]

However it happens, a child who is not gratified remains in rage. If lack of gratification occurs repeatedly, the child becomes locked in rage and cannot get out of it. Chronic deprivation leaves him with an "inability to even partially" believe that someone might care.[34] Instead of trusting his caregiver, he must defend against her.[35] He does not accept love, does not trust, and develops a pathological need for complete control of his life so that he will not have to endure unmet needs.

The word "pathological" implies illness. Whereas the developmental approach views the problem as a developmental and brain problem, the rage cycle approach views it as pathological. The child is sick with an emotional disorder.

How does needs cycle theory affect treatment?

Needs cycle theory, like the systems and developmental theories, holds that the cause of RAD is lack of attachment, so the solution is attachment. Trust is key.

Treatment can vary from the developmental approach because, while the developmental approach assumes that the child *would* comply if he *could*, the pathological view demands that the child *must comply*. After all, taking medicine is not optional for a sick child.[36]

Since lack of attachment was caused by an uncompleted rage cycle, rage reduction therapy is the treatment of choice, used in conjunction with therapeutic parenting.

Rage reduction therapy is only one kind of treatment for RAD. Yet in the 1980s and early 1990s, it was popularized so that it gained the title "Attachment Therapy." It was created by Robert Zaslow and called the "Z-process." Foster Cline, at the Institute for Attachment and Child Development, formerly the Attachment Center at Evergreen, in Evergreen, Colorado, pioneered the therapy for use with children who fit the RAD model.[37] He has been called the founder of attachment therapy.[38] Rage reduction therapy attempts to draw the mad and bad ideas of the child out so that they can be discussed and changed. Treatment shows the child that it is not his fault that he feels badly. Then he learns how to love.[39]

Rage reduction therapy is also called holding therapy. Summarized, through intense verbal confrontation and physical irritation like tickling, he is purposefully made angry to the point of rage while being physically held immobile in a prone position by several adults, thus the term "holding therapy." The idea is that the pain of his past and the hate locked deep within rises to the surface to be dealt with once and for all. He is not released until he submits to the therapist in authority. Then, the reattachment process is begun as the loving parent steps in to comfort the sobbing child. The process is intended to make the patient (the child) work through his rage by recreating the rage/needs cycle in a place where extreme emotions can safely be expressed. Attachment will be produced as the child is forced to complete the cycle.[40]

Most attachment intervention centers do not subscribe to the extreme holding therapy originally practiced. Indiscriminate use of this method has led to the deaths of some children.[41] Also, some researchers in the 1990s began to question whether expressing anger, rather than releasing its energy, actually increases the intensity of it.[42]

In a Nutshell

According to the needs cycle viewpoint, when a child has a need, he calls for help. If the parent helps, the child feels gratified and learns that he can trust his caregiver. If the caregiver does not help, the child enters rage. If needs are consistently not gratified, the child becomes inextricably locked in rage. He learns that caregivers cannot be trusted. To needs cycle proponents, it is because of a lack of trust that he does not attach.

It's All Three: Integration of Theories

Therapists often integrate theories. For example, just as the developmentalists postulate that a pathological environment causes neurological damage, so the needs cycle theorists postulate that a disrupted cycle causes chemical changes in the brain.[43] Perhaps this is because a cyclic view resembles and logically assimilates with the feedback property inherent in Bowlby's systems theory. An example of theory integration is Wilson's explanation of the attachment cycle as the infant's subjective experience of the biological process (Bowlby), which conditions (behaviorism of the needs cycle) the child to see the caregiver as a source of comfort.[44] Chaddock staff incorporate the developmental model (developmentalism), Bowlby's attachment theory (systems theory), and the rage cycle (behaviorism) in their understanding of Reactive Attachment Disorder. But for therapy, they reject holding therapy and use play and narrative therapy. As these examples demonstrate, theories vary and are often blended. There has evolved a wide continuum of interventions. Understanding each separately can aid you in understanding a particular therapist's perspective.

Footnotes
---

1. Bowlby, *Attachment and Loss*, 148
2. Cassidy, "Nature of the Child's Ties," 12.
3. Bowlby, *Attachment and Loss*, 371.
4. Wilson, "Review and Current Status," 38.
5. Karen, *Becoming Attached*, 106, 172-173.
6. Allan N. Schore, "Studies on the Neurobiology of Attachment," foreword to *Attachment and Loss*, 2d ed., vol. 1, by John Bowlby (New York: Basic Books, 1982), xvii.
7. Cassidy, "Nature of the Child's Ties," 6.
8. Bowlby, *Attachment and Loss*, 179.
9. Karen, *Becoming Attached*, 105-106.
10. Wilson, "Review and Current Status," 38.
11. Karen, *Becoming Attached*, 50.
12. Siegel, *Developing Mind*, 2.
13. Peace, *Attitudes*, 37.
14. Author's personal experience with Robert Doman, educational consultant in the early 1990s.
15. Kelly, "Theoretical Rationale."
16. Siegel, *Developing Mind*, 25-26.
17. Ibid., 14.
18. John Medina, *The Genetic Inferno: Inside the Seven Deadly Sins* (Cambridge, U.K.: Cambridge University Press, 2000), 168.
19. Siegel, *Developing Mind*, 32.

20. Bruce Perry, Ronnie A. Pollard, Toi L. Blakley, William L. Baker, and Domenico Vigilante, "Childhood Trauma, the Neurobiology of Adaptation and Use-dependent Development of the Brain: How States Become Traits," *Infant Mental Health Journal*, 16 (1995): 272-280.

21. Wilson, Kelly, "Nurturing Love," 5A.

22. Perry, et. al., "Childhood Trauma," 275.

23. Siegel, *Developing Mind*, 16.

24. Buckwalter, interview.

25. Ibid.

26. Siegel, *Developing Mind*, 20.

27. Kelly, "Theoretical Rationale."

28. Siegel, *Developing Mind*, 119-120.

29. Buckwalter, interview.

30. Kelly, "Theoretical Rationale."

31. Siegel, *Developing Mind*, 77.

32. Buckwalter, interview.

33. Magid and McKelvey, *High Risk*, 75. Verrier, *Primal Wound*, 6.

34. Kelly, "Theoretical Rationale."

35. Ibid.

36. Buckwalter, interview.

37. Carol Lynn Mithers, "Seeking Cures, but Finding Anguish," *Los Angeles Times*, 6 May 2001, http://www.rickross.com/reference/rebirthing/rebirthing16.html (31 Jan. 2005).

38. Shannon-Bridget Maloney, "Be Wary of Attachment Therapy," Revised July 24, 2003, *Quackwatch*, http://www.quackwatch.org/01QuackeryRelatedTopics/at.html (31 Jan. 2005).

39. Magid and McKelvey, *High Risk*, 94.

40. Ibid., 205, 209, 212-213.

41. Howard Pankratz,, "Court Upholds Conviction in 'Rebirthing' Death," *Denver Post* 29 Aug. 2003, http://www.rickross.com/reference/rebirthing/rebirthing25.html (31 Jan. 2005); Carla Crowder, "Evergreen Chock-full of Therapists: Calif. Therapist Taught Technique that Ended in Girl's Death," *Rocky Mountain News* 21 May 2000, http://www.rickross.com/reference/rebirthing/rebirthing4.html (31 Jan. 2005).

42. Kelly, "Theoretical Rationale."

43. Advocates for Children in Therapy, Inc., "Attachment Therapy: Child Abuse by Another Name," Linda A. Rosa, Registered Agent (711 W. 9th St., Loveland, Colo. 80537) http://www.childrenintherapy.org/essays/overview.html (31 Jan. 2005).

44. Wilson, "Review and Current Status," 39.

Chapter 19
What Brain Researchers are Saying

What does the brain research show? Some proponents of attachment theories speak as though research proves chemical and genetic causes for RAD behavior. Note that this claim presupposes that attachment, as defined in the technical sense of attachment theory, is a real phenomenon. For the views of psychologists who deny this premise, please read chapter 21.

In an effort to understand the brain-behavior connection, many are diligently researching brain chemistry and structure and how relationship experiences impact them. Some studies are specific to RAD. Others investigate general social attraction ("I like you and want to stay close to you") and dissociation ("I don't like you and want to stay by myself"). In these latter studies, the word "attachment" often means intense affiliation rather than Bowlby's technical definition targeting infants. Studies utilize humans, animals, blood tests, and imaging equipment. Animal researchers understand that although they gain hints about how brain processes and development in humans *might* occur, animal research cannot be conclusive for humans.

It's the Chemicals

The chemistry of liking people

Why does Polly Parrot prefer Paco Parrot and not Pepe? Animal studies indicate that Polly's behavior may have a chemical basis, especially through chemicals called neurotransmitters. Neurotransmitters are chemicals that nerve cells use to transfer messages across the synapse from one nerve cell to the next in a circuit. Some neurotransmitters include dopamine, oxytocin, norepinephrine, and serotonin. The circuits make up systems. So, for example, serotonin is used in the serotonergic system, dopamine in the dopaminergic system, etc.

Researchers are finding evidence that some neurotransmitters are necessary for animals to be social, bond, and mate. For example, norepinephrine appears to be necessary for rat pups to attach to their mother.[1] Without oxytocin, ewes won't claim their lambs.[2] Bonding of prairie voles, which are innately monogamous, requires oxytocin in females and arginine vasopressin (AVP) in males.[3] Oxytocin in females mediates mating behavior, maternal care, and mother-infant bond formation.[4]

Dopamine, oxytocin, and endogenous opioids are said to process a sense of reward.[5] When something feels good (reward), we learn to do it again. So, one animal may stay affiliated with another animal because of the pleasure of close proximity to that individual; it may be conditioned learning of partner preference.[6] Some researchers propose that social attachment parallels narcotic addiction. Both use brain reward circuitry and chemistry,[7] such as, the use of the dopaminergic system. This provides a biological basis for the idea that love is an addiction.[8] In addition, when the good feelings are active, circuits that process negative emotions and critical assessments of others are suppressed. This correlates with the adage "love is blind." [9]

The chemistry of not liking people

In animal research on social inhibition, tests show that fearful primates use less serotonin and dopamine while showing hyperactive HPA axis activity.[10] The HPA axis is a system which includes the hypothalamus, the pituitary gland, and the adrenal gland. Among other things, the HPA axis regulates fear and anger responses, such as increased heart rate, increased adrenaline, contraction of blood vessels, muscle sensitization, and dilated pupils.

The HPA axis is more reactive in children labeled with RAD.[11] It is hypothesized that since brain reward pathways (like the dopaminergic system) play a role in reinforcing selective social contact, those pathways are dysfunctional in socially-inhibited individuals (like RAD children).[12] Children rated more inhibited to the unfamiliar show higher salivary cortisol levels and quicker heart rate acceleration when exposed to stress than children rated less inhibited.[13] Anxiety disorders occur at a higher rate in people who were socially inhibited as children, noticeably in children labeled with RAD.

However, roles of brain systems are not so simple. There is evidence that reward circuitry may mediate stress as well as reward. Pruessner,

Champagne, Meaney, and Dagher tested dopamine release in adults enduring a stressful situation. Adults who reported suboptimal maternal care in childhood were found to have elevated dopamine (reward) levels under stress conditions. Researchers suggest that neural systems, such as the dopamine system, that modulate reactions to stress may be permanently altered according to maternal care.[14]

It's the Genes

What role do genes play in RAD? One group of researchers from Hungary claims evidence for a genetic predisposition to RAD. They say that a polymorphism on the DRD4 gene which affects the dopamine D4 receptor predisposes some children to disordered attachments.[15] This receptor is a receptor specific for dopamine. "Polymorphism" indicates that more than one form of the gene exists.[16] Receptors are molecules on the cell surface with an affinity for a particular neuropeptide.

They reported that disordered attachment is more likely in infants carrying a certain DRD4 gene construction (polymorphism). Generally, they conclude that in the presence of adverse parenting, biological vulnerability may contribute to disordered attachment.

Research is Inconclusive

Despite all of the brain research, the exact working of the neural circuitry of social affiliation is unknown. Research reports make extensive use of statements of uncertainty, such as "may be" and "studies suggest that," revealing the hypothetical nature of neurodevelopmental theories.[17] Although the Hungarian researchers posit an association between particular gene polymorphisms and attachment organization or disorganization, no other group has duplicated their results, and Bakermans-Kranenburg and Ijzendoorn published research refuting the Hungarian study.[18]

Bartels and Zeki label their own conclusions about neural correlates of love as tentative because, they say, so little is known about brain processing of social interactions.[19] Insel and Young, in an article entitled "The Neurobiology of Attachment," state that "the study of infant attachment in mammals has not identified a specific neural circuit or predominant neurochemical system." [20] Socioenvironmental factors are considered vital for brain development, yet the specific effect of social attachment on brain development is unknown.[21] Research professor Regina Sullivan cautions, "While the human attachment literature fits well with our animal abuse model, there is insufficient information on human brain development to discuss the neural circuitry of human attachment." [22]

Therefore, when considering neurodevelopmental theories and brain research, it is important to keep in mind that while data is being gathered, our understanding of the neurobiological process of social affiliation is still meager. Researchers don't really know.

Footnotes

1. Regina M. Sullivan, "Developing a Sense of Safety: The Neurobiology of Neonatal Attachment," *Annals of the New York Academy of Sciences* 1008 (2003): 125.

2. Eric E. Nelson and Jaak Panksepp, "Brain Substrates of Infant-Mother Attachment: Contributions of Opioids, Oxytocin, and Norepinephrine," *Neuroscience and Biobehavioral Reviews* 22, no. 3 (1998): 443.

3. Larry J. Young and Zuoxin Wang, "The Neurobiology of Pair Bonding," *Nature Neuroscience* 7, no. 10 (Oct. 2004): 1048.

4. Larry J. Young, Miranda M. Lim, Brenden Gingrich, and Thomas R. Insel, "Cellular Mechanisms of Social Attachment," *Hormones and Behavior* 40 (2001): 133.

5. Nelson and Panksepp, "Brain Substrates," 439-440, 446.

   C. Sue Carter, "Neuroendocrine Perspectives on Social Attachment and Love," review of neuroendocrine and behavioral perspectives of love and social attachment, *Psychoneuroendocrinology* 23, no. 8 (Nov. 1998): 783, 787.

   Aron Weller and Ruth Feldman, "Emotion Regulation and Touch in Infants: The Role of Cholecystokinin and Opioids," *Peptides* 24, no. 5 (May 2003): 779-788.

6. Young and Wang, "Pair Bonding," 1049-1051.

7. Young, Lim, Gingrich, and Insel, "Cellular Mechanisms," 137.

8. Young and Wang, "Pair Bonding," 1052-1053.

9. Andreas Bartels and Semir Zeki, "The Neural Correlates of Maternal and Romantic Love," *NeuroImage* 21 (2004): 1164.

10. Mathew J. Sanjay, Jeremy D. Coplan, Jack M. Gorman, "Neurobiological Mechanisms of Social Anxiety Disorder," *American Journal of Psychiatry* 158 (Oct. 2001): 1558.

11. Judit Gervai, Zsofia Nemoda, Krisztina Lakatos, Zsolt Ronai, Ildiko Toth, Krisztina Ney, and Maria Sasvari-Szekely, "Transmission Disequilibrium Tests Confirm the Link Between DRD4 Gene Polymorphism and Infant Attachment," *American Journal of Medical Genetics Part B (Neuropsychiatric Genetic)* 132B (2005): 126-127.

12. Sanjay, Coplan, and Gorman, "Neurobiological Mechanisms," 1560.

13. Ibid., 1561-1562, 1563, 1559.

14. Jens C. Pruessner, Frances Champagne, Michale J. Meaney, and Alain Dagher, "Dopamine Release in Response to a Psychological Stress in Humans and Its Relationships to Early Life Maternal Care: A Positron Emission Tomography Study Using [11C]Raclopride," *The Journal of Neuroscience* 24, no. 11 (Mar. 17, 2004): 2825, 2089.

15. K. Lakatos, Z. Nemoda, I. Toth, Z. Ronai, K. Ney, M. Sasvari- Szekely, and J. Gervai, "Further Evidence for the Role of the Dopamine D4 Receptor (DRD4) Gene in Attachment Disorganization: Interaction of the Exon III 48-bp Repeat and the -521 C/T Promoter Polymorphisms," *Molecular Psychiatry* 7, no. 1 (2002): 27.

16. Woody Wendling, "Gene Polymorphism," 4 Feb. 2005, WWWendling@aol.com (4 Feb. 2005).

17. For example, see Siegel, *The Developing Mind*, and research studies.

18. M. J. Bakermans-Kranenburg and M. H. Van Ijzendoorn, "No Association of the Dopamine D4 receptor (DRD4) and -521 C/T Promoter Polymorphisms with Infant Attachment Disorganization," *Attachment & Human Development* 6, no. 3 (September 2004): 211-218. With discussion, Judit Gervai and Krisztina Lakatos, "Comment on 'No Association of the Dopamine D4 receptor (DRD4) and -521 C/T Promoter Polymorphisms with Infant Attachment Disorganization' by M.J. Bakermans-Kranenburg and M.H. Van Ijzendoorn," 219-222.

19. Bartels and Zeki, "The Neural Correlates," 1164.

20. Thomas R. Insel and Larry J. Young. "The Neurobiology of Attachment," review of research on the neural basis of attachment, *Nature Reviews Neuroscience* 2, no. 2 (Feb. 2001):129.

21. Ibid., 130.

22. Sullivan, "Developing a Sense of Safety," 127.

Chapter 20
Why Not Accept the Explanations of Psychologists?

Part 1

No one questions that there is normally a close social affiliation between parents and infant and that it has a profound impact on the child. What can be called into question is the substance of what is called "attachment," the driving force in the child, its absolute necessity, and the inevitability of severe psychological problems when that affiliation is broken.

Who can speak authoritatively to this topic? Psychologists develop philosophies and models to explain people and problems. The field of psychology is manmade and sits in the realm of philosophy, not science. A philosophy is a set of theories and views, not necessarily facts.

There is no one authority to declare which philosophy is true. Psychologists themselves don't agree with one another. At present, there are over 350 different psychologies, or philosophies. So the word "psychology" does not signify a single unified set of doctrines, let alone truths. Some of the views of secular psychologists who object to attachment theories are explained in chapter 21. While they raise some serious considerations, it still amounts to one man's view versus another's.

Often, there is an appeal to science. Scientific logic and experimentation can rightly be applied to many fields of study. In some cases, we discover or verify facts. Psychologists are skilled at scientific observation and categorization. It is in interpretation where they step out of science into philosophy. When psychologists use science to develop behavioral theories, they employ science outside of its jurisdiction. Science is a system or methodology, not a moral being, so it is incapable of revealing moral truths and has no authority to arbitrate in the realm of morality and relationships.

In contrast, the Bible is given by God. Therefore, the Bible is the exclusive authority on morality and relationships. In this chapter we are going to hang that plumb line of truth beside the attachment theories of the psychologies.

People are not evolved mammals.

Animal researchers say that their results cannot be conclusive for humans, yet attachment theorists apply animal research *diagnostically and prescriptively* to humans. They do so because of their foundational presumption that evolution caused the development of attachment in humans.

It is on the basis of animal research, like Lorenzo's work on imprinting in fowl, that Bowlby formed his foundational attachment theory which dominates thought today. He taught that attachment behaviors were incorporated into the human species because those who used the behaviors survived.[1] Erikson's idea that it is necessary for a child to mature through one developmental stage before a new psycho-social quality can emerge is also based on evolution.[2] Harlow's rhesus monkey research was, and still is, used to reinforce and promote human attachment and mother-love. What was an analogy has become evidence.[3] Treatment programs are built on these evolution-based theories.

What does it matter? By equating the material with the immaterial, evolution-based theories deviate from the core problem—moral choice. True, animal research can lead to a limited understanding of the brain-behavior interplay and uncover causes of brain-damaging diseases. But diseases are physiological. Behavioral choices are moral (Gen. 2:17; Exod. 20:2-17). By reducing human behavior to the biological, evolution-based theories erase motive, desire, will, and God from the equation. Children are reduced to genetically programmed machines and trainable blank slates.

Unlike animals, people were created in God's image (Gen. 1:26-27). Therefore, mankind has a moral aspect to his immaterial inner man that animals do not have. His behaviors do not derive from animalistic biological drives, but from moral desires with moral consequences (James 1:13-14). Attachment theories completely miss this vital factor.

Unlike animals, people have a moral law to obey, the commandments of God (Exod. 20:2-17; Rom. 2:13; 3:31; 1 John 3:4). People have knowledge of right and wrong (Gen. 2:17; Exod. 20:2-17; Rom. 2:14-15). Man has an accountability to God that animals do not have

(Gen. 2:17; John 6:23). While Scripture describes human maturation (1 Cor. 13:11), it never limits humans to climbing the ladder of developmental stages. People are unique from animals in ways that evolution cannot explain.

The mind is not the brain.

Attachment theory is part of a larger debate about what shapes human personality—nature or nurture. "Nature" refers to the physical brain. The premise is, since man is an evolved mammal, the material generates the immaterial. The brain generates the mind. Your brain cells produce your thoughts and without your brain you would have no mind.

In creating their theories, attachment theorists begin with this false presupposition that the brain determines the mind. For example, they speak of a baby's propensity for nearness to a mother arising from a biologically based mechanism,[4] or that the baby stops calling when "the system's sensors indicate" that Mom is near.[5] Siegel says, "Human connections shape the neural connections from which the mind emerges."[6] In a paper about the neurobiology of brain development, Perry, Pollard, Blakley, Baker, and Vigilante write, "It is the brain that mediates all emotional, cognitive, behavioral, social and physiological functioning. It is the human brain from which the human mind arises, and within that mind resides humanity."[7] While the brain may mediate or effectuate that which the heart desires and will determines, that flows in the direction opposite to the mind arising from the brain.

Theorists interpret research by their mind-arises-from-brain presumption. Because they do, they fail to take critical factors into account. It is highly significant that the two most crucial variables in behavior, desire and will, are nearly nonexistent in the data in RAD scientific research reports. With rare exceptions, the words "choice," "want," and "desire" are conspicuously absent from much other attachment literature also. In the brain-equals-mind approach, *the child himself is missing.* He is an evolved neuro-biochemical machine. The unattached child is a malfunctioning machine; the broken cog at the root of the problem is lack of attachment.[8] Organize the parts (neurons) and repair attachment, and the machine is repaired.

In contrast, Scripture teaches that in humans the mind is not the brain, nor does it originate therein. In 2 Corinthians 5:8, Paul says that he prefers "to be absent from the body and to be at home with the Lord." He knows that without his brain he would still be conscious and able to think. So, thought is not necessarily dependent upon the brain.[9] The material influences but does not exclusively determine the immaterial. Therefore, it is important to distinguish between material and immaterial, brain and mind.

As the Bible speaks about the mind, it commonly interchanges the words "mind" and "heart," both of which refer to the immaterial aspect of man, not the material. The mind and heart plan (Prov. 16:1, 9). The mind and heart learn (Prov. 15:14; 2:10). The heart imagines and holds secrets (Prov. 7:25; 1 Cor. 14:25). The heart thinks, intends, instructs the mouth, and controls where we go (Heb. 4:12; Prov. 16:23; 7:25).

If Perry et al. are right that the mind arises from the brain, then we ought to watch over the brain, for from it arises the life that is lived. Instead, Proverbs 4:23 says, "Watch over your heart [not your brain] with all diligence, for from it flow the springs of life." Jesus said that material man is not the source of moral thoughts and deeds, but "from within, out of the heart of men, proceed the evil thoughts ... deeds of coveting ... deceit ... envy, slander ..." (Mark 7:18-22). Genes, neurons, and chemicals neither generate nor prevent choices in moral thoughts and behaviors. Those originate in the heart (immaterial), not the body (material).

It is true that while we dwell in bodies, genes determine and/or influence us. Babies coo rather than bark. Men and women exhibit gender-specific characteristics. The adrenalin active in the expression of fear could not be produced if the genes for it did not exist. It may also be true that we have inherited personality traits that produce what we call temperaments. So, it could be that tendencies toward boldness or inhibition, joviality or solemnity, arousal or lethargy, alertness or dullness are inherited.[10]

But it cannot be said that genes produce moral ideas. So far, science knows of no gene for greed and identifying one would still not explain what motivates greed in a given situation. No gene, nor even a brain region, has been discovered which causes anxiety, anger, obsessive compulsive disorder,[11] or schizophrenia.[12] Although body and spirit interact, because the immaterial is different from the material, what psychologists call behavioral disorders cannot be understood exclusively by empirical science. If a gene for appetite is discovered, it will not change the fact that obesity from overeating is a consequence of moral volition, not genetic coercion.

There may be physiological components to psychology's behavioral disorders, but no one has determined whether physiology caused the behavior pattern or the behaviors caused the change in physiology. There is some evidence that some schizophrenia may have a genetic component. Even so, the Bible speaks authoritatively to the fear, thoughts, imaginations, irrationality, guilt, behavior control, and self-focus characteristic of it.

In his book *The Genetic Inferno,* John Medina uses the motif of "The Purgatorio" in Dante's *Divine Comedy* as a clever forum for exploring the mind-brain-behavior connection. The initial idea is to explain the genetic and neurological connections underlying the seven deadly sins: lust, gluttony, avarice, sloth, wrath, envy, and pride. What he really (and admittedly) explains is the physiology of sexual arousal, appetite, fear, insomnia, aggression, a depressed state, and self awareness—all physiological states. When discussing lust, Medina says, "Exactly what is the biology behind sexual feelings? How does it create subjective feelings of desire? As will become obvious, finding the answer to the first question is comparatively straightforward, and finding the answer to the second practically impossible." [13] Science has no full explanation of the nature of mind or consciousness as they relate to the brain.[14]

Science can be helpful for observing and classifying behaviors, and for uncovering debilitating diseases (like Huntington's) or genetic abnormalities that hinder right thinking. Medicine may even help control the physiology that predisposes or tempts someone by physical tendencies. But the topic of human behavior carries the dialogue into the realm of morality and the intangible inner man (heart). Science is not equipped to explain moral behavior because man cannot decipher the immaterial heart. This has been known for centuries. About 2500 years ago, Jeremiah noted that the heart of man is deceitful. So he asked, "Who can understand it?" implying that no one can. God answered, "I, the LORD, search the heart, I test the mind" (Jer. 17:9-10). Only one being can understand and explain man's heart and behaviors—God. Science is neither adequate nor authoritative for explaining behavioral categories like RAD because the mind is not the brain.

Genetics and brain damage cannot overrule the mind.

Moral choice is not generated by the brain. Therefore, attachment theory is wrong in its doctrine that a brain problem incapacitates the antisocial child so that he cannot behave sociably. Genetics and chemistry influence, but they do not rule. First Corinthians 10:13 says that "no temptation has overtaken you but such as is common to man, and

God is faithful, who will not allow you to be tempted beyond what you are able but will, with the temptation, provide the way of escape." If neurological damage determinatively prevents right moral choices and causes sinful choices, then 1 Corinthians 10:13 cannot be true.

Perhaps we ought to reconsider what Jesus said, as recorded in Mark 7:18-22. If it is the heart of man, not his brain, that generates sinful thoughts that lead to sinful words and behaviors, then in the realm of morality the sequence is the reverse of what the psychologists say. The heart (including the mind) initiates the brain chemistry. The brain provides the means to, or mediates, if you will, heart expression in our physical bodies.

This is not to say that genetics have no role in social behavior. God made us to be relational creatures, first with Himself (Gen. 2:16; 3:8), also with each other (Gen. 2:24-25). We are to love God and love one another (Matt. 22:37, 39). It would not be surprising that He genetically wired us to facilitate that purpose. So, it could be that some children may be genetically predisposed to be more or less social.

Thinking is expressed in brain chemistry and changes that chemistry, which in turn may influence thinking. So neural pathway development may play a role in thought associations or mood habits. Memory of a party pops a smile on the face. There may be positive or negative physiological responses at the thought of a particular person, or a category of persons like authorities and subordinates, mother and father. A friendship may cultivate a habitual sensation of pleasure associated with that person. An antagonistic relationship may produce associated feelings of discomfort with that person.

Sensitization and development of neural pathways may be a factor in habituation and the difficulty of habit change. It could be that habit change grows new neural pathways. If so, the body may provide some resistant influence, making it harder to change.

But God has not left morality dependent upon biology. Physiology does not control man; the heart does (Mark 7:21-23). A temperament of persistence does not require that the child develop a trait of stubbornness rather than one of patient endurance.[15] Neurons do not conclude that the mom hates the child. Soft neurological damage from emotional abuse does not cause a child to spray toothpaste on the wall or to steal coins off of his parents' dresser. No gene causes a person to lie, to plot how to manipulate others, or to look at a human target and pull a trigger. It is the immaterial (desire and volition) that initiates moral actions. The brain simply supplies the physical medium for the execution.[16]

God commands obedience, not neural development therapies. This is great news because it means that no temptation can prevent a person from obeying God by His power. Might physiological habituation make it harder or easier? Possibly. Are therapies necessarily wrong? No. The point is, since behavior is not exclusively determined by a physiological cause (Mark 7:21-23), genes and brain damage cannot overrule the mind set on pleasing God. Since 1 Corinthians 10:13 is true, then right moral behaviors like speaking truth and choosing to love others are not *dependent* upon the development of neural pathways. Change is possible with God!

Responsibility is not outside the child.

In attachment theory, the child is presumed to be innately good, just sick, brain damaged, developmentally-delayed, or victimized. He *would* comply if he *could*, but he cannot because of his disorganized brain development.[17] By this philosophy, responsibility is shifted to forces outside the child's control. The child is both exonerated and incapacitated. The logical conclusion is aptly conveyed by the title of a book about RAD-type children—*It's Nobody's Fault.*[18]

Moral culpability is not so easily escaped in God's courtroom. Romans 6:23 says that "the wages of sin is death." Behavior that violates God's law is sinful and each person is accountable for what he does (Col. 3:25). Emotional pain is not an excuse for rebellion (Job 40:2; Rom. 9:20). All people have a sin nature (Rom. 3:23). Therefore, children are *not* innately good and they *are* responsible for their selfish behaviors.

Culpability is good news! It implies possibility. If, as the psychologists say, the child has a brain structure problem with no neural capacity for trust, for a conscience, or for showing remorse, then hope for change is severely limited. Contrast that with God's ways. Inherent in His commands is the assumption that there is a way to obey them. The child can do right, and can start immediately. Yes, adults are responsible to help, but since ultimate responsibility rests on the child and not on others there is reason to hope that he can radically change.

Hope is not in man's therapies.

Attachment theories and therapies are based upon hope in man's analysis and ways of handling moral and relational problems. God warns against following man's ideas and ways in those areas. Psalm 1 teaches that God's Word is sufficient counsel for abundant life while the advice of those who do not counsel God's Word does not lead to life. This is because man's judgment is twisted so that men are likely to make mistakes in discerning what is true. While believing their ways to be right, those ways actually result in trouble (Prov. 16:25).

According to Psalm 19:8, it is God's Word which is the reliable attestation on reality. God's Word has the power to bring to the person who heeds it all the truth that is necessary to make him skilled at living. Therefore, it is God's solutions, explained in His Word, that work. By "work" I mean that the person succeeds at glorifying God, loving others, and living wisely. God's Word can transform the whole inner person (Ps. 19:7). What psychologist can make that claim about his own counsel?

Okay, so we consult our Bibles. As long as something else also works why not use every means possible? Perhaps we should define the term "works." A person in bondage to alcohol achieve can achieve sobriety through a twelve-step program, but that does not mean that he has pleased God or solved the heart problem that will drive him back to alcohol or produce other troubles. So if he becomes sober, did the therapy work?

Say that therapy persuades the child to trust his parents and improve behavior. This makes life easier. What of eternal value has been gained? The only essential change has been a shift from trust in self (man) to trust in parents (man). Trusting in other people is no more pleasing to God than is trusting in himself (Jer. 17:5-8; Prov. 3:5). His heart is still not trusting Christ. Attachment therapy cannot transform the heart because only Christ can (2 Cor. 5:17).

Worse, he can be inoculated against the gospel. The gospel begins with the news that people are sinful at heart (Rom. 3:23), but the child's therapist tells him that he is "good." No longer "bad," he determines to behave better. He has fixed himself. How? He replaced self-sufficient bad deeds. Behavior improved, but has the child's eternal destiny changed? His core problem of self-sufficiency—independence from God—remains.

In addition, his resistance is now compounded because he considers himself a good person. What need has a good person of a savior from sins? "It is not those who are healthy who need a physician, but those who are sick" (Matt. 9:12).

Now, any message of the church declaring him a sinner contradicts his therapist's teaching that he is good. The authority of the Bible and church leaders is compromised. His authorities tell him contradictory messages. And they want his trust?

His parents risk undermining their testimony. Will they oppose the "goodness" doctrine of psychologists or adopt it? Will they side with the therapist at the office and the Bible at church? Will they treat it like some do like Santa Claus? "Son, we wanted you to believe the therapist because we knew you would be happier, but now that you are behaving better we will tell you the truth."

Attachment theory undercuts hope because forgiveness is not available. An alienated child is considered to be sick, and a sick person needs healing, not forgiveness. *Remove God and guilt from the picture and forgiveness also vanishes.* A new and improved, better-behaved child is that much less in need of forgiveness. On the other hand, if guilt is admitted to the equation, forgiveness also becomes a possibility (Col. 2:13), as does freedom from guilt and a new heart reconciled to God (Rom. 6:23; Rom 8:1; 2 Cor. 5:17; Rom 5:1).

Shifting responsibility from the child disables him. A sick or damaged child is dependent upon what other people do *to* him. God's way capitalizes on accountability. Scripture, while not diminishing the importance of help from godly parents and counselors (Prov. 3:1; Gal 6:1), calls upon the child himself to change by God's enablement (1 Cor. 10:13; Gal. 5:16).

> *Any behavior or mental attitude that God requires may be obtained through the Lord Jesus Christ.*

If there is genetic influence or brain damage, God offers the wonderful hope that even when the intellect is hindered, the heart can be renewed and then taught moral right and wrong (2 Cor. 4:16; 2 Tim. 3:16). When the child is held morally responsible for his own behavior he may, because of the cross of Christ, hope for freedom from guilt and the fear it produces (Tit. 2:11-12). He can hope for relationship with God and the powerful enablement of the Holy Spirit for change.

God's ways always work when we do them. They glorify God and transform our desires, thoughts, and actions. The person is reconciled to God and others and produces the fruit of the Spirit. Should the rebellious child remain rebellious, God's ways work to enable parents and siblings to glorify God, remain steadfast in godliness and joy, and present the best influence upon the child.

Temporal change is not true change.

The goal of attachment therapies is a well-behaved, or at least a better-behaved, child. This is a temporal goal. The therapy success who becomes a well-behaved sinner instead of a "dysregulated" sinner is still an unforgiven sinner with the same eternal destiny. While thoughts and behaviors change, the old autonomous desires remain and will again demand expression in times to come, either in reversion to old ways or in some new self-focused way. Still not under God's authority, he is only a new and improved autonomous child, repackaged to be socially acceptable.

God is no plastic surgeon. He does not settle for better behavior and thoughts. He knows that the only way to deal with a cancer like sin is to, as in a bone marrow transplant, radically change the dead core of our being for a new, spirit-born living nature. Jesus came not to provide behavioral nor even moral improvement. He came to provide new life in reconciliation with God through His death and resurrection (John 10:10; 1 Pet. 3:18; 2 Cor. 5:17; Tit. 3:5). God's goal is a transformed heart that bears fruit in good works done for God's glory (2 Cor. 5:9; Eph. 2:10).

Summary and Conclusions

Because men and animals are of similar construction, animal research may give hints about man's physiology. However, because man is unique, made in God's image as animals are not, behavioral research cannot be diagnostic or prescriptive for human behavior. The mind is not the brain, so genetics and brain damage must not be unneccessarily credited with power to control behavior. The brain is not responsible; the child is responsible for his desires and behavioral choices. Children are not innately good. Hope is not found in man's methods. Temporal change is not true change.

One of the core disabling miscalculations of attachment theories is the equation that nature is equivalent to the biological. They equate mind to brain and propose that behavioral problems are caused by either nature (brain), nurture (caregiving), or a combination thereof. By failing to hold a biblical view of the immaterial aspect of a person, attachment theories miss the fundamental cause of RAD.

The nature versus nurture debate (where "nature" is defined in the physical), also removes morality from the purview. The truth is, the brain (nature) influences, but does not deserve credit for moral choices and behaviors. Caregivers (nurture) bear a great responsibility for their influences, but they are not responsible for a child's choices. At the end of the day, when considering the alienated child who steals, what we still have to reckon with is, "You shall not steal" (Exod. 20:15).

Footnotes

1. Bowlby, *Attachment and Loss*, 6, 224-225.

2. Peace, *Attitudes*, 37.

3. Diane E. Eyer, *Mother-Infant Bonding: A Scientific Fiction* (New Haven: Yale University Press, 1992), 92-98.

4. Cassidy, "Nature of the Child's Ties," 3-4.

5. Bowlby, *Attachment and Loss*, 373.

6. Siegel, *Developing Mind*, 2.

7. Perry, et al., "Childhood Trauma, the Neurobiology," 274.

8. Eyer, *Mother-Infant Bonding*, 85.

9. Street, "Biblical View of Child Development," 2005.

10. Adams, *Christian Counselor's Manual*, 174.

11. Medina, *Genetic Inferno*, 142.

12. Ibid., 110, 137, 142, 180.

13. Ibid., 25.

14. Ibid., 61.

15. Adams, *Christian Counselor's Manual*, 174.

16. Welch, *Blame It on the Brain?*, 48.

17. Buckwalter, interview.

18. Koplewicz, *Nobody's Fault*.

Chapter 21
Why Not Accept the Explanations of Psychologists?

Part 2

While Scripture sufficiently refutes errors in attachment theories, this chapter gives a nod to other angles that also reveal flaws. It provides an introductory sampling of serious discrepancies in theories and how conclusions are constructed on faulty research. Many secular psychologists disagree with attachment theories.

They are Constructed with Defective Evidence

Theories are laced with inconsistencies. Diagnosis has no scientific or medical basis and diagnostic criteria are debated. Research is biased and often fails to adhere faithfully to an objective scientific method.

Theories are incongruent with reality.

In their commendable efforts to understand and help severely troubled children, psychologists make some accurate observations. However, not all of their conclusions fit the evidence. For example, they theorize that developmental delay causes a failure to develop that sense of self in relation to objects, time, and a sense of what ought to come next, or to develop in the areas of behavior, relationships, conscience, and understanding of cause and effect.[1] Impulsivity and lack of self-regulation are attributed to thought disorder, developmental delays, minimal brain dysfunction, and neural disorganization.

Now, if antisocial children's brains are so disorganized, their skill at theft, vandalism, and concealment of evidence are truly amazing feats. Memory of the location of a stolen object demonstrates a sense of self in relation to objects. When arguing, their accurate relating of an incident or conversation shows a well-developed sequence in time. When they plan how they want to hurt others, they demonstrate accurate anticipation of the future and a strong understanding of cause and effect.

As an illustration of thought disorder, Magid and McKelvey relate the story of a counselor who took a firm stand with a maladaptive fifteen-year-old boy. At the next appointment, the boy brought an attorney to intimidate the counselor. The attorney had been totally beguiled by the boy. The authors conclude, "Thought disorder plays a large role in how uncontrollable unattached kids become."[2] Thought disorder? Any minor who can think out the obtaining of a lawyer, then fool the lawyer enough that he cooperates to be used in a plan against a counselor is thinking in an ordered manner. As Samenow states, antisocial children exhibit a strong sense of self in relation to others and calculatingly misrepresent themselves in order to victimize others.[3]

Even attachment researchers themselves make note of the calculated thinking. A 2003 study report on lack of empathy says,

> The tendency for children with RAD to show indiscriminate affection toward strangers yet withdraw from attempts by family members to show affection indicates that these children may be engaging in self-monitoring; that is, they appear to be able to alter their behavior according to their own desire.

In the data, children labeled RAD rated significantly higher on self-monitoring than children not labeled RAD. They conclude:

> Evidence suggests that children with RAD may consciously attempt to present themselves in a socially-desirable manner rather than an accurate manner. Because of this significant tendency to engage in (perhaps) conscious self-monitoring behavior, these individuals pose unique problems for people who deal with them.[4]

According to this description, a sense of self in relation to others, what ought to come next, and predictive outcomes is well developed.

If anything, children labeled with RAD are skilled at reading people and situations. Magid and McKelvey describe Nancy, a RAD-type child, by saying, "Nancy was an obnoxious and demanding child. Her covert ways of controlling were much more intellectually astonishing than her overt mechanisms."[5] Any child who can manipulate others, especially to an "astonishing" degree, has developed thought order and understands cause and effect. The case is not so much a lack of understanding as it is a matter of which effect the child desires.

Attachment theorists' own observations contradict their own theories. Alienated children are not ruled by biology. They have desires that motivate toward a goal and are "able to alter their behavior" accordingly.

Diagnosis is problematic.

Author Harold Koplewicz says that behavioral symptoms in the maladapted child's history "allow us to diagnose a brain disorder as precisely and as reliably as physicians diagnose diabetes and hypertension." [6] This is a bold statement. How exactly does one measure behaviors? More fundamentally, how can one diagnose what has not been proven even to exist? RAD has no medical basis. Physical diseases can be diagnosed through biological tests such as blood tests, x-rays, and brain scans, but there are no valid biological diagnostic tests that can identify any so-called mental or behavioral disorder, including RAD. Instead, diagnosis is based on observed behaviors, and those observations are not objective, measurable, or well-defined.

RAD is not even clearly defined in psychology's diagnostic standard, the *DSM-IV*, and there is debate over the label and its criteria. The listing provides few criteria, which is why practitioners privately create lists of behaviors which might better fit other diagnoses such as conduct disorder or ADHD. The criteria focus on social behavior instead of the attachment itself. Quantification of severity is not enumerated in measurable standards, and the maximum age (five) by which children are to exhibit the behaviors is arbitrary and unfounded by research. No one has produced more than theories and associative evidence as to the cause. The label is ambiguous. No standard assessment protocol is provided. Other than the Adult Attachment Interview for adults and the Strange Situation test for children, no standard method of assessment is available. [7]

Research is flawed.

If diagnosis holds a basket of problems, behavioral research holds a barrelful. There are difficulties in identifying variables, in measuring them, and in interpreting data.

Measurement is not quantifiable. Research on RAD is ambiguous and subjective. Simply put, relational phenomena cannot be directly measured. How can maternal responsiveness or child inhibition be measured? They can't. So researchers must use indirect observations like behavioral interactions, physiological reactions, visual tracking of the attachment figure, behavioral and endocrine responses to separation and reunion, and maintenance of proximity. How many feet or inches qualify as "proximity"? To measure inhibition, Lakatos et al. timed what they called "latency to smile at stranger" and "latency to accept toy."[8] How many seconds equals "latency"?

Mary Main, at Berkeley, used adult interviews to identify and quantify variables and label attachment categories. Yet, adult memory about childhood is highly unreliable. Also, raters disagreed on how to classify people, and many individuals did not fit into any category.

Numbers can be manipulated. Main's interviews were considered 70-80% accurate. Well, that also means that 20-30% of the information could be inaccurate, a significant amount. Data was unreliable and the conclusions subjective.

Variables are not all identifiable. In behavioral research, a multitude of variables cannot be known and many are subjective. For example, something like emotions cannot always be known by the researcher to incorporate as data. Even if they could, how would they be quantified? The study by Lakatos et al. illustrates. It identifies a possible genetic influence involving dopamine reuptake.[9] The researchers used the Strange Situation to test twelve-month-old infants. Therefore, they started with a twelve-month mass of data missing. There is nothing in the report to indicate whether researchers knew if some of the infants were accustomed to meeting new people while others led more secluded lives, or whether some may have felt shy but looked bold because they were used to getting toys on demand. Perhaps some mothers encouraged independence and self-control of emotions more than others. It is unknown whether any of the infants endured a frightening experience with a stranger that may have predisposed them to a fear reaction or "latency to smile at stranger." The already active imaginations are not taken into account. The study does not explain the general home atmospheres already being absorbed, especially family attitudes to novelty or new people. It does not relate the moods of the mothers on the day of the experiment or how intensely one mom or another wanted to please the researchers. What if the infants noted with "latency to accept toy" simply did not like the toy? The mass of variables influencing behaviors overwhelms behavioral studies.

One variable almost entirely missing from behavioral research studies is motive. This may partially explain why words like "desire" and "want" are almost nonexistent in study data and reports. Yet this is the key variable in behaviors!

Freud assumed that the motive for seeking the mother in attachment was satisfaction of the need for food. Bowlby did not allow for motive at all but assumed behaviors to be the natural working of a biological mechanism on the order of the imprinting instincts of a duckling. Whose counsel shall we follow?

Motive is almost impossible to test. It cannot be quantified. A one-to-one correlation of motive to behavior does not exist. Motive can't even be reliably identified. No person, especially a child, is always conscious of why he behaves as he does. Because dishonesty is endemic to RAD children in particular, data based upon their statements of motive remain unreliable.

Interpretation is not objective. Researchers must contend with the fact that their own subjectivity biases analysis of the data. In the mid-1970s, Mason and Berkson published a study of rhesus monkeys comparing the impact of warm, stationary cloth surrogates to that of moving surrogates. The babies of moving moms grew to behave like normal monkeys while the babies of stationary moms did not. Mason and Berkson hypothesized that motion stimulates the nervous system to respond to changes in physical position. Therefore, motion helps to develop the nervous system. Also, unpredictability in the mom requires that the baby think about how to approach her.[10] So, what Harlow saw as a need for attachment, Mason and Berkson demonstrated as a need for movement and thought.

Bias can be found in what is missing. For example, Harlow's surrogate-raised babies were deprived of not just a mom but all animal contact. Therefore, his studies did not test the importance of mothering but of total social deprivation. Rene Spitz argued for attachment from his observation of the high percentage of infants who died in a foundling home, yet there is reason to suspect that those children died in a measles epidemic.[11] Bowlby developed attachment theory partly in response to the antisocial behaviors of orphans he observed. He concluded that absence of mothering was the cause. What might be the conclusion if it was discovered that those orphaned children were being mistreated in the orphanages?

Interpretative bias results when behavioral researchers selectively overlook species differences, as in Harlow's studies. Rhesus monkeys show marked maternal affiliations, but baby capuchinss are not strongly connected to their mothers. Cotton top tamarins cling to the family member that spends the most time with them. Fluffy titi adults partner for life and mate connection is much stronger than mother-baby connection. The females show no noticeable maternal instinct; males are the caregivers 80% of the time.[12] Had Harlow used fluffy titis instead of rhesus, he might have preached that fathers should stay with the kids while mothers bring home the bananas.

Others see many Discrepancies

Many psychologists do not accept the theory that attachment is an innate, determinative mechanism in babies. Instead, some picture a child shaped by both temperament and experiences.[13] Some view attachment theory itself as a product of social and psychological trends, recognize many exceptions to the attachment model, and maintain other paradigms for child social behavior.

Social history is influenced by trends.

In her book *Mother-Infant Bonding: A Scientific Fiction*, Diane Eyer depicts attachment as a cultural theorem instead of an empirical fact and says that research is conducted to validate that bias. For example, paternal bonding is not researched, and that is because it does not fit attachment theory's paradigm.[14] Both the model and the research discount the social influences of fathers, siblings, grandparents, friends, teachers, music, television, churches, temperaments, and the influence that children themselves have on those around them.[15] Researchers are trying to explain how the widget works before proving that the widget exists.

Eyer looks at culture's historical inclinations to stress the roles of experience (nurture) and temperament (nature). Some psychologists are temperamentalists. They view inherited temperament as the dominant influence on a child's development. Attachment theory, by its emphasis on neurological wiring, also sketches nature into its template. What makes it different from temperamentalists' view is that it connects this prewiring with a physiological attachment mechanism, not with temperament. The child is prewired to attach (an amoral necessity), yet is still a blank and morally neutral good slate. (Yes, that is contradictory.) The slate is shaped by the environment. Nurture, not nature (temperament), determines character.

Eyer views attachment theory as a product of the trend to emphasize nurture (experience) rather than nature (temperament) in child development. She documents how emphases on nurture dominated-social trends in the last century and affected debates over spanking, reward, day care, and legislation of early childhood intervention programs. It influenced the trend to remodel the hospital birthing scene back into a pseudo-home, with birthing rooms, a present father, bonding time, and breast feeding skin-to-skin.[16] Present day nursing books still emphasize the need for attachment and instruct nurses on how to facilitate the bonding process.[17]

The nurture philosophies construct a passive child shaped by his environment, interacting but not initiating. Therefore, it became popular to overly blame parents and view hurt people as victims in an adaptation of the "sins of the fathers visited upon the children." [18] Attachment theories have not been empirically validated; they are a collection of philosophies swirling in the ocean of social currents.

Attachment theories are insufficient explanations.

Dissenting psychologists find that many children do not fit the attachment paradigm. When a study labels 85% of those mistreated as insecure, there are 15% who managed to become secure despite mistreatment, evidence that the theory is hardly definitive fact. Jerome Kagan, a temperamentalist, cites a study of 229 Korean girls, some severely malnourished, who were adopted in America at ages two to three. All of them adapted well. He also notes a woman who was abused and shifted through foster homes. She first reacted as the attachment model would predict, but in adolescence, she rejected her RAD responses and later became a loving mother of her own son.[19]

Samenow, psychologist and author of books on the criminal mind, also sees discrepancies. In his book, *Before It's Too Late*, he cites several examples. One is the situation of two brothers removed from severe inner-city poverty when found in a state of neglect. Placed in an affluent home, they had nurturing and opportunities for extensive education. One became a lawyer, the other a convicted armed robber. The severe deprivation was the same, but two different paths were chosen. Moreover, the criminal received more attention in remediation (which should have filled his love tank fuller) than the one who chose to be law-abiding.[20]

Child researcher and temperamentalist Carol Kaufman challenges attachment categories. Regarding a child who fit the label avoidant or disorganized, Carol thought her confidently independent. She was highly skilled at sensing when to avoid her mother and when and how to approach her. Kaufman describes her as creative, curious, and confident in independent play.[21]

Kagan notes that some mothers encourage self-confidence and self-control over anxiety and fear. Their children may not cry or seek comfort, and appear to be avoidant. The overprotected child may cry and run to the mother for comfort, and would be labeled secure.[22]

So then, what the attachment theorist labels ambivalent, the temperamentalist considers an inherited tendency to anxiety or inhibition. What the attachment theorist calls secure or anxious attachments, a temperamentalist views as the expression of inborn traits of confidence or inhibition, respectively. Where the attachment theorist sees a need for consistent, responsive care, the temperamentalist sees a need to be respected.[23]

Temperamentalists dispute developmentalism, objecting to the idea that new stages are dependent upon experience and successful completion of a previous stage. Rather, stages occur through the maturation of the brain independent of experience. For example, puberty is not a response to experiences. Neither is separation anxiety in infants. Anxiety appears between seven and fifteen months across the board irrespective of positive or negative experiences.[24] If not all new qualities result from response to experiences, then developmentalism is not a sufficient explanation for emotional and behavioral maturation.

The child is not a passive receptacle.

In non-attachment models, the child rather than the environment makes the difference. While abuse can pressure a child toward a negative direction, children can also analyze and disagree with caregivers' messages, can influence relationships or find alternate relationships, and can profit by meeting and surmounting the unfortunate adversity of maltreatment.

Steve and Sybil Wolin, in *The Resilient Child*, use the term "Damage Model" to label theories predicting that abuse in childhood necessarily leads to psychological problems later. They note that in the damage models children unquestioningly accept the "bad child" messages conveyed by parental mistreatment.[25]

The Wolins refute that a child will automatically trade truth for safety, saying, "I accept that young children sometimes purchase pseudo-safety at the cost of truth, but they also can be psychologically sophisticated—even at very young ages—and sense their parents' flaws." For example, seven-year-olds can verbalize skepticism of their parents' behaviors.[26] If children can verbalize skepticism by age seven, then they are observing, analyzing, and drawing their own conclusions long before then. Even very young children judge fairness: "That's not fair!"

Kagan states, "All children have the capacity to generate ideas about good and bad states, actions, and outcomes."[27] Curiosity may lead a child to consider options. He may decide at some point that he is not the problem and that the parent's maltreatment has very little to do with himself. Perhaps he chooses to believe the teacher who says, "You're clever," or a neighbor who says, "You were a big help." Perhaps he notices that some attempt of his succeeded and decides, "I am competent."

Three children of a paranoid schizophrenic mother demonstrate the power of young children to analyze, disbelieve their parents, and determine their own destinies. Because the mother was convinced that the food at home was being poisoned, she always ate at restaurants. The eldest daughter accepted her mother's ideas and stayed with her for meals. The middle daughter ate at home with the father when he was there, but otherwise ate with the mother. The seven-year-old son bought his own food, fixed it, and ate at home even if he was alone.[28]

Besides choosing beliefs, young children are capable of influencing relationships toward what they want them to be. Sandra, in an abusive family, used trial and error to find a technique of joke telling that aroused her severely depressed mother enough to prepare dinner. Later, when she was nine years old, she initiated and gained a friendly relationship with an elderly male neighbor. By pursuing a friendship with a neighbor woman, she gained surrogate mothering. She created siblings by using her school recess time to read to the kindergarten class.[29] In their practices, the Wolins have found many cases of children who turned adversity to the good and gained a greater sense of competency by overcoming the challenges of an abused childhood.[30]

Samenow shifts the focus away from both nature (genetics/temperament) and nurture. He states unreservedly that antisocial children are "behaving monstrously by choice." The cause is not parenting, poverty, or peers. Most abused and poor children do not become criminals, and those pressured into crime by peers have chosen their peers. Children are not unformed clay "haplessly molded by parents." Regardless of parenting or temperament, children make choices.[31]

Samenow says that hypothesizing the why of the behavior just coaches a child to more excuses, so Samenow turns the discussion from why to how. He asks how the child is choosing to deal with whatever genetics and environment he has been dealt, and advocates that parents and therapists focus less on the reasons and apply themselves more to helping the child become responsible regarding his present problems. Samenow and others who reject attachment theory suggest that we start to view children as active participants in their own development.[32]

Footnotes

1. Buckwalter, interview.
2. Magid and McKelvey, *High Risk*, 89.
3. Samenow, *Before It's Too Late*, 25.
4. Hall and Geher, "Behavioral and Personality Characteristics," 150, 157, 159.
5. Magid and McKelvey, *High Risk*, 89.
6. Koplewicz, *Nobody's Fault*, 55.
7. Rochelle F. Hanson and Eve G. Spratt, "Reactive Attachment Disorder: What We Know About the Disorder and Implications for Treatment," *Child Maltreatment* 5, no. 2 (May 2000): 139-140.
8. K. Lakatos, Z. Nemoda, E. Birkas, Z. Ronai, E. Kovacs, K. Ney, I. Toth, M. Sasvari- Szekely, and J. Gervai, "Association of D4 Dopamine Receptor Gene and Serotonin Transporter Promoter Polymorphisms with Infants' Response to Novelty," *Molecular Psychiatry* 8, no. 1 (Jan. 2003): 90-97.

9. Lakatos, et al., "Association of D4 Dopamine Receptor Gene," 92.

10. Blum, *Goon Park*, 186-189.

11. Eyer, *Mother-Infant Bonding*, 67.

12. Blum, *Goon Park*, 185, 279, 278.

13. Christopher Shea, "The Temperamentalist," Boston Globe, 29 Aug.2004
    http://www.boston.com/news/globe/ideas/articles/2004/08/29/the_
    temperamentalist?pg=full (4 Jan. 2006).

14. Eyer, *Mother-Infant Bonding*, 108.

15. Ibid., 199-200.

16. Shea, "The Temperamentalist," Boston Globe.

17. Sally B. Olds, Marcia L. London, Patricia A. Wieland Ladewig,
    Michele R. Davidson, *Maternal-Newborn Nursing and Women's Health Care*,
    7th ed. (Upper Saddle River, N.J.: Pearson Education Incorporated, 2004),
    848-853-854, 981-982, 997-999, 1037-1038.

18. Steven J. Wolin and Sybil Wolin, *The Resilient Self: How Survivors of Troubled
    Families Rise Above Adversity* (New York: Villard Books, 1993), 20.

19. Jerome Kagan, *The Nature of the Child* (New York: Basic Books, 1984), 101, 254.

20. Samenow, *Before It's Too Late*, 19.

21. Kagan, *Nature of the Child*, 117-118.

22. Ibid., 60-61.

23. Karen, *Becoming Attached*, 298-301.

24. Kagan, *Nature of the Child*, 78, 47.

25. Wolin and Wolin, *Resilient Self*, 74.

26. Ibid., 74-75.

27. Kagan, *Nature of the Child*, 130-131.

28. Wolin and Wolin, *Resilient Self*, 67-71.

29. Ibid., 119-122.

30. Ibid., 18.

31. Samenow, *Before It's Too Late*, 200-202, 3, 13, 1-15.

32. Ibid., 200-202, 6, 71.

Chapter 22
Cautions Regarding Therapies

Those who manage treatment programs work hard to find solutions to help children become able to lead peaceful and productive lives. Treatment programs look appealing to parents because they offer the possibility of a fix. If attachment therapies improve the child even a little, why not use them? There may be some reasons to do so.

It is beyond the scope of this book to evaluate therapies. This chapter is intended to outline only a few principles to guide your own evaluation. More elaboration on biblical truths regarding attachment, and therefore attachment therapies, can be found in Part 1 and chapters 20 and 21.

Source of answers

From what source does this treatment program draw its answers and solutions? God's Word lacks nothing that we need for godly living (2 Pet. 1:3). Scripture is able to restore, to make wise, to enlighten, and give hope (Ps. 19:7-8). It is able to teach, correct, and train people to be equipped to live godly lives (2 Tim. 3:15-17). The Bible gives a hope for change beyond anything the world can offer (1 Cor. 6:9-11; Phil. 4:13). If it is true that the Bible has sufficient effective solutions to any interpersonal or relational problem (and it is), the logical corollary is that any therapy that offers answers outside of what the Word says is either superfluous or wrong. This is not to say that the Bible offers comprehensive specifics on methods. It does mean that the Bible holds the principles out of which methods should be developed.

Goal for change

What is this program's central goal for change? Scripture presents a child as a unique creation formed for worship through relationship. Therefore, the goal in counseling and parenting the alienated child is not attachment, not trust in the parent, and not healing. Even if brain structure affects behavior, God's goal is not neural development. Improved behavior must be secondary. The foremost goal is to lead the child to glorify God in relationship with Him and others through trust in Christ (1 Cor. 10:31; Matt. 22:37-39; Jer. 17:5-8).

Source of problem

What is presumed to be the child's foundational underlying problem? The source of the problem is not a lack of attachment, not a lack of brain development, not incompletion of a needs cycle, not a lack of identity or self-esteem, and not a lack of trust. According to Jeremiah 17:9, the source of the problem is a wicked heart. It is untrained, easily swayed by various feelings and beliefs, holds inaccurate perceptions, and does not understand or accept truth (Eph. 4:14, 18-19). It has become morally insensible (Eph. 4:19). That heart is enticed by lusts (James 1:14). People sin because they want (lust for) things (James 4:1-3). People do what they do because they think what they think because they want what they want. Any God-glorifying solution must see the source of the problem primarily as the child's corrupted heart.

Solution to problem

Psychologists in treatment programs disagree on methodology because they disagree on etiology.[1] Behavioral geneticists, seeing cause in genes and chemicals, find at least partial solutions in drugs and, perhaps in the future, genetic manipulation. Developmental behaviorists, seeing cause in brain development, find at least a partial solution in trying to develop new neural circuits. Behaviorists offer hope based on rewards and changing the environment. Cognitive counselors try to change thinking. Psychoanalysts try to change a subconscious self. Almost all programs emphasize persuading the child to esteem himself, and at least one residential program in the States centers its treatment on developing identity. Many counselors mix and match.

Attachment therapists almost universally agree that getting the child to trust the therapist or parents and getting him to attach are necessary goals. Since rage reductionists believe that a disrupted bonding cycle created a pathology, "the only hope for [normalcy is] in a rebonding process."[2] Through holding therapy, the child is put through bonding cycles until he trusts and attaches.

Because developmentalists add to the broken bonding cycles idea a close connection to brain development, their therapy is different. Through talk and play, developmentalists try to stimulate the neurons which mediate trust. They want to rebuild the brain, to build neural pathways for expressing trust in order to achieve the child's trust in/ attachment to the therapist and parents.

There is strong evidence that experiences affect brain development. It might be that habit is explained by neural pathways, construction, and chemistry. It may be that learning of new habits involves formation of new cells or increased sensitized firing of certain cells in certain brain locations. It may be that guided repetition of words and behaviors is a valid means to develop new neural pathways.

Nevertheless, morality is not dependent upon chemistry. Scripture does not command us to develop nerves. It calls us to obey and promises that choosing morally right behavior is possible. Therapy or parental guidance helps, but the Holy Spirit can enable the child even when an adult is not there or is not guiding.

Habit is an important biblical principle. Perseverance to practice new right behaviors so that they become habit is a biblical mandate. If practice of obedience develops the nerves, fine. If it does not, fine. What is needed is to pursue the majors, not the minors. Obedience to God's Word is the major.

Pursuing neural development is not wrong, but can distract from seeing the solution God's way. It encourages dependence upon man's methods to reshape the brain rather than upon the Holy Spirit to renew the heart. It covers the central issue—that an alienated child's behaviors are a *moral*, not a *physiological*, issue.

Scripture teaches that what the alienated child needs is a new heart. Anything short of that just shuffles the "dysregulated" sinner into a well-behaved sinner. Can secular programs programs "work," as in improve the child's behavior? Yes, but they cannot "work," as in produce permanent spiritual and eternal change. Secular approaches fall short because they do not lead to salvation that provides the child with a cleansed heart through forgiveness in Christ (Heb. 10:22).

Scripture says to renew the mind, put off old ways, and put on new ways (Eph. 4:22-24). Anyone who helps must call upon the child to put off his love of safety, revenge, and control, and to put on trust in God.

Secular therapies sometimes help to change behavior. They can help because they have stumbled upon principles that God originated. For example, practice of right behaviors is a part of (not all) of the put-on method in Ephesians 4 for rehabituation. Therapists' use of an even tone of voice follows Proverbial guidelines like, "a gentle answer turns away wrath" (Prov. 15:1) and that being slow to anger pacifies contention (Prov. 15:18). The calm demeanor of cognitive therapists may make knowledge acceptable (Prov. 15:2). Residential programs are strong in structure, an Ephesians 6:4 principle. They apply consequences, a Galatians 6:7-8 principle, more rigidly and consistently than most parents. They try to instill a practice of reciprocity, self-control, and self-awareness, all helpful habits.[3]

It could be that developmentalist techniques like play therapy help to ease fears and woo the heart to want change. Play therapists emphasize fun and enjoyment of relational interactions and try to transform tense moments into continued engagement with the child.[4] Like advertisements to consumers, play may entice the child with something good that he might want enough to try letting go of his negative ways.

Holding therapy, or rage reduction, is not a method to use for several reasons. First, the basis is wrong. If anyone can be stuck "helplessly" in rage, then 1 Corinthians 10:13 is not true. A so-called "need" for control is not pathology, but idolatry. Second, because gratification and trust are matters of the heart, they cannot be forced. What can happen is forced compliance or cooperation just to gain relief (wrong motive). This point does not preclude that some children might go on to choose to trust their parents. Third, by deliberate provocation while keeping the child helpless to stop it, the therapist has set up an unreasonable situation intended to provoke the child to anger, if not despair. Resentment and hatred would also be likely accompaniments. How does such treatment encourage godliness in the child? How is the therapist upholding the holiness of God? Provoking another to sin is what Satan did in the Garden (Gen. 3:1-8). In contrast, we are to take great care to make sure that we do not provoke others to sin (Rom. 14:13; 1 Cor. 8:9). Furthermore, Hebrews 10:24 commands that we "provoke one another to love and good works." Provoking to good works means prompting and challenging the other to do what is right and good. Fourth, the attempt to force the child to trust a particular person contradicts Jeremiah's warning that "cursed is the man who trusts in mankind" (Jer. 17:5). Directing the child to trust in a parent detours the child from the ultimate priority, trusting in God. The child is not called to repent from sin and love God. Fifth, God nowhere coerces people to trust Him.

Practices in residential treatment centers will generally not be founded on Christian principles. If the claim is made that the methods are biblical, check it carefully. Most centers base their approach on psychological theories rather than Scripture.

You might opt to send your child to a center for a variety of reasons. Improved behavior is an acceptable intermediary goal. Keep in mind that most centers will not call upon the child to view Scripture as authoritative for living, to repent from sin, to trust Christ, or to depend upon the Holy Spirit for change, in accord with the "discipline and instruction of the Lord" (Eph. 6:4). After treatment, you will need to correct lies that the child was taught, like self-esteem or self-righteousness (because he changed for the better without Christ). You will need to teach him about goals, sin, the true source of our sinful behaviors, and God's solutions done God's way for God's reasons. If he was taught differently in treatment, he may resist your teaching. In the end, you are responsible for the spiritual training of this treasure that God has granted to you.

Footnotes

1. Hanson and Spratt, "Reactive Attachment Disorder: What We Know," 142.
2. Magid and McKelvey, *High Risk*, 209.
3. Ibid., 46.
4. Wilson, "Nurturing Love," 5A.

Chapter 23
Hope to Spare

Even after children leave home to build their own lives, their choices can affect the rest of the family. Parental responsibilities change, and parents' love and counsel may still have some influence on the child.

I want to reiterate that whether our children give grounds for joy or grief, there is something more important than the outcome and more important than whether we are happy or sad. While we rightly desire that our children trust and obey God, our central focus must not be on how they turn out so much as whether we parented to please God. We cannot make our children change, but we can obey the Lord ourselves. Loving and glorifying God is a parent's first priority (Matt. 22:37; 1 Cor. 10:31; 2 Cor. 5:9).

I was once a "Mrs. DeSpare." Then I learned truths from God's Word that changed me. I now handle difficulties differently. What a treasure the Bible is! When couples like the DeSpares see the difference God's Word and Spirit make in their lives, marriage, and parenting, their names change. Mrs. DeSpare becomes "Mrs. Hope TuSpare."

I hope that your view of God is higher than when you began this book and that your thinking has become more biblical. If you are a believer, be absolutely convinced that God has, with love, sovereignly and wisely planned your family situation so that He might do good to you by conforming you to the image of His Son, that He might be glorified (Rom. 8:28-29). You have great cause to rejoice.

If you are a friend, pastor, or counselor of the parent or sibling of an angry, alienated child, pray for the family. Think biblically before you speak. Support the weak and correct with gentle grace.

I hope that as you, Reader, apply the truths from God's Word in a gentle, loving manner under the rule of Christ, the alienated child you love will soften his or her heart. I pray that the Holy Spirit will open your child's eyes to God's gracious way of salvation so that your child might no longer be enslaved to anger and selfishness and that you may enjoy a richly rewarding relationship with him or her. May all of your children learn and apply God's Word so that they make the most use of their trials as opportunities to grow in the knowledge of God, wisdom for living, and compassion for others.

It is my strong hope that by God's grace you will have hope "TuSpare" for others, sharing the principles of God's Word regarding the heart, change, parenting, and trials. May your greatest ambition be to love the Lord your God, to be pleasing to Him, obedient in your responsibilities while gratefully trusting Him with His will for your family (Matt. 22:37; 1 Cor. 10:31; 2 Cor. 5:9; 1 Thess. 5:16-18).

Appendix
Resources for Parents

Since the alienated child is full of fear and especially anger, resources that address those problems will be useful to you even if those resources are not specific to Reactive Attachment Disorder. The following are outstanding resources for parenting in a biblical way:

- Priolo, Lou, *Teach Them Diligently: How to Use the Scriptures in Child Training.* Woodruff, S.C.: Timeless Texts, 2000.

- Priolo, Lou, *The Heart of Anger.* New York: Calvary Press Publishing, 1997.

- Priolo, Lou, *Getting a Grip: The Heart of Anger Handbook for Teens.* New York: Calvary Press Publishing, 2007.

- Tripp, Tedd, *Shepherding a Child's Heart.* Wapwallopen, Penn.: Shepherd Press, 1995.

The following are resources for building parents' understanding of biblical principles on the heart, change, marriage, and parenting:

- Adams, Jay, *From Forgiven to Forgiving.* Amityville, New York: Calvary Press, 1994.

- Baker, Amy. "Reactive Attachment Disorder." National Association of Nouthetic Counselors Annual Conference, 2005. [CD N0507]. Chesterton, Ind.: Sound Word. (5 Nov. 2005). *This can be ordered online at http://www.soundword.com/national-association-of-nouthetic-couselors—baker—amy.html*

- Bridges, Jerry, *Trusting God: Even When Life Hurts!* NavPress, 2008.

- Gundersen, Dennis, *Your Child's Profession of Faith.* Sand Springs, Okla.: Grace & Truth Books, 2010.

- Mack, Wayne, *Your Family God's Way*. Phillipsburg, New Jersey: P & R Publishing, 1991.

- Sande, Ken, *The Peacemaker*. Grand Rapids, Mich., Baker Book House, 2004.

- Welch, Ed, *When People Are Big and God Is Small*. Phillipsburg, New Jersey: P & R Publishing, 1997.

- Welch, Ed, *Blame It On the Brain?: Distinguishing Chemical Imbalances, Brain Disorders, and Disobedience*. Phillipsburg, New Jersey: P & R Publishing, 2001.

About the Author

Linda J. Rice

Married since 1980, Linda Rice and her husband have a biological daughter, an adopted daughter, and an adopted son. They have lived in Virginia, Missouri, Malaysia, Nevada, and Illinois.

With an M.A. in Biblical Counseling from The Master's College in Santa Clarita, California, Mrs. Rice has been a biblical counselor at Gateway Biblical Counseling and Training Center, Fairview Heights, Illinois since 2007.